Th
NEW POLITICS
of
INEQUALITY

12/86

Blick —
   worTk reading —
it dumps on everyone,
including reformers . . .

         Phil

The
NEW POLITICS
of
INEQUALITY

Thomas Byrne Edsall

W. W. NORTON & COMPANY
New York   London

Published simultaneously in Canada by
Penguin Books Canada Ltd,
2801 John Street, Markham, Ontario L3R 1B4
Printed in the United States of America

The text of this book is composed in 11/13 Bembo,
with display type set in Bembo.
Book design by Nancy Dale Muldoon

First published as a Norton paperback 1985

Library of Congress Cataloging in Publication Data
Edsall, Thomas Byrne.
The new politics of inequality.

1. Income distribution—United States. 2. United
States—Economic policy—1971–1981. 3. United States—
Economic policy—1981– . 4. Equality—United States.
5. Political parties—United States. I. Title.
HC110I5E36 1984 338.973 83–25507

ISBN 0-393-30250-4

W. W. Norton & Company, Inc.,
500 Fifth Avenue, New York, N. Y. 10110
W. W. Norton & Company Ltd.,
37 Great Russell Street, London WC1B 3NU

4 5 6 7 8 9 0

To Mary
without whom this book would not have been written

Contents

Acknowledgments

AMONG my editors at the *Washington Post* to whom I am indebted are Peter Silberman, Frank Swoboda, Peter Behr, and Peter Milius, who have given me both latitude and guidance. At the *Baltimore Sun*, William F. Schmick III, now chief of the Ottaway News Service in Washington, has been both an editor and a good friend.

Burt Hoffman provided specific help on the manuscript, and, over the years, repeated insights into the political process. James W. Wetzler, deputy chief of staff of the Joint Committee on Taxation, read the manuscript with care, not only correcting factual errors but suggesting substantial improvements in the content and structure. Karl W. Deutsch, my father-in-law, lent the wisdom and perspective of a lifetime committed to the acquisition of knowledge, to the teaching of political science in the broadest possible sense, and to the improvement of the world around him. Each of these three people was invaluable to the production of this book; its shortcomings are, however, my own.

For anyone attempting to understand federal tax legislation, the Joint Committee on Taxation is a critical resource. Among those on the staff who have been particularly helpful are David H. Brockway, Mark McConaghy, Lin Smith, and Randall Weiss.

Robert S. McIntyre and Charls E. Walker, two lobbyists who

disagree on almost every issue, have shared some of their expertise with me.

Over the years, there have been a number of fellow reporters, editors, politicians, lobbyists, academics, friends, and professional staff members who have shared, often generously, sometimes inadvertently, their understanding of elections and the legislative process. Among these are: Robert Healy, Richard Ben Cramer, David Broder, Adam Clymer, Frank A. DeFillipo, Joseph Foote, David Rogers, Frederic B. Hill, Jerome Kelly, G. Jefferson Price, Jr., Phil Evans, Ernest Imhoff, Robert Keller, Marvin Mandel, Walter S. Orlinsky, Dick Conlon, Neil Newhouse, Robert Lighthizer, Adam Spiegel, Abby Trafford, Don Neff, Stephen Luxemberg, Stanley Plastrik, Ward Sinclair, Gloria Borger, Tom C. Griscom, Thomas J. D'Alesandro III, Alan Spector, Carl Leubsdorf, Martin Tolchin, Helen Dewar, Peter Reuter, Mark Kleiman, Stephen Nordlinger, Parren J. Mitchell, William Donald Schaefer, Irvin Kovens, Stephen Sachs, John Salmon, Peter Davis, Nancy Mathews, Douglas Hibbs, Murray Levin, Howard Zinn, William R. Pitts, Ernest S. Christian, Jr., Mark Bloomfield, John Petrocik, Harold Carroll, Ari Weiss, Kirk O'Donnell, Caroline Atkinson, James Talbert, Joe Raymond, Dominic Mimi DiPietro, Margaret Carroll, Troy Brailey, Dale Hess, Harry Rodgers, and Art Pine.

At Norton, I would like particularly to thank George Brockway, who readily accepted the idea for this book, and Donald Lamm, whose editing and critical insights were greatly beneficial.

For the past fifteen years, Judy Milliken has been a good friend, providing unfailing support and a second home. My thanks to Ruth Deutsch, and to my uncle and aunt, John and Margaret Edsall. My late parents, Katherine Byrne Edsall and Richard Linn Edsall, created a foundation upon which much of this book has been built. Special thanks to my daughter, Lexa. Most important of all, however, has been my wife, Mary, who shared the burden of this book from the beginning, bringing to what has been a joint project her editing skill, social vision, compassionate intelligence, and endurance.

The
NEW POLITICS
of
INEQUALITY

Introduction

THIS book attempts to describe a major shift in the balance of power in the United States over the past decade, and to describe the consequences of that shift in the formulation of economic policy. The two—power and policy—are irrevocably linked, as public policy is made by, and in behalf of, those with power. In the United States in recent years there has been a significant erosion of the power of those on the bottom half of the economic spectrum, an erosion of the power not only of the poor but of those in the working and middle classes. At the same time, there has been a sharp increase in the power of economic elites, of those who fall in the top 15 percent of the income distribution.

This transfer of power has coincided with an economic crisis: productivity growth, which for the three decades following the Second World War had been the source of a continuing rise in the standard of living, slowed to zero by the end of the 1970s; the median familiy income, which had doubled in real, uninflated dollars from 1950 to 1973, declined during the next ten years, paralleling a decline in the average factory worker's weekly earnings; and inflation and unemployment, instead of acting as counterbalancing forces, rose simultaneously.

This mounting economic crisis provided an opportunity for newly ascendant representatives of the interests of the business community and of the affluent to win approval of a sea change in economic policy. For nearly fifty years, since the formation of the New Deal coalition in the 1930s, there had been a sustained base of support for both social spending programs and a tax system that modestly redistributed income and restricted the concentration of wealth in the hands of the few. These deeply rooted liberal traditions were abandoned during the late 1970s in favor of policies calling for a major reduction of the tax burden on income derived from capital, and for reductions in domestic spending programs directed toward the poor and the working poor. These shifts in tax and spending policies, in combination with inflation, have had enormous distributional consequences, resulting, for the period from 1980 through 1984, in losses for every income group except the very affluent.

Although the election of Ronald Reagan to the presidency has been the catalyst for much of this alteration of policy, its roots run far deeper. The delicate balance of power between elites and larger groups seeking representation in the political process has been changing in almost all quarters, including the Democratic party, the Republican party, the business lobbying community, organized labor, and the intellectual establishment. These changes have been both accelerated and exacerbated throughout the entire electorate by increasingly class-skewed voting patterns. In each of these areas, the changes are resulting in a diminution of the representation of the majority in the development of economic policy, and in the growing leverage of the well-to-do.

Underlying this shift in the balance of political power among economic groups is a changed economic environment that has forced fundamental revisions in political strategies for both political parties. The economic crisis of the past decade has cut to the heart of a tradition in American politics, particularly in Democratic politics, playing havoc with that party's tradition of capitalizing on a growing and thriving economy in order to finance a continuing expansion of benefits for those toward the bottom of the income distribution. Past economic growth had provided the federal government with a fiscal dividend in additional tax revenues with which to finance growth in such broad-based programs as Social Security and Medicare, while simultaneously maintaining popular support, as all wage earners benefited from rising real incomes.

Altered economic circumstances have turned politics into what Lester Thurow has termed a zero-sum process. The balance of power in the competition for the benefits of government has shifted increasingly in favor of those in the top third of the income distribution. In many respects these shifts have pushed the national debate well to the right of its locus ten or twenty years ago. In 1964, the Republican presidential nominee, Senator Barry Goldwater, was decisively defeated while advocating a major reduction in domestic federal spending and a sharp increase in military spending; sixteen years later, Ronald Reagan, one of Goldwater's most ardent supporters, was elected to the presidency on a platform remarkably similar to Goldwater's and succeeded in persuading Congress, including a Democratic House of Representatives, to act into law legislation that would have been politically inconceivable at any time during the previous fifty years.

The roots of this shift to the right are by now deeply imbedded in the political system, severely restricting the scope of choices available to either party, particularly to the Democratic party. Just as the shift to the left in public policy in the early 1960s resulted from fundamental alterations in the balance of power—ranging from rapid postwar economic growth, to the cohesiveness of the liberal-labor coalition, to the political vitality of the civil rights movement—the shift to the right over the past decade has resulted from complex, systemic alterations in the terms of the political and economic debate and in the power of those participating in the debate.

The election of a Democrat to the White House would inevitably slow the conservative initiative; forces pushing the national agenda to the right, however, will retain what amounts to veto power both over the scope of issues admitted to national political discourse and over congressional legislation likely to achieve victory. These conservative forces, as this book will explore, are not only within the Republican party, the right-wing ideological groups, and the business community but within the Democratic party itself. Not only are these forces present in all major elements of the political system; even with economic recovery, lowered inflation, declining unemployment, and growth in the gross national product, the shape of economic and political pressures on the electorate at large would appear to preclude, for at least the near future, the emergence of a consensus in support of a revived liberal agenda.

The genesis of this book lies, in part, in the experience of spending four long days and much of each of those nights covering the proceedings of the Senate Budget Committee in March 1981, in Room 6202 of the Russell Office Building. The Budget Committee was taking up the first major budget initiative of the administration of Ronald Reagan. Since I had taken my first newspaper job, in 1965 with the *Providence Journal,* I had reported on the political process at the county, city, state, and federal levels, as that process expanded to provide legal rights, medical care, workplace protection, integrated education, federal subsidies for those living below the poverty level, student loans, fair housing, programs to reduce hunger and malnutrition, and a variety of other regulatory and legislative benefits to the poor and to those at the margin of society. During those years, Congress enacted the Voting Rights Act of 1965, Medicare, Medicaid, the food stamp program, Supplemental Security Income, the Job Corps, VISTA, Head Start, the earned income tax credit, the Occupational Safety and Health Administration, the Environmental Protection Agency, Legal Aid, the Elementary and Secondary Education Act, the Model Cities Program, fair housing legislation, and the Community Action Program.

In less than a decade, however, the national consensus behind these programs began to crumble. The first strong evidence of this erosion became clear in the mid-1970s, while I was covering Capitol Hill for the Washington bureau of the *Baltimore Sun,* as Congress rejected legislation to create a consumer protection agency, election-day registration, a proposed major revision of the nation's labor laws, and 1978 tax reform legislation. What passed in those years instead was legislation cutting the tax rate on capital gains, a form of income limited almost entirely to the top 10 percent of the population—the first signal that Congress was preparing to abandon the use of tax legislation as a vehicle for the progressive redistribution of the tax burden. The election of November 1980 confirmed a major shift to the right, with the presidential victory of Ronald Reagan and the Republican take-over of the Senate.

It was not, however, until those days and nights in March 1981, two months after Reagan's inauguration, when I was covering the Senate Budget Committee, that the scope of the change in national public policy seemed apparent. The committee had before it the Reagan administration's proposal to cut government domestic spending by $48.6 billion. The cuts, eventually enacted into law, eliminated the entire public service jobs program, removed 400,000 persons from the food stamp program, eliminated the Social Security minimum benefit, and reduced or eliminated welfare and Medicaid benefits for the work-ing poor. Residents of public housing would be required to pay 30 percent of their income toward rent instead of 25 percent. A formula allowing welfare recipients with part-time jobs to retain a portion of their benefits as their income increased, providing an incentive to work, was eliminated. The cuts, in effect, chipped away at the margin of the most marginal incomes. Democrats on the Budget Committee com-plained bitterly. "We have undone thirty years of social legislation in three days," Senator Daniel Patrick Moynihan, Democrat of New York, told his colleagues on March 18. But on March 19, when the final vote of the committee was taken, the panel was unanimous in its support of the package of spending reductions, a unanimity that in-cluded Senator Moynihan; such liberal Democrats as Howard M. Met-zenbaum of Ohio and Donald W. Riegle, Jr., of Michigan; and Senator Gary Hart of Colorado, then plotting his long-shot bid for the presi-dency in 1984.

The full shape of the decade became apparent during the next five months when Congress enacted a $749 billion tax cut. I had moved to the *Washington Post* in July of 1981 and was assigned to cover Congress as it proceeded to abandon what had been a fifty-year-long tradition of tilting tax legislation toward those in the working and lower-middle classes; the Economic Recovery Tax Act of 1981 was the first reduction in individual tax rates since the 1920s that was skewed in favor of the rich. The legislation lowered the capital gains rate, sharply cut the top rate on unearned income, and shrank enormously the power of the sole provision in the tax code designed to restrict a concentration of wealth in the hands of the few, the inheritance tax. As the legislation passed the House, Thomas P. (Tip) O'Neill, Jr., one of the few remaining politicians whose roots remained firmly in the Democratic party of Franklin Delano Roosevelt, sat slumped in a chair far to the rear of the House floor. After twenty-eight years in the House, four of them as Speaker, O'Neill was procedurally and substantively powerless as legislation undermining half a century of Democratic party commitment to limited redistribution through the tax code was enacted. Unquestionably, the balance of power had changed.

The distribution of income and wealth in a democratic country goes to the heart of its political ethic, defining the basic contours of a nation's sense of justice and equity as it pursues economic growth, and determining how the benefits of growth, or the burdens of decline, will be shared by its citizens. In the United States, the issue was first formally posed, but not resolved, in the second paragraph of the Declaration of Independence: "We hold these Truths to be self-evident, that all Men are created equal, that they are endowed by their Creator with certain inalienable Rights, that among these are Life, Liberty, and the Pursuit of Happiness." Inherent in the concept of equality, stressed by the country's founders, is the basic question of income and wealth distribution, permeating political decisions for the past two centuries at every level of government. Not only Congress and the president deal with issues of far-reaching distributional consequence: a contemporary city council zoning decision permitting the creation of a shopping and restaurant area in a decaying urban center may increase the income of those holding the land, reduce the income of those operating corner stores and working in warehouses, dislocate the lives of existing poor residents, create new service industry employment, provide contracts for developers, and create from the commercial investors a new source of campaign contributions for the mayoral administration. At the federal level, the size and mix of domestic spending, the structure and distributional consequences of the tax system, and the permitted rate of growth in the money supply are central factors in determining the rate of inflation, the rate of unemployment, the rate of interest on borrowed money, and the proportion of families living below the poverty level, as well as of those living in great wealth.

Most significant governmental decisions have distributional out-comes—that is, governmental decisions alter the well-being and eco-nomic status of individual citizens, classes of citizens, categories of workers, geographic areas, sets of corporations, and racial and ethnic groups. In the making of governmental decisions, even when ideals of equality are among the desired objectives, a fundamental question arises again and again: how are ideals of equality to be achieved in law and policy? Who will benefit from the decision of the zoning board—the operator of the corner store, or the fast food franchise owner who will replace him? Does an inheritance tax restrict the equal rights of all families to acquire and pass on wealth and property from generation to generation, and the power that goes with wealth and property, or does such a tax reduce inequities in income and wealth, increasing the fairness of economic competition for each new generation? A decision on whether or not to regulate an industry determines the degree to which new competitors will be able to enter the marketplace, prices for the consumer, the quality and availability of goods produced by the industry, the health and safety of the workers and of the surrounding population, and the damage to the environment.

It is within the political process—in campaigns and elections at all levels of government, in debates and votes in the House and Senate, in the competition between political parties, in the power to determine the details of the federal budget, in the ideological convictions of those in office, in political appointments ranging from the judiciary to the regulatory commissions, in the leverage of private sector organizations, in the financing of elections, in the authority of the bureaucracy, and in innumerable other exercises of political strength—that these basic distributional issues are resolved.

Competition for control over the distribution of the benefits and burdens of government is central to the competition for control of government. Both Republicans and Democrats, for example, believe in economic growth; they disagree, however, as to the mechanisms through which to achieve growth, and as to the determination of who will profit and who will lose in the political processes surrounding economic growth.

The first five of the following six chapters attempt to describe how power has shifted over the past decade—both within the political parties themselves and within the broader context of the shifting leverage of major organizations attempting to influence government decisions. Chapters 1 and 2 examine the Democratic and Republican parties, exploring ways in which the power of the affluent has grown in both. In the case of the Democratic party, a constituency increasingly weighted toward those in the bottom third of the income distribution is in direct conflict with party and congressional reforms shifting power to those in the upper-middle class, a conflict exacerbated by the shift in the role of political parties away from voter mobilization and toward fundraising, and exacerbated as well by a system of politics dominated more heavily each year by television and by new computer-based technologies. For the Republican party, these changes have all coincided with, and reinforced, a GOP increasingly weighted toward the affluent. There has been a growing class and income-based distribution of voters, with the GOP attracting the more affluent and the Democrats attracting the poorer voters. However, the ability of the Democratic party to represent, in terms of enacted policy, the interests of its constituents has declined, while the ability of the Republican party to represent its supporters in this regard has grown rapidly.

Chapter 3 traces the rise in power and the increasing sophistication of the business community. Over the past decade, the community of corporate interests has achieved an unprecedented political mobilization, its members joining forces—in grass-roots lobbying efforts, in the funding of conservative intellectual institutions, in the financing of a broad spectrum of political campaigns, in the formation of ad hoc legislative lobbying coalitions, in the political organization of stock-holders and management-level personnel, and in de facto alliances with conservative, ideological groups—to convert what had been in 1974 an anti-business Democratic Congress into, by 1978, a probusiness Democratic Congress; and to change in general the terms of the national tax and spending debate, preparing the way for the election of Ronald Reagan and the sharp shift to the right in 1981.

Chapter 4 takes up the decline of organized labor that has paralleled the rising strength of the business community. During the past two decades, organized labor has continued to lose strength, both as the representative of men and women in the workforce, and as a political force in Congress and within the Democratic party. The growing weakness of organized labor, which can be traced back at least to the mid-1950s, sharply accelerated in the early-1970s, when big business abandoned what had generally been a cooperative relationship with labor, to challenge a completely unprepared trade union leadership, in the marketplace as well as in the legislative arena.

The fifth chapter describes in detail what have become increasingly class-skewed patterns in voting. The general decline in voter turnout between 1964 and 1980 was weighted heavily against those on the bottom half of the income distribution, increasing the voting disparity between rich and poor, to the political advantage of the rich. In turn, there has been a strong correlation between the growing class disparity in voting and the increasing conservatism of Congress.

The sixth and final chapter attempts to describe how the cumulative impact of these changes in the political system—and in the intellectual climate that provides a basis for the practice of politics—has been to contribute to an extraordinary alteration in economic policy, which produced, as a result of tax and budget legislation passed in 1981 and 1982, increased taxes and lost government benefits for every income group except for those making in excess of $75,000 a year. For a family earning over $200,000, the net gain over four years from this legislation has been about $17,000, largely in reduced taxes, while the marginal family making $8,000 to $13,500 a year—the working poor—had a net loss of just under $1,000 in lowered benefits and increased taxes over the same period. Transformations of the political system during the past decade have had extensive consequences, not only in terms of the distribution of the tax burden and of government benefits, but in the application of the federal regulatory system, in the extent of government intercession in the private marketplace, and in the negotiation of the difficult terrain between traditional American ideological commitments to equality and increasingly inequitable policy outcomes.

Perhaps most important of all, the adoption of recent government policies in a series of congressional decisions approved by members of both the Democratic and Republican parties has given political legitimacy to legislative and administrative initiatives undermining a relatively recent and fragile American tradition of government participation in the market system in order to protect those at the bottom of the income distribution and to encourage the advancement of those moving through the middle of the economic ladder.

1

The Democratic Party

The Party in Conflict

THE Democratic party has held majority status over the past two generations in large part because a majority of the American people have relied upon it to act as a forum for debate and resolution of the central issues before the country. The Democratic party has functioned, in the description of Samuel Lubell, as an energy-generating political sun: "Our political solar system, in short, has been characterized not by two equally competing suns, but by a sun and a moon. It is within the majority party that the issues of any day are fought out; while the minority party shines in reflected radiance of the heat thus generated. . . . As the party of the past, the Republicans have been ideally situated to attract all the voters who felt the Democratic majority had pushed too far, or who sought to evade the vexatious issues which have wracked the Democrats."[1]

This dominant status has been achieved in a uniquely American way. The Democratic party is not ideological, nor is it controlled by any single interest, such as trade unionism. The Democratic party has, rather, loosely functioned as the representative of those on the bottom half of the economic spectrum, while the Republican party has represented those on top. For the past two generations, the most exhaustive study of voter allegiance[2] shows that the Democratic party's strength has been among all demographic groups except upper-status northern white Anglo-Saxon Protestants. Catholics, blacks, Jews, poor, and lower-middle-class northern and southern Protestants have all provided Democratic pluralities. The details of this general outline have shifted significantly over the years, and partisan voting on the basis of class is much weaker than it was forty-five years ago, but the general outline remains constant into the present. After the 1980 election, an ABC exit poll of 9,341 voters found that the 16 percent of voters with incomes below $10,000 were split 53–40 in favor of Jimmy Carter, while those at the top of the income scale, making $30,000 or more, gave Ronald Reagan a 60–28 margin of support.[3] A more detailed regional analysis based on 12,782 voters by CBS/New York Times found Carter winning among voters making less than $15,000 a year, while among very well-to-do voters making more than $50,000 in the West and South Reagan's margin reached, respectively, 78–16 and 73–21. Similarly, during the 1982 congressional elections, extensive exit polls by all three networks, with sample sizes ranging from 5,785 voters to 24,438 voters, showed a steady increase in GOP support moving up the income ladder and the steady growth of Democratic support moving down the ladder. The findings by CBS, which were paralleled by ABC and NBC,[4] were:

Table 1.1 PERCENTAGE OF DEMOCRATIC AND REPUBLICAN VOTERS BY
INCOME CATEGORIES

	CBS	
Income	*Democratic*	*Republican*
Less than $10,000	70	28
$10,000–19,999	59	39
$20,000–29,999	59	40
$30,000–50,000	46	49
Over $50,000	36	64

Numerous forces, including both the major alterations of rules governing the Democratic party's presidential selection process, and the rise in real incomes throughout the 1950s and 1960s, have functioned to lessen over the past twenty years the strength of these economic divisions. But these divisions have deep historical roots within the two parties, and have significant consequences for the tactics each party has had to use to gain majorities on election day. Without competing ideologies along the lines of European political parties to act as a cohesive basis both for governing and for electoral support, American political parties, and the Democratic party in particular, have been forced to function as bargaining agents between often conflicting minority interests. The essence of Democratic party campaigning has been the struggle to forge a collection of minority interests into victory on election day. This coalition of minorities has included in its membership union members, Jews, city political organizations, most Catholic ethnic groups, blacks, southerners, and, in the most recent shift in voting patterns, women.

Although often unacknowledged, an underlying characteristic of all these groups has been a shared sense that each is outside of the mainstream, insofar as the mainstream has been defined in large part by that social group that is Republican, upper status, and white. Historically, the Democratic party's representation of those groups seeking entry into the mainstream has forced it to be the party challenging the economic, legal, and social status quo, while the Republican party has, in the main, been the defender of the status quo. White southerners, for example, were a vital part of the Democratic coalition for as long as the region was substantially poorer than the rest of the country, and before the civil rights movement turned many of these same white southern voters into proponents of the status quo and, in increasing numbers, into Republicans. Although women are not a minority, those who have switched to the Democratic party are those seeking both changes in the workplace and the intervention of government in their behalf.

For the Democratic party to win within this diverse and changing constituency, and within a narrow range of acceptable economic choices prohibiting challenges to liberal/free market tenets, requires a special brand of politics: the ability to make deals. In the pre-television era of politics, this meant that politicians first promised, during elections, to distribute the benefits of office to key support groups and then, if successful and trustworthy, to pass them out after victory. These benefits ranged from the appointment of postmasters in rural towns to the creation of Jewish and black seats on the Supreme Court; from granting labor veto power over National Labor Relations Board (NLRB) appointees to private assurances that defense contracts in factories within the districts of key congressional supporters would not be cut back.

While these kinds of commitments are characteristic of both parties, they are, for complex reasons, more important for the Democratic party, involving, as they do, the kind of wheeling and dealing essential to the conversion of a collection of minority factions into a working political coalition. It is this kind of politics that produced a steady transfer of jobs and power in major cities from Protestants of English ancestry to the Irish, Italians, Poles, and, most recently, to blacks. For all of its faults, for all of its inherent potential for corruption, for all of its use as a mechanism to keep political power out of the hands of the politically weak, it has been a vital element toward social change and economic mobility, providing an avenue first for a job and then for entry into the middle class for countless citizens who, without politics, would have remained on the margins.

Although present at every level of government, this redistributive function of politics is most apparent at the city and state level. What reformers have disparagingly called the spoils of politics have been stepping stones not just into menial, make-work jobs at the lower echelons of city and state government, but into all aspects of employment and production in the private sector.

From 1797 to 1903, to use the example of just one city, the mayors of Baltimore were men with names like Thorowgood Smith, George Stiles, Samuel Hinks, Robert T. Banks, and William Pinkney Whyte. As political power was held by this old-guard Anglo-Saxon establishment, the benefits of office went to the old-line banks, which held the city's interest-free deposits; to the established insurance companies, which bonded all construction work and provided coverage for all buildings; to the downtown architectural and engineering firms that designed the buildings and roads; and to the construction firms with ready access to bank financing. In Baltimore, as in the United States at large, status and economic power were not fixed as in a European class-stratified society. Nonetheless, control over both the private sector —partnerships in the prestigious law firms, executive positions in insurance companies, banks, and stock brokerage firms, management of the industries in Baltimore's port—and control over the public sector —the mayoralty and City Hall—were held by the same elite.

Shortly after the turn of the century, however, the names of the mayors of Baltimore began to change: McLane, Timanus, Mahool, Broening, McKeldin, Grady, D'Alesandro (Jr. and III), and Goodman. With the change in names came a steady change in the distribution of the benefits of office. Firms with the names Piracci, Frenkil, Flanigan, and Callahan began to dominate municipal and state construction and road work. Jewish, Italian, Irish, Polish, and, later, black architectural, engineering, law, and insurance firms began to get larger shares of both bid and nonbid contracts. The ethnic composition of the multitude of city and state regulatory boards—the Board of Barber Examiners, the Board of Examining Engineers, the Workmen's Compensation Commission, the Home Improvement Commission, the Bank Commission —changed with each administration, and with the changes came successive new sets of entrepreneurs, with different racial or ethnic backgrounds.

In certain respects, the political system at all levels of government functions as a backdoor antitrust mechanism, breaking up established power and allowing the entry of new groups into the political-economic system. Traditional Anglo-Saxon establishments in cities like Baltimore and Boston were by no means eliminated by changes in ethnic, class, or cultural origins of those holding political office, but old-guard control over profits derived from the political marketplace was substantially diluted. The ability to force the transfer of jobs, contracts, and a host of other government benefits from an established elite to a challenging group—Irish, Italian, Jewish, or black—is based on the wide discretionary powers of those in control of government. A housing inspector can treat the building code as a set of rigid regulations or as a set of general guidelines. Even under federal civil service merit requirements, a supervisor can write a job description to fit the résumé of a party loyalist. Political officials in agencies ranging in size from the Defense Department to a rural county board of supervisors have the power to decide whether the burden of unanticipated cost overruns should be borne by a contractor or treated as legitimate "extras" to be paid for by government. The award of almost all architectural and engineering contracts at the federal, state, and municipal levels is made on a nonbid basis. Selecting the location for a major construction project will determine, in many cases, whether it is built by union or by nonunion labor. The choice of appointees to the Justice Department, Securities Exchange Commission, Federal Trade Commission, and other executive and regulatory bodies significantly defines the rules of the marketplace.

At the federal level, the use of the discretionary power of political office to alter the economic balance of power is far more complex, severely restricted in some areas, while in others far broader than at the city or state level. In the case of the presidency of Lyndon B. Johnson, for example, the use and manipulation of the discretionary powers of government produced such diverse results as the appointment of Thurgood Marshall as the first black on the Supreme Court, and the less publicized conversion of Brown and Root from a minor Texas construction firm into an international corporate giant.[5] More than any other president since Franklin Delano Roosevelt, Ronald Reagan has consciously set out to use the federal government to alter the balance of power between labor and management through his appointments to the Department of Labor and to the National Labor Relations Board; through the weakening of the regulatory functions of the Occupational Safety and Health Administration (OSHA); and through cutbacks in unemployment benefits and public service jobs and in special assistance to those thrown out of work because of foreign competition.

Much of the source of presidential power rests in two areas. The president has the authority to define the scope and direction of federal spending through the presentation of a budget to Congress, which may in turn modify the budget proposal but which most often follows the general outline. Secondly, the president has the power to make key appointments throughout the executive branch, the judiciary, the system of regulatory agencies, and the Federal Reserve. Together, these and other executive powers can determine which cities get urban grants, which defense contractors get work, which complaints to the National Labor Relations Board are dismissed and which aggressively pursued, which mergers are challenged on antitrust grounds and which permitted. At the same time, the entrenched powers of Congress and of the bureaucracy, along with the highly sophisticated use of political influence by organized interest groups, place severe restrictions on the exercise of discretionary power by the president.

Congress, in this context, is not only the forum for the debate and resolution of national policy issues; it is also the arbiter in a host of marketplaces. It has guaranteed blacks 10 percent of the subcontracts on major mass transit projects; it has granted independent oil producers a tax advantage over major oil producers; it sets the terms for the competition between the three major television networks and such insurgent companies as Cable News Network; it can insulate industries as diverse as baseball and shipping from provisions of the antitrust code; congressional tax code decisions determine the relative costs of production by labor or machinery, while an increase in the foreign aid appropriation creates a larger marketplace for such firms as Caterpillar Tractor and TRW, which are assured customers under provisions of the law requiring foreign aid recipients to buy American products. The scope of this ability to influence the marketplace is reflected in the rules defining the jurisdiction of just one committee in the House of Representatives, Energy and Commerce, a jurisdiction that includes all interstate commerce, national energy policy, railroads, health care, television, and the network of telephone systems. These powers have made Energy and Commerce, along with the Ways and Means Committee, which has jurisdiction over tax and trade legislation, the two most sought-after committee assignments among junior members of the House.

Between Democrats and Republicans at all levels of government, there is a significant difference in the use and importance of the discretionary power of government. As the party that, in very general terms, has represented the bottom half of the economic spectrum, the Democratic party has been more dependent on using discretionary political power to alter the status quo in favor of its constituent groups. On matters of broad social policy, this process has resulted in Democratic advocacy of Section 7a of the National Recovery Act, affirming that "employees shall have the right to organize and bargain collectively," in the creation of the Social Security System in the 1930's, and of Medicare and civil rights legislation in the 1960s.

The achievement of a base of popular support for these broad social initiatives has required a special brand of parochial politics: the promise, implied or direct, of giving each constituent group appointments to key regulatory and policy-making positions—for example, to blacks, seats on the Civil Rights Commission and on the judicial bench; to labor, key posts in the Department of Labor and on the NLRB; to Jews, appointments ranging from a seat on the Supreme Court to influential posts within the State Department; to women, parity with men at the presidential nominating conventions and appointments to positions of power ranging from cabinet posts at the Departments of Housing and Urban Development, Commerce, and Education to seats on the federal bench; to big-city contractors with ties to local Democratic organizations, commitments to build regional offices and new branches of federal agencies outside of Washington.

In a number of respects, the Republican party has sought to undercut the Democrats in this political terrain with, for example, the appointment of women to the cabinet at the Department of Transportation, the Department of Health and Human Services, to the ambassadorship to the United Nations, and to the Supreme Court; and with the appointment of a black to the cabinet at the Department of Housing and Urban Development. The recent Republican appointment of minorities and women seems to have been motivated, however, more by tactical attempts to avoid alienating significant constituencies than by an attempt to construct a political party committed to the inclusion of groups outside of the mainstream of society, groups historically excluded from the politically determined distribution of economic benefits.

While the partisan differences then clearly are not absolute, Democrats have tended over a long period of time to open the marketplace up to new groups challenging the status quo, while Republicans have tended to protect the governmental marketplace for those who are already benefiting from the system. This Democratic bias has generally been in favor of individuals, groups, and businesses less equipped than others to capitalize on the inequities in the private sector—in some cases, for example, denied access to adequate bank financing and to other financial resources. Historically, the large demographic groups denied this access have been the Catholic ethnic groups—Irish, Italians, Poles—as well as Jews, blacks, and Hispanics. Each of these groups, before achieving middle-class status, has been a key component of the Democratic constituency. In this marketplace structure of government, a central distinguishing characteristic of Democrats and Republicans is the determination of what set of companies, individuals, and groups will profit most from government. This difference is more a tendency or a divergence in direction than a substantive, ideological division. Both parties have overwhelming ties to established institutions and interests in society, and both are dependent for victory on the receipt of broad support from the middle class. The Democratic party, facilitating the entry of its constituents into the middle class, can in no way be described as a party of social and economic insurgence.

Undermining of the Democratic Party

Over the past decade, a combination of self-imposed reforms, changes in the substance and style of political campaigns, economic stagnation, and a paralyzing conflict over strategies to be used to regain majority status have placed the Democratic party in a serious dilemma. Throughout the 1970s, a dominant theme of many political analysts and of a strong segment of the Democratic party was that the future lay with the middle class, particularly the once solidly Republican neighborhoods and districts that, in reponse to Watergate, to the rise of environmentalism, and to a disenchantment with the right-wing dominance of the GOP, had become prime targets for Democratic conversion.[6]

Proponents of this strategy found sustenance in the waves of freshmen Democrats elected to the House of Representatives in 1974 and 1976, many taking seats away from seemingly secure Republican incumbents. More recently, however, polls and analysis of the 1982 election results suggest that if there is a mechanism through which to regain ascendancy, it is through an expansion of the electorate, an expansion not into the middle and upper classes but among black and white poor, working and lower-middle-class voters. In 1982, for example, sharply increased black turnout in Chicago converted the Illinois gubernatorial contest from a GOP rout into a tight battle; in Texas, a massive outpouring of poor and working-class blacks, Hispanics, and whites cut a nascent Republican party off at its knees and resulted in an underdog Democrat, Mark White, winning the governorship by 231,933 votes.

In fact, as will soon be shown in more detail, there is a strong element of truth in both analyses: at one and the same time, the Democratic party is heavily weighted toward the poor and the working class, a base economically similar to that of the New Deal coalition; and it is stronger than the GOP in what used to be firmly Republican constituencies: among much of the upper-middle class, white-collar professionals, and the college educated. This strength among previously Republican constituencies is, however, very fragile, reflected in party allegiance but not in firm voting habits. Democratic strength is far more deeply rooted among those in the bottom third of the income distribution, voicing itself not only in party identification but in consistently strong Democratic voting majorities. This central class ambiguity has been a major factor in the inability of the Democratic party to develop a political strategy that serves the party's historical roots—a core allegiance to those in both the lower and middle classes struggling to move up the rungs of the economic ladder—while developing policies appropriate to contemporary economic complexities and to the interests of those already above the median income.

The difficulties of governing for any party in a stagnating economy, in a nation losing business to foreign competitors, are immense. But the Democratic party has, almost systematically, tied itself into knots just at a time when there has been a revival of intense conflict over the distribution of the costs and benefits of government, a battle the Republican party is singularly well equipped to fight; when pressures to shift the balance of power through the formulation of a national economic policy have intensified; and when the tax system, the fiscal core of an active federal government, is under severe attack. Not only is the Democratic party, whether or not it holds the presidency, and whether or not it holds a Senate majority, facing difficulties in staking out its own public stance, but, through accident and design, it has become vulnerable to almost the same political weaknesses that have debilitated the Republican party for fifty years: favoritism toward elites and the failure to function as a broadly representative party. The forces and developments contributing to this process grow out of a number of political and historical developments.

First, in Congress, the Democratic party in the mid-1970s initiated a series of reforms that transferred power to junior Democrats elected in the post-Watergate elections of 1974 and 1976. Many of these members of Congress won election in previously Republican districts, and their first priority was to prevent largely middle- and upper-middle-class voters from returning to the GOP fold. These congressmen had little or no interest in taking legislative steps to expand the electorate or, at a more controversial level, in strengthening the power of organized labor with the long-range goal of providing institutional support to Democratic voting blocks. Such actions and votes in behalf of blue-collar, lower-middle-class, and poor constituents have the potential to alienate just those voters that these members of Congress saw as most likely to bolt back into the Republican party.

Second, coinciding with, and preceding, congressional procedural reforms of the 1970s, the Democratic *party* itself undertook a series of political reforms that functioned to dilute and to weaken the power of nonelite groups, particularly of those voting groups that provide the strongest Democratic margins, including those with low incomes, those without college educations, and blacks. The requirement that states adopt either open primaries or highly regulated caucuses for the selection of delegates to the Democratic presidential conventions created systems for delegate selection that tilted the balance of party power toward an activist upper-middle class whose interests are often in direct opposition to the interests of less active, but larger, blocks of Democratic voters.

Third, two fundamental changes in the structure of politics have wounded the ability of the Democratic party to direct appeals to those minority voting blocks that together in the past have combined to give the party's candidates periodic election-day majorities. Television, and to a lesser extent the shifting role of the parties away from voter mobilization and toward fundraising, both function to restrict the effectiveness of campaigning directed toward specific voting groups: blacks, union members, leaders of urban political organizations, women, and ethnic groups such as Jews, Italians, Hispanics, and Poles. Without the ability to target specific groups, a television commercial directed at any one of these groups is, in fact, visible to all, and consequently can cost a candidate as many votes as it wins.

And fourth, the collection of scandals that fell under the general heading of Watergate all functioned to severely disrupt the national political process.[7] As Kevin P. Phillips has argued in his book *Post-Conservative America*,[8] Watergate may have halted what would have been the natural emergence of a Republican majority. For the Democrats, however, Watergate provided a false respite for a party under siege. Watergate provided the Democratic party with an electoral bonanza—Democrats in the mid-1970s won House majorities unprecedented since the 1964 Goldwater debacle and, before that, the 1936 election—while allowing the Democratic party to postpone addressing internal and external conflicts over both policy and political strategy, conflicts that blossomed into debilitating weaknesses by the end of the decade.

Together, these forces, developments, and postponed decisions combined to push the ideological midpoint of Congress toward the right, to facilitate the Republican victory of 1980, and to encourage the adoption of increasingly conservative economic policies by the administration and by Congress, beginning well before Ronald Reagan took office in 1981. These forces represent only an aspect of the nation's changing political structure, but their consequences extend beyond the outcome of elections and beyond individual contests for power in Congress and the executive branch. Working in tandem with other developments—the rise of the business lobby, the continuing decline of organized labor, a decline in voting participation among the poorer half of the electorate, the emergence of the South as a focal point for party competition, and the growing power of unrepresentative elites —these political developments have resoundingly echoed into the nation's economic policy.

Political and Economic Power

No matter which issues and theories dominate the economic debate —Keynesian or neo-Keynesian policies, monetarism, supply-side theory, capital formation, industrial policy, objectives of equity and efficiency—ultimately economic decisions are made by, and in behalf of, those who hold political power. A failure of economic policy sooner or later results in political defeat, but in the meantime the party that gains office will shape its policies to the benefit of those who have power within the party. A basic argument of this book is that the tenuous balance between elite control and broad representation critical to governing in this country has been distorted by a growth in the power of elites at the expense of the political and economic representation of larger groups. As politics and economic decisions are irrevocably linked, this distortion of the political process has had profound consequences for economic policy. Changes in the balance of political power not only affect who holds power but set the terms of the debate on such questions as the distributon and size of the tax burden; the scope of government commitment to education, welfare, military spending, public works, civil rights, and the administration of justice; and affect additionally the manipulation of the money supply, inflation, economic growth, employment, and interest rates.

The period after Watergate provides at least a starting point for an exploration of the intersection in Congress of political change and the formulation of economic policy. The first post-Watergate election in 1974 raised the Democratic margin in the House from 243–192 to 291–144 and in the Senate from 57–43 to 62–38. Both margins held firm through the 1976 election when the Democrats also won the presidency with Jimmy Carter. It was an extraordinary rebound for a party that had been on the ropes after the 1972 election, when the Democratic presidential nominee, George S. McGovern, carried only Massachusetts and the District of Columbia. Party strength in the House in 1975 was only four votes short of the majority Lyndon B. Johnson had in 1965 to push through legislative enactment of his Great Society program, and twenty-one votes short of the majority available to Franklin D. Roosevelt in 1933.

The Democratic strength of the mid-1970s did not, however, represent the kind of positive mandate that gave the party in 1964 and in 1932 the opportunity to alter substantially the relationship of government to society. Instead, the Democrats in control of Congress in 1975, and, by 1977, in control of the White House, were there in strength as a result of a powerful historical accident, Watergate and the political sea change that surounded it.

The evidence of internal rot within the Democratic party was, in fact, present on almost every front. In 1968, Alabama Governor George C. Wallace had won 9.9 million votes and 46 electoral votes in a display of the unwillingness of many white southern and working-class voters to support the Democratic party. Four years later, Richard Nixon had defeated George McGovern by 18 million votes, in a demonstration of the vulnerability of the Democratic coalition when the nominee represented the hybrid liberalism of the early 1970s. Organized labor, a core element of the Democratic party, had continued to lose its hold on the working man and woman, as the percentage of the workforce represented by unions fell by about a third of a percentage point each year after 1955. The Republican foothold in the South and Southwest had turned into a formidable beachhead, as the GOP's 1964 House victories in deep southern states held firm and as the Republican base expanded to include both senators from Oklahoma, a state known for its yellow-dog Democratic voters,[9] North Carolina and Virginia

Senate seats, and a total of nine House seats in such Democratic bastions as Mississippi, South Carolina, Arkansas, Texas, and Louisiana.

The Ambiguous Victories of Reform

THE fluke of Watergate and the temporary discrediting of the Republican party gave the Democratic party a unique set of choices, none exclusive of the other. The easiest was to take up the banner of procedural reform and to capitalize on public outrage over the legal transgressions and over the flagrant abuse of commonplace ethical standards that had characterized the Nixon administration.

In politics, the concept of reform can have many meanings. In this case, the two types of reform under examination are procedural reform and substantive reform. *Procedural* reform refers to the making of changes in the legislative or political process, usually with the intent of achieving some kind of ethical, moral, or at least behavioral improvement in the conduct of politicians. These include, earlier in this century, among many possible examples, strict rules for voter registration and off-year nonpartisan municipal elections, and, more recently, an expansion of the use of primaries, the imposition of ethics codes on public officials, regulation of campaign finance, and the reduction of the power of committee chairmen. Often, the goal of procedural reform is to reduce the power of politicians, although the goals often do not coincide with the results. *Substantive* reform usually involves an attempt to use government to correct a compelling social or economic problem and often involves the alteration of the relationship between government and citizen. Historically, laws prohibiting child labor, laws requiring the availability of public education, and laws setting minimum health and safety standards for food and housing are examples of substantive reform. More recently, such measures as the civil rights laws of the 1960s and Medicare were substantive reforms that now have widespread acceptance.

In 1974, the pursuit of procedural reform was an attractive political choice. After that year's election and in the wake of Watergate, however, there was a far more difficult choice available as well—substantive reform—that is, to attempt to use the power of majority control of Congress and, later, of the presidency to enact legislation designed both to strengthen the party's base among voters and to lessen the divisiveness that had emerged between such Democratic core constituencies as the poor and working class—a divisiveness arising over a combination of escalating tax burdens and a network of programs exclusively devoted to the poor.

The choice of specific legislation to relieve some of the pressure resulting from increasingly heavy taxes and from means-tested social programs was then, and is still now, highly controversial. Furthermore, it can be argued that a critically important step for the maintenance of a healthy Democratic party in the mid-1970s would have included legislation to strengthen the protections of both workers and unions in representation fights against hostile management. The importance of a healthy labor movement to the Democratic party is hard to overestimate. A second logical strategic step would have been legislation to expand the electorate and either to slow or to reverse the steady decline in voter turnout, a decline that cut away at Democratic votes and served as a boon for the GOP.[10]

A more complex question involved the two-tiered structure of social programs that had been enacted into law by the Democratic party over the past fifty years. On the first tier were programs perceived as beneficial to large segments of society, including much of the Democratic voting base. These included Social Security, unemployment compensation, Medicare, college scholarship and loan assistance—programs that provide assistance to a broad segment of society; and programs that alleviate temporary hardships, such as short-term job loss. The broadest of these programs is Social Security, which, as of 1979, provided benefits to 92.5 percent of those over sixty-five.

At the second tier were those social programs directed specifically toward the poor and toward those with the most marginal jobs—jobs paying, in 1983 dollars, a maximum wage of about $13,000 a year. These programs included food stamps, Supplemental Security Income, Aid to Families with Dependent Children (AFDC), and Medicaid. To a certain degree, the first tier of broad-based programs was created during the depression, and the second tier of programs, targeted toward the poor, was enacted under Lyndon Johnson's Great Society of the mid-1960s, but this distinction is not absolute.

The two-tiered structure of social programs has functioned in practice to divide working-class Democrats from poor Democrats and has exacerbated racial splits within the party. In 1980 the entire population of the United States was 11.7 percent black. The median black family income in 1980, however, was $12,674, or 57.9 percent of the median white family income, $21,904. This split became apparent in the distribution of benefits within the tier-two programs, those specifically directed toward the poor. Recipients of food stamps are 62.6 percent white and 35.1 percent black. For subsidized housing, the distribution is 58 percent white, 34.4 percent black; for Aid to Families with Dependent Children, 52.6 percent white, 43 percent black.[11]

The formulation of mechanisms to reduce the division between these two sets of programs, if not to integrate them, remains essential to the Democratic party if it is to lessen this conflict within its own constituency. Throughout the 1970s, a growing block of once-solid working-class Democratic voters, their party allegiance eroded by inflation, wage and work-rule concessions, and the threat of unemployment, no longer saw programs directed toward the poor as an integral part of the broad Democratic commitment but as a source of personal, social, and economic depletion. This conflict had its origins in the 1960s, when organized labor, particularly the construction trades, was under pressure from liberal politicians, the courts, and the Justice Department to open up its ranks to blacks. It was compounded by a collision of the lifestyles of the anti-war protestors with the burghers of Queens, N.Y.; Natick, Mass.; East Baltimore; South Philadelphia; Cicero, Ill.; and Lubbock, Tex. The conflict might have abated with the decline of the new left, except that the sustained economic growth of the 1960s came to a dead halt in the 1970s. The median family income—translated into 1981 dollars and accounting for inflation—grew from $17,259 in 1960 to $23,111 in 1970, an increase of $5,852, or 33.9 percent, in real, before tax dollars. The growth was felt through all income classes as the percentage of families making $10,000 or less (in 1981 constant dollars) fell from 24.3 percent in 1960 to 15.5 percent in 1970, while affluent families, those making $25,000 or more, grew from 24.7 percent to 44.2 percent. From 1970 to 1980, however, median family income grew, in 1981 dollars, by only $93, or 0.4 percent, from $23,111 to $23,204.[12] What had been a society of extensive income mobility in the 1960s became a society of income and economic stagnation in the 1970s. Such stagnation, in turn, eroded the fragile consensus behind Democratic domestic spending programs.

In the mid-1970s, historical circumstances created by Watergate permitted Democrats in Congress and in the White House to disregard schisms within the Democratic party constituency, as well as the declining bases of essential support, and to concentrate instead on procedural reform. The concentration on procedural reform not only resulted in a diversion of attention and energy from the substantial problems facing the party but created a network of new difficulties.

The reform agenda had strong appeal, especially to the two waves of House Democrats elected in 1974, when the party's freshman class numbered seventy-five, and in 1976, when there were forty-six Democratic newcomers. Procedural reform, unlike the advocacy of substantive legislation, is the terrain of the junior member, often providing immediate and direct access to newspaper and television coverage. It takes years of experience before a member of Congress begins to acquire increments of legislative power and is able to influence, for example, tax legislation or the revision of the criminal code. A demand, however, that Congress adopt an ethics code to prevent conflicts of interest, or that restrictions be placed on campaign contributions to prevent special interests from buying elections, provides, at moments of intense public concern with official malfeasance, access to news coverage in the home town press, sometimes in the national press, and occasionally, twenty seconds on the network news. Perhaps most important, advocacy of procedural reform, in contrast to participation in debates over the tax code, labor law, or welfare programs, alienates no important block of voters. For junior members intensely fearful of electoral challenge, the political safety of procedural reform makes it highly attractive.

A second, and parallel, element of congressional reform was the establishment in the early and mid-1970s of House rules weakening the power of committee chairmen, who had gained their posts through seniority. This was achieved by transferring much of their authority into the hands of a host of junior members through an expanded and strengthened subcommittee system. At the behest of reformers, the number of subcommittees was increased, but more significantly, members were prohibited from holding the chairmanship of more than one subcommittee; full committee chairmen lost the power to select the membership of subcommittees; and subcommittee jurisdiction was determined by the Democratic members, not the committee chairman. The effect of these changes was to grant new legislative power to the subcommittees and to spread the chairmanships of the subcommittees among many of the junior members. While a seemingly arcane element of the legislative process, this dispersion of authority to a host of subcommittees meant that the power to initiate legislation, to stop a proposal in its tracks, and to amend key provisions was distributed on a geometrically widening basis.

Before these reforms, the number and authority of subcommittees (with the major exception of the thirteen House Appropriations subcommittees) were such that the Congressional Directory for the first session of the Eighty-ninth Congress, 1965, did not list them. By the Ninety-fifth Congress in 1975, the directory listed 164 standing committees and subcommittees in the House and 149 in the Senate. Leadership had been spread so thin that all but two Democratic senators and half of the House members held committee or subcommittee chairmanships.[13]

Historically, the drive to weaken the powers of committee chairmen had its roots in the liberal wing of the Democratic party. During the late 1950s and early 1960s, this increasingly strong wing of the party repeatedly ran into a stone wall—autocratic chairmen who overruled House majorities to bottle up civil rights, health, and education legislation, such chairmen as Representative Howard W. (Judge) Smith, Democrat of Virginia, the arch-conservative chairman of the Rules Committee, who, for the decade from 1955 to 1964, singlehandedly stymied civil rights measures, aid to education, and other progressive initiatives. The conflict was between the more liberal national (or presidential) wing of the party and the entrenched southern conservative wing, which often aligned itself with the GOP.

In 1965, for example, the House voted to give the Speaker power to force legislation out of the conservative-dominated Rules Committee onto the House floor, if the majority of the House supported the action. This procedural rules change permitted the House, and ultimately Congress, to enact the Elementary and Secondary Education Act of 1965, and insured that the Voting Rights Act of 1965 and the creation of Medicare were not halted by a single House committee against the will of the majority. In 1969, the Democrats changed internal caucus rules to permit groups of Democratic representatives, and not just the leadership, to place items on the caucus agenda, increasing the possibility that House Democrats would take party positions on substantive issues. This change was key to the 1973 adoption of a House amendment calling for the withdrawal of U.S. military forces from Indochina, and, in 1975, in forcing a House floor vote on the oil depletion allowance.

By the time, however, the challenge to the chairmen reached full strength in 1975, when the Democratic caucus voted to unseat three aging chairmen—Wright Patman, 81, Banking and Currency; F. Edward Hebert, 73, Armed Services; and William R. Poage, 75, Agriculture—the politics of the House had changed markedly. Many of the arch-conservative southerners who had held an iron grip on the chairmanships had died, retired, or were about to retire, and the national, or liberal, wing of the Democratic party was on the ascendancy among committee chairman. In effect, even without reform, the seniority system itself was pushing the committee leadership of the House to the left, and only the remnants of the southern old guard remained. By 1977, fifteen of the twenty-two House committee chairmen had favorability ratings of 80 percent or more from the AFL-CIO, and all but two could be described as "national" Democrats. As a result, the reforms of the committee system led not to the transferring of power from a recalcitrant, conservative old guard to the party's liberal wing; rather, much of the transfer of power was away from the party's liberal elders who become, through seniority, eligible for chairmanships, to an ideologically mixed, if not confused, collection of junior members.

The goal of the earlier House reformers was, then, to change the rules to strengthen the power of the majority to take action on substantive legislation. By 1975 the goal of reformers had shifted away from enactment of substantive legislation. The new aim was to clean up government, to impose a system of ethical norms on elected officials, to require public disclosure of financial interests and of the source of all campaign contributions, to restrict the size of campaign contributions, to insure public access to official proceedings, and to accelerate the decentralization of power from committee chairmen to a host of new, and much more junior, subcommittee chairmen. These changes unquestionably increased public access to both the legislative and executive branches of government, although it is curious to note that there are still no representatives of the general-interest press and television at the overwhelming majority of congressional committee sessions. Instead, public access to these meetings is used primarily by lobbyists and publications catering to special-interest groups. Similarly, the Freedom of Information Act is used far more by corporations seeking to gain an advantage over, or information about, competitors than for the disclosure of governmental activity to the general public. Along the same lines, campaign reforms have made information on sources of political financial support more accessible, but, as chapters 2 and 3 will explore in more detail, these reforms have given institutional legitimacy to many of the practices reformers were struggling to restrict.

In some respects, the reforms of the 1970s strengthened the hand of the House Speaker, giving him control of the critically important Rules Committee, which sets the terms and timing of debate on the House floor, and considerable leverage within the Democratic Steering and Policy Committee, which proposes all committee assignments and nominates committee chairmen. With the accession in 1977 of Thomas P. (Tip) O'Neill, Jr., Democrat of Massachusetts, to the House Speakership, the combination of reforms diffusing power to junior committee members and strengthening the hand of the Speaker in theory presented the possibility of an alliance between a deeply experienced Boston-Irish politician knowledgeable in the ways of Washington and an energetic group of junior Democrats unafraid to challenge tradition.

In fact, however, the combination produced a deep tension. The junior members, dominated by their interest in procedural reform, correctly saw in O'Neill a politician with little or no interest in supporting their attacks on the institutional structure of the House of Representatives, particularly when those attacks resulted in the undermining of the ability of the House to enact legislation and, on a more personal level, when such attacks meant gutting the powers of friends, colleagues, and allies who had begun their congressional careers with O'Neill in the 1940s and 1950s. O'Neill's willingness to support a code of ethics, financial disclosure, and the like was based on a pragmatic need to shore up his own base of support among House Democrats and to contribute to the public perception of the Democrats as a party willing to keep its own house in order, in contrast to the momentarily discredited Republican party.

More important, O'Neill and the junior Democrats came from two separate generations whose experiences of the potential of politics to mobilize voters were different, if not antithetical. O'Neill not only came of political age in the depression when he developed a deeply rooted belief in the social obligations of government, but he had also seen, from the vantage point of political self-interest, what happened when working-class nonvoters began to go to the polls. In O'Neill's formative years—during his adolescence and his twenties—cities across the country went through an extraordinary transformation. From 1924, when he was twelve, to 1940, when he was twenty-eight, turnout in such cities as Camden, Cleveland, Akron, and St. Louis grew by 10 to 28 percentage points. Over the same period, the Democratic party went from minority to majority status, with margins of victory in 1940 approaching or exceeding two to one.[14]

In contrast, the experience of the young Democrats elected in 1974 and 1976 was markedly different. They had seen voter turnout steadily decline, dropping from 63.8 percent nationwide in 1964, when many were just starting their political careers, to 55.8 percent in 1976, a decline of 8 percentage points.[15] This decline reflected a steady lessening of Democratic voting power at the polls, halted only by Watergate. In this context, it is interesting to take for study the four Democratic members of the reform-minded classes of 1974 and 1976 who have subsequently emerged as leaders both in Congress and in the national debate: Representatives Norman Y. Mineta of California, Timothy E. Wirth of Colorado—both were elected in 1974—and Richard A. Gephardt of Missouri and Leon E. Panetta of California, both elected in 1976. Of the four, three were elected from suburban districts that had, until their elections, been represented by Republicans, and the fourth, Gephardt, represents the more conservative, white half of St. Louis and the suburbs to its south. None of the four represents a district that had experienced a surge among black voters during the civil rights movement in the 1960s: the percentage of blacks in these four districts in 1974 and 1976 ranged from 0 to 6 percent.[16]

In effect, the domination of Congress by the procedural reform agenda pitted two generations of Democrats against each other, rather than functioning to unite the party for the brief moment during which it had the votes to achieve substantive reform. The attitude of the junior Democrats toward O'Neill and toward the rest of the party's senior officials was reflected, in part, by a comment of Gephardt's in 1977: "You know, there is nothing the leadership can offer me, really nothing." In this atmosphere of defiance and distrust, the question of the two-tiered structure of social programs was neglected entirely, allowing it to become a major electoral liability by the latter half of the decade, when the combination of continued inflation and high unemployment—stagflation—laid the economic groundwork for a sustained Republican attack on Democratic spending programs for the poor. Legislation substantially reforming the nation's labor laws, a preliminary step in reviving organized labor, was allowed to die in 1978 in a Senate with sixty-one Democratic members when stalled by the filibuster of a freshman Republican, Orrin Hatch of Utah, supported by seventeen Democratic senators.[17] Legislation to permit voter registration on election day, which, short of registration initiated by government, is a key step toward an expanded electorate, was killed before it reached the House floor.

Just as power had shifted in Congress in the mid-1970s to junior Democratic members oriented toward suburban, middle-class concerns, and whose interest lay in procedural reform, not in substantial reform, power among the organizations influencing Congress also shifted. As the leverage of organized labor, civil rights groups, and such organizations as Americans for Democratic Action and the American Civil Liberties Union began to wane, Common Cause took center stage. Capitalizing on public reaction to Watergate, Common Cause[18] effectively set principal elements of the national agenda from 1974 through 1977. Within Congress, the reform organization successfully forced adoption of rules and legislation providing for a code of ethics, public disclosure of outside income, ceilings on earned income other than congressional salaries, and limitations on the receipt of honoraria. In the regulation of campaigns, Common Cause led the fight for public financing of presidential general elections and matching public money in presidential primary elections; limitations of $1,000 on the amount any individual could give to a candidate and $5,000 on the amount a political action committee could give to a candidate; and the creation of the Federal Election Commission (FEC) providing for extensive public access to contribution and spending records. The power of Common Cause to set the agenda at that time exceeded the power of any other organization, including that of both business and labor.

The emergence of Common Cause as the single most influential organization in the Congress of the mid-1970s was important primarily as a reflection of the changing allegiances of the Democratic party. Although the organization is technically nonpartisan, in fact it is far closer to the Democratic party than to the Republican party. At the same time, Common Cause is an organization identified with the upper-middle class. Supporters of Common Cause are generally far more affluent than the general population, with incomes averaging

$45,000 a year, and are highly educated, with an average of one year of postgraduate education, according to studies of their direct-mail supporters. With the waning of the civil rights and anti-war movements at the beginning of the 1970s, Common Cause provided an avenue for continued political participation by affluent whites, many of whom had been active in the presidential campaigns of Robert Kennedy and Eugene McCarthy in 1968, and of George McGovern in 1972. Although a part, and a significantly influential part, of the Democratic constituency, the views of Common Cause activists epitomize elite distrust of a basic element of politics, and of Democratic politics in particular: the bartering and trading of votes, favors, jobs, and other benefits, often behind closed doors, which make the negotiation and resolution of much larger issues possible, facilitating those compromises essential to the operation of government, particularly in the pluralistic, nonideological politics of the United States.

Although proponents of procedural reform have been a constant presence in the political debate, the key difference in the mid-1970s was that procedural reformers, principally Common Cause, briefly gained majority support, and succeeded in imposing their agenda on Congress. This assertion of power substantially undermined what had been a central, if unacknowledged, aspect of the Democratic party's system of governing. In this context, if government is, in large part, an economic marketplace with the two political parties competing over control of the distribution of benefits, then procedural reform takes on new meaning. A fundamental goal of procedural reform is the regulation of the political process to achieve such goals as technical efficiency; the elimination of favoritism; the establishment of a legislative process in which decisions are based on unbiased consideration of information publicly disclosed at open hearings; and the selection of employees and contractors on the basis of merit, price, and the quality of work, not because of political loyalty or campaign contributions. These goals, while clearly laudable in theory, make the assumption that a "neutral" political system is in fact neutral and will lead to increased equity, fairness, and representative distribution.

However, a political system "neutral" according to the definition and terms usually applied by procedural reformers will reinforce and affirm inequities in the private sector. At the municipal level, for example, a strictly enforced system of competitive bidding gives major advantage to the established paving contractor with ready access to bank financing at favorable rates over underfinanced competitors, whose lack of financial backing may be based as much on ethnic or racial prejudice as on merit, allowing the established firm to underbid contracts, absorb brief losses, and force competitors into bankruptcy. In a system where the established contractors have, in the main, been Republicans, while those challenging them have, in part, tied their futures to the Democratic party, procedural reform functions to protect Republican interests. The growth of the trade union movement in the 1930s would have been severely retarded without the enactment of laws granting labor organizations special treatment in the private market-place: the right of an employer in the free market to hire and fire was sharply restricted. A major part of the history of the Democratic party over the past fifty years has been the enactment of laws and the use of discretionary political power to alter accepted norms in the private sector in behalf of the party's political supporters.

It is this tradition of Democratic party governance that collides with the emergence, over the past decade, of the suburban/procedural reform wing of the Democratic party. This conflict surfaces not only in the distributive policies of the Democratic party once in office but in the style of Democratic party campaigning, and in the basic economic allegiance of the party to its supporters.

For the procedural reformer, the binding together of a collection of minorities through the piecemeal making of promises to groups as diverse as organized labor, small businessmen, blacks, urban ward leaders, teachers, family farmers, city contractors, and women reduces the political process to a system of special-interest bargaining. This brand of politics, in the view of the procedural reformer, results in corrupt forms of compromise and accommodation; the willingness to compromise, in turn, encourages the clouding of such critically important issues as abortion, the nuclear freeze, and the protection and preservation of the environment, and facilitates the suppression of principle in favor

of legislating on the basis of campaign contributions and the paying off
of political debts.

The Old Guard versus the New Class

THE economic consequences of the internal upheaval that had transferred party power to a more affluent, younger, professional, upwardly
mobile, and reform-minded class of Democrats did not become apparent until the latter part of the 1970s. This transfer of economic power
meshed with a generational split, and the conflicts between economic
groups and age groups are by now beginning to shape Democratic
presidential politics, as reflected in the struggle between Gary Hart and
Walter Mondale for the 1984 nomination. The roots of this upheaval,
however, lay in conflicts that dominated the 1960s. By the end of that
decade, the central conflict within the elite of the Democratic party was
between, on the one side, labor union and traditional political leaders,
epitomized by AFL-CIO president George Meany and Chicago Mayor
Richard Daley, and those who for lack of a better descriptive phrase
have been referred to as the new-class Democrats.

The leaders of the new class were those who had earned their
political spurs in the civil rights movement and later in the anti-war
movement, not in union halls or in Democratic clubhouses. The civil
rights movement had encouraged much of the labor movement—
particularly the white-dominated construction trades unions facing
court orders to admit more blacks into their ranks—to adopt a reac-
tionary, defensive posture. The subsequent anti-war movement compounded this trend, as an elderly generation of union members and
leaders whose international vision had been formed in the anti-communist heyday of the 1940s and 1950s saw in dress, language, and style of
the protesters against the Vietnam War, many of whom were first-
generation college-educated children of blue-collar workers, an intoler-
able challenge not only to patriotic values but to the family structure,
religion, ethical norms, and neighborhood stability.

Over the past twenty years, foreign policy has been a consistently divisive issue for the Democratic party, cutting diagonally across traditional economically based alliances. Détente with the Soviet Union, Vietnam, the invasion of Afghanistan, El Salvador, Nicaragua, Lebanon, Grenada, relations with Cuba, the neutron bomb, the MX missile, the B1 Bomber, the production of nerve gas—each of these issues has functioned to place such domestic liberals as Lane Kirkland of the AFL-CIO and the late Senator Henry M. Jackson of Washington on the far right of the Democratic party center on foreign policy issues —including, most recently, Tip O'Neill on the question of the initial deployment of American marines in Lebanon. Conversely, the anti-interventionist, anti-militaristic wing of the Democratic party consists of an amalgam of such domestic and foreign policy liberals as Senator Edward M. Kennedy of Massachusetts and Chris Dodd of Connecticut, with such lesser-known junior members of the House as Panetta and Gephardt, who have little interest in liberal domestic spending programs but whose suburban districts are wary of American military involvement abroad.

Equally divisive for the Democratic party during this period was the issue of court-ordered busing. Busing, more than any other issue, represented what was perceived as the imposition of social goals by a liberal elite on the white working class. The burden of school integration was carried by white and black city dwellers, while much of the elite remained insulated from the process, with children in overwhelmingly white suburban public school systems or in private schools.

The animosity between the old and new guard of the Democratic party was only peripherally economic, where there was a substantial conflict between proponents of economic growth and those seeking to protect the environment. Rather, the focus of the animosity was on social and cultural questions. A survey comparing the views in the early and mid-1970s of old-guard Democrats—those over fifty, in blue-collar jobs without college training—with new-class Democrats— those under forty, with college degrees and holding professional or managerial jobs—produced the following results. Of new-class Democrats, 73 percent favored abortions for a married woman who does not want more children, while only 32 percent of old-guard Democrats held this position. Among old-guard Democrats, 80 percent opposed extramarital sex and 89 percent opposed homosexuality, while only 38 and 27 percent of new-class Democrats were opposed to extramarital sex and homosexuality, respectively. Similarly sharp divisions were present on questions of divorce, racial intermarriage, and discrimination in the sale of housing.[19]

The animosity between these two groups of Democrats, the old guard and the new class, turned into open warfare at the 1968 Democratic convention in Chicago, in proceedings marked by abuses of political power within the convention hall and by abuses of police power in the streets of the city. It was a battle won by the old guard with the nomination of Hubert H. Humphrey and the defeat of Eugene McCarthy. In the November general election, however, Humphrey lost the popular vote by a margin of 500,000 votes out of 63 million cast. With the burden of defeat falling on the Democratic party's traditional wing, the new-class Democrats were able to take over the party machinery and to force approval of a set of reforms that radically shifted power within the Democratic party.[20] The Commission on Party Structure and Delegate Selection, which became known as the McGovern Commission after its chairman, Senator George S. McGovern (D–S. Dak.), was formed in February 1969. Its subsequent report was adopted by the Democratic National Committee in 1970, so that it set the rules for the 1972 convention.

The goals of the McGovern Commission were to prevent the denial of representation to major blocks of Democratic voters, not only to proponents, for example, of peace, but also to traditionally excluded groups—women, Hispanics, and blacks—and to insure that no one claiming to be a Democrat would be denied access to the Democratic presidential selection process. Underlying the commission report, however, was the implicit belief that political organizations, if left to their own devices, would deny democratic representation to those not favored by party leaders. The commission prohibited altogether the selection of convention delegates by closed-party caucus systems, which had been, until then, the most common mechanism of delegate selection, and prohibited as well "blind" delegate primaries. In blind presidential primaries, voters were given the power to choose the delegates to the convention, but the ballot gave no indication as to the presidential preference of those seeking to become delegates. The effect was to encourage the selection of well-known local leaders and politicians as delegates, who went to the convention free to vote for the presidential candidate of their choice. In many of these primaries, voters were able to cast a separate ballot reflecting their choice among the presidential nominees, but their decisions were not binding on the delegates.

The McGovern Commission reforms prohibited as well the practice of granting automatic, or ex-officio, delegate status to elected officials such as governors, senators, and members of Congress or to the party chairmen and national committee members; the discretionary power of state parties to appoint delegates was restricted, as well, to no more than 10 percent of the state's convention delegation, and even that 10 percent had to be picked under highly regulated procedures. In effect, the commission required that the states use either open primaries where voter choices are defined on the basis of the candidates for the presidential nomination, not by the competing delegates, or that they use open convention systems in which participation is accessible to any voter in the state claiming to be a member of the Democratic party.

There were a number of significant consequences to the McGovern Commission reforms. The first was the near-exclusion of Democrats elected to federal office from active participation in the presidential conventions. The percentage of Democratic senators serving as delegates or alternates fell from 68 in 1968 to 36 in 1972, to 18 in 1976 and to 14 in 1980; the percentage of incumbent House members participating fell from 39 to 15 percent from 1968 to 1972 and stayed there through 1980.[21]

At the same time, the explosion of primaries and caucuses functioned to weaken the ability of the Democratic party, and of its presidential candidates, to develop lasting coalitions. The incentive in a nomination system dominated by primaries is to form momentary factions in which the upper-middle-class voters who turn out in strength for primary elections are given disproportionately large roles. The primary system encourages presidential candidates to gear their campaigns toward an elite constituency significantly different from the general election constituency, and, if there are three or more serious candidates competing in a given state primary—or caucus—the first goal is not to gain a majority of the primary vote but a plurality. In other words, the primary system encourages candidates to seek support from a minority of a minority.

The political problems created by Democratic party reforms have been the subject of extensive analysis, not only in the press and in academia but within the party itself, which in turn has been struggling to at least partially reverse the thrust of the McGovern reforms and to restore a share of the nominating powers to elected and party officials. A succession of Democratic party commissions under the direction of Representative Barbara A. Mikulski of Baltimore in 1974, Michigan Democratic party chairman Morley A. Winograd in 1978, and North Carolina Governor James B. Hunt in 1982 has succeeded in increasing the leverage of party and elected officials at the conventions, although they will remain a distinct minority. Under the most recent changes, 10 percent of the delegate slots will go to Democratic officials in a process insuring that every party chairman and vice-chairman, up to three-fifths of the Democratic members of the House and Senate, and most large-city mayors and governors, will be able to serve as un-pledged delegates.

While the political consequences of the McGovern Commission reforms were quickly recognized, the economic consequences of the procedural reforms of both Congress and the Democratic party have been subject to far less examination. Perhaps the most significant consequence of the reforms was to create a new economic elite with much of the power to pick delegates to the Democratic presidential convention. Departing from a network of delegate systems dominated by state political party leaders, the McGovern Commission rules forced states to choose between open primaries or open conventions. Most states chose primaries. Those that already had primaries changed the rules according to McGovern Commission guidelines to restrict severely the number of local elected and party officials assured of becoming delegates. The number of primaries rose from seventeen in 1968 to twenty-three in 1972 to twenty-nine in 1976 and thirty-one in 1980.

The result of this shift was to establish a Democratic electorate in the presidential primaries that is radically different from the Democratic constituency in general elections. The extreme disparity between the Democratic primary and general electorates compounds one of the most severe problems facing the Democratic party: the class bias of voter turnout. If the increasingly low turnout levels in general elections are weakening the strength of less affluent, and more Democratic, voters, the turnout in primaries is even more class-skewed.

In terms of income and education, there is a sharp class disparity between the turnout in primaries and that in general elections, with the poor and the less educated turning out in primaries at rates significantly lower than those of the general election. Similarly, in the case of black voters, turnout in primary elections is far below that of general elections. The following table demonstrates the comparative primary and general election turnout pattern in the case of income.[22]

Table 1.2   PERCENTAGE OF DEMOCRATIC VOTERS IN PRIMARIES AND GENERAL ELECTIONS WHO EARN MORE THAN $20,000 A YEAR

State	Primary	General
California	35	23
Florida	26	16
Illinois	25	21
Indiana	17	11
Massachusetts	24	24
Michigan	16	17
New Hampshire	15	14
New Jersey	37	19
New York	32	16
Ohio	23	17
Oregon	15	23
Pennsylvania	20	9

In effect, the Democratic party promoted a system for the selection of delegates to the presidential convention that undercut in varying degrees the party's most loyal voting blocks. In primaries compared to general elections, the affluent are *over*represented by a margin of 41.8

percent, the better educated by a margin of 94 percent, and blacks are *under*represented by a margin of 35.6 percent.

This distortion of the party's own constituency was then translated into the income and class backgrounds of the delegates who go to Democratic conventions and cast the ballots for the presidential nominees. In 1972, the year in which the McGovern Commission reforms were to have opened the process to those who had been excluded from the exercise of political power in the past, power was in fact transferred to a new, and affluent, elite. In a *Washington Post* study of the economic background of the 1972 Democratic delegates,[23] 31 percent of the delegates had incomes exceeding $25,000 a year (the equivalent of $55,000 by 1983), while in the general population, persons this well off made up only 5 percent of the total. In other words, the well-to-do were *over*represented by slightly better than a 6 to 1 ratio. At the opposite end of the spectrum, those with incomes below $15,000 (the equivalent of $32,500 in 1982) made up 36 percent of the delegates, while 77 percent of the population were in this income range. The poor and middle class were *under*represented by a ratio of just over 2 to 1.

A significant class bias among delegates to both party conventions has been traditionally characteristic of conventions before and after the 1972 reforms.[24] The difference, however, is that the political marketplace in which the delegates were selected shifted from the party structure and leadership in all the states to an elite group of voters who turn out in disproportionately large numbers and who have no direct interest in seeking representation for political and economic goals that diverge from their own. In terms of income and status, there may be only slight differences between these two elites, but the political survival of party and elected officials depended at least in part on their ability to represent a broad cross-section of the Democratic party.

If political parties have always been organized and run by elites, then the question becomes: how representative an elite? The difference in the composition of the delegates before and after the McGovern reforms is reflected in the disparity between the views of the delegates and rank-and-file Democrats on economic and social issues. In 1956 the mean difference between the two groups when asked fourteen questions on domestic and foreign policy was 11.6 percentage points. In 1972, after the reforms, this difference rose to a 54.9 percentage point difference. In 1976 the difference fell to 31.4 percentage points but remained far above the pre-reform period.[25]

The result of these changes has been an indirect, but significant, shift in the kind of pressures felt by ambitious Democrats once in office. In the heart of all but the most crusty senior members of Congress lurks the thought that their party might one day select them for, if not the presidency, then, in a ticket-balancing move, for the vice-presidency.[26] As a consequence, these ambitious politicians are highly attuned to the presidential selection procedure, to the make-up of the electorate selecting delegates to the presidential convention, and to the interests of the delegates themselves. The ideology, class, and social status of the delegates and the demographics of the primary election electorate consequently play a substantial, if formally unacknowledged, role in the decisions made in Congress. This interrelationship is clearly present on the Republican side of the aisle in the Senate, where a number of essentially moderate but ambitious members have felt pressure to move to the political right to prevent alienating what has become an increasingly conservative body of convention delegates and activists.[27]

For the Democratic party, the policy-making effect of the changing delegate selection process has been more complex. At one level, it has probably helped to sustain support among the presidentially ambitious for a liberal stance on such social issues as abortion, school prayer, and the Equal Rights Amendment, despite the intense controversy within the electorate over these questions. The willingness to stick with these positions has undoubtedly been a factor in the growing support for the Democratic party among women. At an economic level, however, the shift to a more elite and affluent constituency in the delegate selection primary system weakens support for the interests of the working and lower-middle class in the formulation of tax legislation, for the maintenance of government benefits to the poor and to those in the lower tax brackets, and for a strengthening of the power of organized labor to expand its representation among service workers and other low-paid personnel. These are the groups that have lost leverage through the expansion of the primary system and the consequent intensification of class-skewed voting, and these are the groups that are least equipped to protect themselves in a time of federal budget cutbacks.

The Power of Ascendancy

In politics, and in the setting of economic policy, the absolute level of power—votes, money, public visibility—of a group, class, or special interest is not the only critical element in the ability to influence events. An equally important factor is whether the organization is ascendant or in decline. Organized labor, for example, is by any statistical standard a major force. In 1980, 22.49 million workers were members of labor organizations, and in the 1982 elections, organized labor gave $16.2 million to House and Senate candidates. Organized labor's ability to influence Congress, however, does not approach the leverage these figures would suggest. This results, in large part, from the fact that organized labor is on the wane, as its representation of the workforce declines by about a third of a percentage point a year, reaching a low of 23.6 percent in 1978, the lowest level since 1937.[28] Similarly, the power of blacks in Congress, whose political strength reached a high point in the 1960s as the civil rights movement produced a sharp increase in voting, has dropped steeply. The reasons for this decline are complex, but a contributing factor has been the changing shape of the black vote. In the North, the black vote has sharply declined from a high point in 1974. Most white Democratic congressmen for whom an alliance with blacks is politically possible are from the North, but, with the decline in black turnout, there is less pressure on these white Democrats to form such partnerships. In the North, voter turnout among whites in presidential elections fell from 74.6 percent in 1964 to 61.0 percent in 1980; for northern blacks during the same period, turnout fell from 72.0 percent to 52.8 percent, a far sharper decline. In the South, in contrast, the total vote turnout has effectively remained constant, with black turnout increasing slightly from 44 to 48.2 percent from 1964 to 1980, and white turnout declining, from 59.5 percent to 57.4 percent.[29] Two of the most significant variables for Democratic politics during the next decade will be the success or failure of efforts

to increase black voter turnout—and black political power—in both
the North and the South, through such presidential candidacies as that
of Jesse Jackson, through black candidates at the state and municipal
level, and through local voter registration drives; and the degree to
which organized labor can counter the decline in the strength of its
numbers with increased political participation in the Democratic presidential selection process and in increased participation in general election campaigns at all levels.

In this light, Democratic party reforms have functioned not only to
give disproportionate power to an elite group of Democratic voters
whose affluence and economic interests do not coincide with the majority of Democratic voters but have also granted ascendant status within
the party to this same group. This, in turn, has been translated into
disproportionate leverage over the making of policy. This leverage was
demonstrated in the power of the upper-middle/new-class Democrats
to set the reform agenda of the Democratic party in 1969 and 1970 and
to set the parallel Democratic reform agenda in Congress, particularly
in the mid-1970s.

The Democratic party reforms were by no means the sole cause of
the rising leverage within the party of its upper-middle-class wing. Of
the two parties, the Democrats were unquestionably more receptive to
both the anti-war and pro-environment movements, each of which
resulted in expanding the number of the relatively well-to-do within
the party's ranks. In addition, the relative economic decline of the
Northeast and Midwest created an entire region of the country more
sympathetic to the Democratic tradition of government intervention
and government subsidy, creating coalitions of geographic interests
cutting across class lines. At the same time, the general increase in the
nation's standard of living from the 1950s through the early 1970s
lessened the ties of the Democratic party to its traditional constituent
groups.

It is, however, dangerous to make the commonplace assumption that
since the entire electorate has become more middle-class, the Democratic party, which retains the nominal allegiance of a majority of
voters, is no longer the working-class-based party of New Deal coali-

tion days. This analysis, while superficially accurate, masks a series of highly complex and conflicting trends in the long-range make-up of the Democratic party.

There are two basic ways to look at the Democratic party, or at any political party. The first is to attempt to determine the demographic make-up of the party itself and the changes in the composition of the party over time. This approach asks, in effect, how persons who identify themselves as Democrats are distributed among different income groups, religions, socioeconomic classes, regions, types of employment, racial groups, and union and nonunion families, and how the distribution of Democrats among these various groups has changed. The second vantage point is to examine the Democratic party in terms of competitive strengths and weaknesses in comparison to the Republican party. Among the rich, poor, black, white, Protestants, Jews, Catholics, southerners, northerners, which party has a stronger base of support? For the purposes of this book, the key demographic groups are economic: principally groups defined by income and status, although other groupings—such as those by culture, gender, religion, attitudes toward race and toward war and peace—are clearly important.

The location of voters in the distribution of income goes to the heart of the politics of economic policy. The fundamental debate during consideration of every major tax bill centers on the allocation of the tax burden to different income groups. At the same time, income is the principal determinant of eligibility for such social programs as Aid to Families with Dependent Children, Medicaid, and food stamps; and proposals to reduce or increase spending for these programs often involve tightening or liberalizing the income restrictions. At both ends of the Social Security system—the taxes raised to finance the program, and the benefits distributed to elderly recipients—income determines the amount paid in taxes as well as the amount received in benefits.

For the Democratic party, changing income patterns over the past thirty years have been highly contradictory. Democrats, just like everyone else, have been the beneficiaries of real gains in earnings. From 1950 to 1980, the median family income, calculated in 1981 dollars, rose from $12,539 to $23,204, an increase of $10,665, or 85 percent, in real, spendable income.[30] At the same time, however, the distribution of Democratic support among different income groups has been changing, as the percentage of Democrats who are in the bottom third of the income distribution has grown, while the percentage from the top third has declined. The following table 1.3 traces the distribution of persons who identify themselves as Democrats among income groups for the period from 1952 through 1980. Voters have been divided into three income groups—the bottom, middle, and top thirds—and the periods covered are 1952–58, 1960–68, 1970–78, and, for the most recent trends available from these statistics, 1976–80. In the period from 1970 to 1978, for example, 35 percent of those who called themselves Democrats fell into the bottom third of the national income distribution; another 35 percent fell into the middle third of the national income distribution, and the remaining 30 percent fell into the top third.

Table 1.3 [31] THE DISTRIBUTION OF DEMOCRATS BY INCOME FROM 1952 TO 1980

Income group	1952–58	1960–68	1970–78	1976–80
Bottom third	34%	35%	35%	38%
Middle third	34	33	35	33
Top third	32	32	30	29

These figures suggest that what could be called the shape of the Democratic party is shifting toward those at the bottom of the income distribution. Over the three decades, the percentage advantage of the bottom third over the top third has grown from 2 percentage points to 9. This trend is supported not just when the Democratic party is looked at in terms of the distribution of its supporters among income groups but when the party's strength is compared to that of the Republican party within these same income groups. Table 1.4 compares the strength of the two parties in each income group for the same time period, with the first percentage figure showing Democratic allegiance and the second Republican allegiance, so that, for example, in the 1970s, among those in the bottom third identified with one party or the other, the Democratic to Republican margin was 69–31.

Table 1.4 [32]   DEMOCRATIC AND REPUBLICAN VOTER ALLEGIANCE AMONG
DIFFERENT INCOME GROUPS

Income group	1952–58	1960–68	1970–78	1976–80
Bottom third	64–36	66–34	69–31	71–29
Middle third	63–37	65–35	64–36	63–37
Top third	56–44	58–42	53–47	53–47

These figures show that over the past three decades, the percentage advantage of the Democratic party among voters in the bottom third has grown significantly, from 28 percentage points to 42 percentage points, while the Democratic edge in the top third has declined from 12 percentage points to 6 percentage points, as divisions in the middle have stayed roughly the same.

However, the figures in table 1.4 point to a central factor in the ideological ambiguity of the Democratic party. For the past thirty years the Democratic party has held a relatively consistent edge among all voters over the Republican party—53 percent to 33 percent.[33] The Democratic party is weighted toward those in the bottom third of the income distribution, and this trend appears to be growing, but the Democratic party, by the sheer weight of its numbers, simultaneously has an edge over the Republican party in each third of the income distribution. The Republican party gains a majority only in the upper reaches of the income distribution. A 1983 poll by the National Opinion Research Center of the University of Chicago shows, for example, that among the 80 percent of those surveyed with incomes below $35,000, Democrats outnumber Republicans by a margin of 65 to 35; but for the 20 percent of the sample with incomes above $35,000, Republicans outnumber Democrats by a margin of 58 to 42. Among the top 10 percent with incomes in excess of $50,000, the Republican margin grows to 69–31.

These dual characteristics, increasing dependence on support from the bottom third of the income distribution combined with continued diffuse support from all income groups, made the formulation of economic policy particularly difficult for the Democratic party in the mid- and late 1970s. This period was marked by a combination of high inflation, high unemployment, and a failure of the median income to grow. The lack of growth prevented the Democratic party from maintaining its traditional strategy of increasing benefits for the poor and working poor and providing tax breaks for other income groups while simultaneously receiving the indirect political benefits of rising real incomes in the private sector. By the mid- and late 1970s, this political-economic equation no longer worked.

This Democratic dilemma was compounded by the fact that the party had become increasingly dependent for support on groups that do not turn out well at election time, and by the fact that the high margin of voter self-identification with the Democratic party among the middle and upper-middle class does not translate into actual votes on election day. In 1980, for example, turnout among those making less than $10,000 was 34 percentage points below that among persons making more than $30,000. At the same time, those with incomes below $10,000 supported Democratic House candidates over Republicans by a margin of 64 to 36, while those making in excess of $30,000 voted Republican by a margin of 55 to 44.[34]

To summarize, then, the argument thus far, the increased leverage of an elite segment of the Democratic party grows in large part out of the changed rules of the Democratic party, and also from parallel developments in election turnout. Not only has the turnout in elections become increasingly class-skewed in favor of the affluent, but the growth in primaries has compounded the class skewing. In general elections, those with incomes above $20,000 comprised 17.5 percent of the electorate, but in primary elections this share grew to 23.8 percent. Similarly, the strength of those with college educations grew from 14.5 percent of the electorate in general elections to 27.1 percent in the primaries, while black voting strength fell from 15.1 percent to 10.2 percent.[35]

Altogether, the Democratic party of the 1970s was a pluralistic party with extensive, if often nominal, support among a wide range of income groups. It was, however, pushed into two divergent directions. In terms of voter allegiance, it was gaining strength among those in the bottom third of the income distribution; in terms of elite control, party rules and reforms had significantly magnified the power of the affluent and the well educated. For a party struggling to formulate economic policy at a time of severe strain, this combination was a formula for inaction.

The Policy Consequences

The reform-induced ascendancy of upper-middle/new-class Democrats within the party has been only a part of a series of changes, both within the party and within society at large, changes that contributed to Democratic decline in the late 1970s, culminating in the election of Ronald Reagan. Reforms, as pointed out earlier in this chapter, contributed to the distortion of the Democratic electorate through the proliferation of primaries, and encouraged Democratic elected officials to shift their attention to the concerns of the upper-middle-class segments of their constituencies. Following upon Watergate, the choice of issues for a Democratic party handed majority status in the middle of the 1970s was in the direction of least resistance: procedural reform. Such reform alienated no blocks of voters, including traditional bases of Democratic support; it provided a large group of young and aggressive Democrats in Congress with a vehicle for publicity and for the creation of an appearance of effectiveness; it briefly kept the focus of public attention on the central weakness of the Republican party at that time, corruption; and it met the standards of the party's new-class Democrats, who had wrested from old-line Democrats control of political clubs in cities and suburbs, from New York to Los Angeles, across the nation.

In turn, these developments in combination acted as disincentives for the Democratic party to address far more substantial problems, including an increasingly discontented working class that saw the average gross weekly earnings for production and nonsupervisory workers fall in 1977 dollars from $198.35 in 1973 to $172.74 in 1980;[36] including turnout patterns undermining the party's base of support; and including a growing inability to form a party consensus behind an economic strategy to counter the seemingly intractable combination of unemployment and inflation. The diversity of the Democratic party makes it particularly difficult for it to develop a working consensus on any issue, much less a broad economic policy. While reformism and the rules-induced ascendancy of upper-middle-class voters within the party have compounded this difficulty, these two developments have worked in tandem with two seemingly separate changes in the political system —the decline of traditional political organizations and the emergence of television—to erode further the strength of the Democratic party.

In sum, procedural reform, Watergate, and demographic changes over the past twenty years created an ascendant wing within the Democratic party of the mid- and late 1970s composed, in Congress, of a wave of junior Democrats who saw the preservation of their political futures in the firming up of support among suburban, middle-class constituencies. The strength of this congressional wing was buttressed by the ascendancy of upper-middle-class voters and by the delegates they sent to presidential conventions. In political terms, this left the Democratic party highly vulnerable to pressures from a business community that had been quietly but effectively mobilizing since 1973, when key corporate lobbying leaders recognized the weakness of business in the wake of disclosures of massive illegal corporate contributions to President Nixon's 1972 reelection campaign, in the wake of charges of bribery by U.S.-based multinational corporations of foreign officials, and in the wake of disclosure of the involvement of ITT in the overthrow of Salvador Allende, president of Chile.

In substantive terms, a Democratic party that conceded dominance to members and organizations placing first priority on upper-middle-class goals, goals often expressed through procedural reform, was unable to enact its own agenda. Not only were labor law revision and election-day registration killed, but consumer protection, common situs picketing (legislation giving construction unions power to shut down building sites), welfare reform, hospital cost containment, and national health insurance—all ended up on the cutting room floor. Nor was the Democratic party able to revise its agenda with the emergence and persistence of stagflation; it was caught instead in a form of legislative paralysis as the suburban-oriented wing of the House Democrats formed a de facto alliance with southern conservative Democrats in a frenetic effort to achieve a balanced budget before the 1980 election, while traditional elements of the party struggled to maintain support for programs benefiting their constituents.

By 1978 the pendulum had swung to the right: Congress, for the first time since the Democratic party achieved majority status in 1932, passed an individual tax cut in which the goal of income redistribution was effectively abandoned and the centerpiece of the legislation, a cut in capital gains rates, was targeted toward the upper-middle class and the rich. The 1978 tax bill presaged, well before the election of Ronald Reagan, the new direction in tax policy, which reached full force with the enactment of the 1981 tax bill. The passage of the 1978 tax bill marked a significant turning point: it was a demonstration of the fact that the flow of economic benefits from government is to those who have political power. The Ninety-fifth Congress (1977–78), with overwhelming Democratic majorities in both the House and the Senate, and with a Democrat in the White House, cut the top tax rate on capital gains, a form of income earned almost exclusively by the very rich, from 48 to 28 percent, while raising the Social Security tax, which, because it is applied to the first dollar earned but exempts entirely income in excess of $37,800 as of 1984, is the most regressive federal levy.

This shift in tax policy, along with the defeat of a host of liberal initiatives, resulted in part from the growing muscle of the business lobby but also from the changing balance of power within the Democratic party. The internal upheaval left the Democratic party in a weakened posture from which it could not mobilize its own forces on what amounted to an economic battleground, when the issues before Congress shifted from questions of procedural reform to taxation, labor law, wage policy, health insurance, the voting franchise, and the structure of social programs.

Most damaging for the Democratic party was not, however, its paralysis, which it had experienced before, nor even its losses in the 1980 election. The most devastating blow was more subtle: loss of the power to set the terms of the national debate. For fifty years, the Democratic party had been the arena in which economic and political questions were raised and resolved. From government programs designed to combat the depression, to the Marshall Plan, to the civil rights, anti-war, and environmental movements, and even to the national response to Watergate—all these issues and crises had been, in the main, fought out, debated, and, to the extent that they were resolved, resolved within the Democratic party. By the time of the 1980 election, the Democratic party had, at least momentarily, lost this centrality. A part of this loss can be attributed to reform-induced conflicts within the party, but only a part.

The following chapters will attempt to examine additional forces contributing to the deterioration of the Democratic party; to delineate a very different set of developments within the Republican party, particularly the circumstances leading to its new-found capacity to set the national legislative agenda; and to examine policy consequences, particularly in the politically determined distribution of economic benefits and burdens.

2

The Republican Party

The Rise of a New Elite:
Conservatives, Businessmen, and Party Regulars

DURING the past thirty years, the composition of the Republican party has been steadily changing. For a generation, the GOP has remained the party of the minority, holding the allegiance of a relatively consistent percentage of the electorate, ranging back and forth, since 1952, from 30 to 38 percent, and averaging about 33 percent.[1] At the same time, however, the make-up of this one-third of the electorate has changed, and the most important changes, in terms of the formulation of economic policy, have involved the conversion of the Republican party into a political instrument increasingly effective in the representation of the interests of an economic elite. Within the Democratic party, campaign fundraising, party rules, and the emergence of a dominant reform wing during the post-Watergate period have resulted in a disproportionate share of power going to an upper-middle-class, professional, highly educated, and relatively affluent elite, a distribution of power that has been at odds with the party's growing base of support among those in the bottom third of the income distribution. Within the Republican party, much of the traditional core of support remains, the cost-conscious, conservative-minded men and women of middle to moderate means representing the traditional social, cultural, and religious values of a large sector of the American population. At the top of the party, however, an alliance of conservative ideological leaders, corporate chief executive officers, sunbelt entrepreneurs, independent oilmen, and key representatives of Washington's business lobbying community has been gaining a broad and legitimate claim to power. Within the GOP, the affluent are not quite a majority, but they have become a strong plurality; they are strongly represented, and all the trends suggest that their influence will continue to grow.

The rising strength of an economic elite within the Republican party has already had enormous consequences in the formulation of economic policy. As the national legislative process has increasingly become adversarial, reflecting entrenched distributional conflicts between income groups, the GOP is far better equipped than the Democratic party to represent the interests of its most powerful constituent block, the affluent. As the core issues in the debate over tax legislation and over domestic social spending focus on which income groups are to receive lessened or enlarged tax burdens and which income groups are to receive larger or reduced government subsidies, the Republican party is prepared to enter the legislative battleground with far fewer internal conflicts than the Democratic party, and in a vastly better position to make choices when such choices require the economic success of one income group to be achieved at the expense of others.

The changing composition of the Republican party, which has been largely neglected as journalistic and academic attention has focused on the larger Democratic party, results from a host of demographic and economic factors. What support the GOP once had among blacks, for as long as the memory of the party of Abraham Lincoln lingered, has all but disappeared. The allegiance to the Republican party of poor and lower-middle-class whites in the North—marginal farmers, clerks, bus drivers, and teachers in small towns and in rural sections of the Midwest and of New England, with ties to the party dating back to the nineteenth century—has slowly eroded. Replacing these groups in Republican ranks have been well-to-do southern and southwestern whites, the more affluent Catholics, and a continuing strong base of support among the highest-status northern white Protestants. Table 2.1, taken from a detailed analysis of the changing composition of the two parties by John Petrocik, of the University of California at Los Angeles, traces the evolving make-up of the two parties, based on a series of voter surveys conducted in the 1950s and another set conducted in the 1970s. In the 1950s, for example, 10.1 percent of the Democratic electorate

Table 2.1 [2]   CHANGING DEMOGRAPHIC CHARACTERISTICS OF THE DEMOCRATIC AND REPUBLICAN PARTIES FROM THE 1950S TO THE 1970S

Groups	Demographics of the Democratic party		Demographics of the Republican party	
	1950s	1970s	1950s	1970s
White northern Protestants				
Very high status	1.4%	3.2%	9.0%	13.9%
Middle-high status	5.1	5.0	19.1	17.8
Lower status	7.4	8.9	18.7	14.7
White border south				
Middle-upper status	1.7	2.3	0.6	3.9
Lower status	2.9	4.6	3.1	3.2
White South				
Middle-upper status	9.0	5.6	1.4	5.0
Lower status	15.5	10.7	3.6	5.1
Immigrants from North to South	2.2	2.2	2.2	5.4
Catholics				
Polish and Irish	3.2	3.4	1.9	1.2
Other high status	2.1	4.0	2.4	5.3
Other middle and lower status	8.0	8.7	5.5	3.9
Jews	4.5	3.2	0.8	0.7
Blacks	10.1	16.2	4.9	2.4
Union members	22.0	19.4	18.0	13.2
Northern farmers	4.9	2.6	8.8	4.3
Total	100	100	100	100

were black; by the 1970s, this had grown to 16.2 percent. Similarly, very high-status white northern Protestants were 9.0 percent of the Republican electorate in the 1950s but grew to 13.9 percent by the 1970s.

Over this period, the general outline of each party has retained certain basic characteristics, but at the same time there have been substantial changes. The largest single group within the Republican party remains northern white Protestants, 46.8 percent of the GOP in the 1950s and 46.4 percent in the 1970s. The percentage of Democrats who are white southerners has fallen, while the proportion of Republicans who are white southerners has more than doubled, from 7.2 percent to 15.5 percent. If the Republican and Democratic parties are examined in terms of the status of their constituencies, strikingly divergent characteristics emerge. Within the Democratic party, the balance between upper- and lower-status supporters has remained about the same, while within the GOP, upper-status supporters have gained tremendous strength. If the following groups from table 2.1 are lumped together into the upper half of the status spectrum: "very high-status" and "middle- and high-status" white northern Protestants, "middle-upper-status" border South, "middle-high-status" and "immigrant" southerners (immigrants to the South tend to be affluent) and "other high-status" Catholics; and if "lower-status" white northern Protestants, border state whites, and southern whites, along with "other middle- and lower-status" Catholics, blacks, and union members are classified in the bottom half of the status spectrum, the following patterns emerge:

Table 2.2   CHANGING STATUS CHARACTERISTICS OF THE TWO PARTIES FROM THE 1950S TO THE 1970S

Status	Democrats		Republicans	
	1950s	*1970s*	*1950s*	*1970s*
Upper	21.5%	22.3%	34.7%	51.3%
Lower	65.9	68.5	53.8	42.5

In effect, the composition of the Democratic party measured in terms of status has remained about the same, while the Republican party has completed a remarkable shift: the proportion of Republicans who could be described as upper-status has grown from just over a third of the party in the 1950s to a majority of the party by the 1970s, as, during the affluent postwar years, the proportion of higher-status members of the electorate as a whole increased. The proportional increase in upper-status Republicans can also be seen when the Republican party is examined in terms of the distribution of Republican voters among the bottom, middle, and top thirds of the income distribution over the past thirty years. The following table is parallel to table 1.3 in chapter 1, which showed how the distribution of Democrats had gone from almost exactly even divisions among the top, middle, and bottom income groups in the 1950s to an increasingly bottom-heavy party by the late 1970s, with 38 percent of those identifying themselves as Democrats coming from the bottom third, while 29 percent come from the top third of the income distribution. In the case of the Republican party, the trend has been in precisely the opposite direction. In the 1950s, the Republican party was divided so that 29 percent of the Republicans were in the bottom third of the income distribution and 38 percent were in the top third of the income distribution. By the late 1970s, the party was divided so that 25 percent of Republicans were in the bottom third and 43 percent were in the top third.

In other words, reading the columns vertically, the percentage point difference between the proportion of Republicans in the top third of the income distribution and the bottom third has doubled from the

Table 2.3 [3]   DISTRIBUTION OF REPUBLICAN VOTERS BY INCOME GROUP, 1952–80

Income group	1952–58	1960–68	1970–78	1976–80
Bottom third	29%	30%	25%	25%
Middle third	33	30	32	32
Top third	38	40	42	43

1950s to the 1970s, from a 9 percentage point difference (29–38), to an 18 percentage point difference (25–43). By each of these measures, then, as shown in tables 2.1, 2.2, and 2.3, the Republican party has become increasingly representative of the well-to-do. In certain respects, these trends are significant political liabilities to the Republican party, functioning to affirm the widely held perception that the GOP is the party of big business and the rich. In the changed economic and political environment of the late 1970s and early 1980s, however, the growing class and ideological identification of the Republican party has produced advantages that, in many ways, compensate for its minority status.

The clearest advantages for the GOP are increasingly class-skewed voter turnout patterns in general elections, as well as turnout patterns that are even more favorable to the affluent in primary elections, both of which function to give the strongest Republican voters, the well-to-do, disproportionate weight at the polls. While the turnout patterns weaken the bottom-heavy characteristics of the Democratic electorate, they magnify the top-heavy characteristics of the Republican electorate. Additional advantages to the GOP stemming from an increasingly affluent constituency include: the ability of the Republican party structure—the Republican National, Senatorial, and Congressional committees—to raise vastly more money than their Democratic counterparts; the parallel ability of the GOP to make far more extensive and effective use of the expensive technology of politics, including television, polling, computerized information bases, and targeted direct mail; the ability of the GOP to compete effectively in the geographic area of most intense partisan conflict, the conservative South; and the ability of the GOP and its network of financial supporters to make significantly better tactical distribution of campaign money to candidates in key races that are won or lost by narrow margins.

The Republican-Conservative Nexus

An essential part of this ability to target money more effectively has been the increasing intersection throughout the last decade of the interests of the right-wing ideological community, the business community, and the Republican party. This conservative convergence or nexus has provided ideological coherence to what had previously been a disparate, and often conflicting, set of forces, and has provided financial backing for a shift in the balance of power in American politics.

While the Democratic party splintered, a network of generally conservative groups, interests, and organizations began in the mid- and late 1970s to coalesce around the Republican party. Such previously hostile and mutually suspicious groups as the corporate lobbying community; ideological right-wing organizations committed to a conservative set of social and cultural values; sunbelt entrepreneurial interests, particularly independent oil; a number of so-called neo-conservative or cold war intellectuals with hard-line views on defense and foreign policy issues who, although sometimes nominally Democratic, provide support for the politics and policies of the GOP; economists advocating radical alteration of the tax system, with tax preferences skewed toward corporations and the affluent—all of these groups found that the Republican party offered enough common ground for the formation of an alliance of both convenience and, frequently, shared interests.

Two key turning points in the process of Republican consolidation were the elections of 1976 and 1978. Before these elections, the two most important contributors to the revival of the Republican party, the right-wing ideological groups and much of the politically active wing of the business community, viewed each other as adversaries. To the business community, the social and cultural right wing was a fringe group, treacherously unsophisticated, and, as such, a political liability in Washington. The tiny faction of right-wing members of the House and Senate at the beginning of the 1970s, most notably Republican Representatives Robert E. Bauman of Maryland, John H. Rousselot of California, John M. Ashbrook of Ohio, and Senator Jesse A. Helms of North Carolina, claimed, at least rhetorically, to be as opposed to corporate subsidies and tax breaks as to food stamps and welfare. Close association with this group of activists ideologically committed to a vast curtailment of the entire federal enterprise, exempting from proposed budget cuts only the Pentagon, was seen by the business community as likely to result in severe reprisals, not only from the Democratic congressional majority but from key moderates in the Republican leadership. Business, in turn, was seen by the right wing as a fair-weather ally, likely under pressure to compromise principle for profit. Business, from the viewpoint of the right wing, was likely to abandon its opposition to federal spending if, for example, a Democratic jobs bill included special corporate tax breaks for job training.

The 1976 election increased the ranks of the Republican ideological right in the Senate, however, with the addition of two solidly conservative members, S.I. Hayakawa of California and Orrin G. Hatch of Utah, along with the only slightly more moderate Harrison H. Schmitt of New Mexico and Malcolm Wallop of Wyoming. Republicans remained a minority of thirty-eight in the Senate after the 1976 election, but the ideological center of gravity shifted significantly to the right. During the next two years—the Ninety-fifth Congress (1977–78)—the conservative Republican additions proved not only not to be a liability to business but a major advantage, as the legislation most opposed by the corporate lobbying community, labor law reform, was killed by a filibuster led by freshman senator Orrin Hatch.

The 1976 election had improved the icy relations between the right wing and business, but some conflict remained. The 1978 election provided the basis for a working alliance. In the 1978 election, the GOP gained ground in both the House and Senate, but the gains were not exceptional for a mid-term election—three seats in the Senate and sixteen seats in the House—leaving the Democrats with solid majorities in both branches of Congress. More significant was the election of three more arch-conservative Republican senators: William L. Armstrong of Colorado, Gordon J. Humphrey of New Hampshire, and Roger W. Jepsen of Iowa. In effect, the hard core of junior, ideologically committed conservative Republican senators had grown from a tiny faction of four in 1975—Jesse A. Helms of North Carolina, James A. McClure of Idaho, Paul Laxalt of Nevada, and Jake Garn of Utah—to eleven in 1979, effectively a major wing of the Senate's Republican membership, particularly when this wing combined forces, as it did routinely, with the GOP's old-guard conservatives, such as Strom Thurmond of South Carolina, Barry Goldwater of Arizona, and John Tower of Texas. The same pattern was emerging among Republicans in the House, where Republicans as a group were becoming more conservative, and where the elections of 1976 and 1978 increased the number of ideologically conservative Republicans by a total of twenty-eight members—an increase of eight in 1976 and an additional twenty in 1978.[4]

From the point of view of the politically active business community, these elections converted the right wing of the Republican party from a small and strategically insignificant minority into a substantial block of votes, of crucial importance if brought in on the side of business on such issues as the regulatory power of the Federal Trade Commission, the lowering of capital gains tax rates, and on most legislative conflicts over the relationship between management and labor. The election of two conservative Republican senators—Humphrey and Jepsen—was of particular significance. Humphrey and Jepsen demonstrated that it was possible to defeat seemingly entrenched Democrats, Thomas J. McIntyre of New Hampshire and Dick Clark of Iowa. Major elements of the business-political establishment, particularly the lobbyists and political strategists for many of the Fortune 500 companies, had come to accept as inevitable the presence of such liberal senators as Clark and McIntyre. The ideological right wing demonstrated the elective vulnerability of incumbent liberal Democrats.

At the same time, the business-political community was growing and changing in ways that facilitated accommodation with right-wing organizations. The growth in this community was toward the sunbelt, as the most active, aggressive, and conservative of the corporate leaders were the entrepreneurs and oilmen of the South, Southwest, and West. Leading this surge to the right within the business-political community have been officials of such companies as Flowers Industries, a major food producer, of Thomasville, Ga.; Milliken & Company of Spartansburg, S.C., one of the largest American textile companies; the Fluor Corporation of Irvine, Calif., an international contracting firm specializing in the development of oil fields, rigs, and related equipment;

Coors Brewery of Denver, Col.; and a network of political action committees (PACs) organized by independent oil entrepreneurs, including the Dallas Energy PAC and the Louisiana National Energy PAC. (PACs are committees set up by corporations, associations, labor unions, ideological organizations, or single-interest groups in order to channel campaign contributions to political candidates.)[5]

Simultaneously, influence within the Washington business lobbying community shifted away from the established lobbyists for such firms as Ford, Procter & Gamble, United States Steel Corporation, and General Motors. The specialty of the men who represented these firms in Washington had been to influence those already in office, both Democrats and Republicans. With memberships in Washington's exclusive clubs, and with highly developed contacts throughout both the executive and legislative branches, regardless of which party held office, these men had no interest in mounting a substantial challenge to, or attack upon, the system. Although most such old-line lobbyists are Republicans, they have traditionally been advocates of bipartisan campaign contributions. In the mid- and late 1970s, however, the ability of the old-line wing of the business lobbying establishment to determine political strategy within the entire business community began to wane. In its place has emerged a network of business advocates, many from the South and Southwest, whose goal has not been to work with those already in office but to replace liberal and moderate incumbents with conservatives.

A large network of corporate political action committees, trade associations, and industry groups, ranging from the Sheet Metal and Air Conditioning Contractors Association to the Business and Industry PAC (BIPAC), saw their political mission as the partisan and ideological conversion of Congress. In practical terms, this meant that a significant segment of industry became a de facto arm of the Republican party. In 1980 the Chamber of Commerce provided independent support to 180 candidates and opposed 34 others. Of the 180 candidates, 165, or 91.7 percent, were Republicans. Every one of the 34 candidates who was actively opposed by the Chamber was a Democrat.[6] In 1982 the ratio of money going from the Chamber to Republicans, compared to Chamber money going to Democrats, was 22 to 1, and almost all of the money going to Democrats was for conservative candidates running in solidly Democratic districts in primary elections against more liberal Democratic opponents—in other words, in districts where there was no chance of electing a Republican. Similarly, BIPAC supported Republicans exclusively in the general election of 1982. In the 1982 election, the Sheet Metal and Airconditioning Contractors gave $189,021 to Republicans and $52,026 to Democrats, with most of the money spent on Democrats targeted to supporters of the Reagan administration's budget and tax cuts.[7]

Overall, these changing patterns resulted in a general shift in the direction of business and trade association political money. In 1976 these groups evenly split their contributions between Democrats and Republicans, as the dominant purpose of campaign contributions was to purchase access to incumbents, not to effect a fundamental change in the composition of Congress itself. Late in the 1978 campaign, however, the flow of business money, and to a lesser extent the flow of trade association money, changed course. Of a total of $9.8 million donated by corporate PACs in the 1978 campaign, $6.1 million, or 62 percent, went to Republicans, and $3.6 million, or 37 percent, to Democrats. With each election cycle, the margin has continued to grow very slightly, while the total has grown very rapidly, making the overall discrepancy between Republican and Democratic receipts increasingly significant: in 1982 corporate PACs gave a total of $27.4 million, of which $18 million, or 66 percent, went to Republicans, and $9.4 million, or 34 percent—that is, only half of the amount going to Republicans—went to Democrats.

The Republican bias of the business community has been more than matched by the partisan bias of the right-wing ideological groups. In 1980 the National Conservative Political Action Committee (NCPAC) channeled $1.9 million in independent expenditures in favor of twelve candidates and $1.4 million in so-called negative campaigns directed against ten candidates. All twelve of the supported candidates were Republicans and nine of the ten opposed candidates were Democrats.[8] Two years later, in the 1982 elections, NCPAC spent $3.04 million in campaigns against eighteen members of the House, all of whom were Democrats, and against twenty candidates for Senate, seventeen of whom were Democrats.[9] In 1982 the Fund for a Conservative Majority spent a total of $119,577 on congressional races, of which $116,502, or 97.4 percent, went to Republican candidates.

In effect, the interests of much of the business community, and effectively the interests of all of the right-wing community, converged on the Republican party. The relatively small amount of money going from these groups to Democrats was almost entirely directed toward conservative, largely southern, Democrats, who were being rewarded for voting with the GOP on key issues before Congress. These Democrats included such representatives as Ralph Hall of Texas, Richard Shelby of Alabama, Sam Hall of Texas, Kent Hance of Texas, and Phil Gramm of Texas, who became a Republican in 1983.

The Power of Affluence

THE shifting pattern of campaign contributions has produced significant and complex consequences for the candidates of both parties, for the formal party structures of both the Democrats and the Republicans, and for the ideological coherence of each party. In this respect, it is important to consider the candidates of the two parties, the actual individuals running for office, separately from the party structures—the Republican and Democratic National committees, and the Republican and Democratic Senatorial and Congressional Campaign committees. In the case of the party structures, the growing domination of the GOP by the affluent and the increasingly strong ties between the GOP, the business community, and the ideological right wing have been major factors in the steadily growing financial advantage of the Republican party committees over the Democratic party committees, an advantage that reached a ratio of 5 to 1 by 1982. This advantage, $214.9 million for the GOP to $39 million for the Democratic party structure in the 1981–82 election cycle, or $175.9 million in favor of the Republican party, understates the difference in the financial situation of the two party structures.

The money received by the Democratic party structure barely covered the cost of staff, the provision of nominal assistance to candidates, office rentals, and the payment of past debts. The Republican party structure, in contrast, has been able to finance extensive polling; television advertising packaging and promoting both the party and its legislative program; a national staff whose function is to recruit, train, and support Republican candidates for office at every level; the purchase and development of increasingly sophisticated direct-mail lists; and the acquisition of computerized links to Senate and House campaigns across the country. A number of the pervasive consequences of the Republican advantage in party fundraising will be explored later in this chapter.

The situation of individual Democratic and Republican candidates is somewhat different. In the case of the individual candidates who run for office, and who receive only a small percentage of their support from the party structures, Republican candidates, as a *group,* on average, have no significant financial advantage over their Democratic opponents, as a *group,* when fundraising *totals* of the two groups of candidates are compared. Democratic candidates have been able to capitalize on a generation of control of Congress, on the power that goes with incumbency, and on strong backing from organized labor, so that when all Democratic candidates are considered, they have been able *in toto* to effectively match Republicans dollar for dollar.

This parity at the candidate level, however, masks far more significant differences for Democrats and Republicans in the allocation of money among marginal and safe seats, and among incumbents. The enormous war chests raised by powerful and safe Democrats obscure the underfinancing of many less well positioned candidates, particularly nonincumbent Democratic challengers. Additionally, the overall parity in fundraising masks the very different ideological and economic pressures placed on the candidates of each of the two parties as a result of the divergent sources of their campaign money. Finally, this rough overall parity at the candidate level masks the vast resources available to all Republican candidates from the Republican National, Senatorial, and Congressional committees, resources often not reported by the candidates themselves.

In the 1982 election, a total of 468 Democratic candidates for the House and Senate in the general election received an average of $333,-618 each, and 426 Republican candidates received an average of $340,-269 each, an insignificant difference of just $6,651 in favor of the GOP. In the House races, Republican general election candidates received an average of $230,241 while Democrats got an average of $215,921, a GOP advantage of just $14,320. Democratic senatorial candidates received considerably more than Republican senatorial candidates, an average of $1.89 million to $1.66 million. Figures for the senatorial races are skewed, however, by the contributions of $8.2 million from the personal fortunes of two Democratic candidates—Mark B. Dayton of Minnesota and Frank R. Lautenberg of New Jersey; and by the disproportionate number of incumbent Democrats up for reelection—nineteen, compared to the number of incumbent Republicans seeking reelection, eleven—since incumbency provides a major fundraising advantage. If these factors are accounted for, in senatorial contests the GOP would appear to have a modest edge.

When, however, the distribution of money between congressional candidates is examined more closely, a major difference between the two parties and the groups supporting them begins to emerge: while individual candidates for both parties receive about the same amount of financial support in total, the cash is put to far more effective use by Republicans. For example, 1980 was a year of high Democratic vulnerability, with both inflation and interest rates in double-digit figures, and with a weak candidate, Jimmy Carter, at the head of the ticket. In the House, twenty-five incumbent Democrats seeking reelection were defeated. In nineteen of those races, or 76 percent of the total, the challenging Republican was significantly better financed than the incumbent Democrat, despite all of the presumed financial advantages of incumbency. In two of the races, the Republican and Democratic candidates raised virtually the same amount of money, despite the fact that these two contests involved challenges to incumbents who were chairmen of major House committees—Al Ullman, Democratic chairman of the Ways and Means Committee, and Harold T. Johnson, Democratic chairman of the Public Works Committee. In all twenty-five of these races, Republicans raised a total of $9.7 million, compared to $7.2 million raised by the incumbent Democrats.[10]

In 1982 the general political situation was reversed, as the deepest recession since the Second World War, taking place under a Republican administration, made the GOP vulnerable. In that year, the Democrats gained twenty-six seats in the House. Twenty-one of these new seats were won by Democratic challengers beating incumbent Republicans, while the rest resulted from contests in open districts where the incumbent had retired or from contests where two incumbents were thrown together by redistricting. In the twenty-one contests where Democratic challengers beat Republican incumbents, the Democrats raised more money than the Republican incumbent in only four, or 19 percent, of the contests. In other words, the financial situation of successful Republican challengers in 1980 was the opposite of the financial situation of successful Democratic challengers in 1982. In 1980, when the momentum was with the GOP, 76 percent of the Republican party's successful challengers were able to back the momentum with more cash than their Democratic opponents. In 1982, when the tide shifted to the Democratic party, the party's successful challengers were able to outspend their incumbent Republican opponents in only 19 percent of the races. In these twenty-one 1982 races, the Democrats raised a total of $6.4 million, compared to $9.1 million raised by the Republicans.[11] These figures also fail to reflect the far more extensive technical and political support—provided all Republican candidates, particularly challengers, by the Republican Congressional Campaign Committee, much of which does not show up in the individual candidate reports of receipts and expenditures.

The financial contrast between the two parties is more striking when the strong 1982 Democratic challenges to GOP incumbents are examined. There were twenty-nine congressional contests where Democrats came within 10 percentage points (45–55 or closer) of victory but failed to win. In these twenty-nine races, the Republican incumbents outspent their Democratic challengers, by a ratio of 2 to 1—or $5.7 million spent by the Democrats and $11.1 million spent by the Republicans.

For the Republicans, money tends to go to incumbents who are in trouble and to challengers with a strong chance of winning a seat. For the Democrats, a disproportionate amount of money goes to safe incumbents, while those in need, particularly challengers who have none of the advantages of holding office, are shortchanged in the distribution of support. The difference in the pattern of contributions to the two parties results in part from the fact that the GOP has a base of supporters who see the GOP as integral to their own economic interests, or to their ideological interests, or to both. This base or network of supporters, which includes major elements of the business and right-wing ideological communities—along with such influential trade association PACs as the American Medical Association, the National Association of Realtors, the Associated General Contractors, the Chamber of Commerce, and BIPAC—is prepared to direct money for the purpose of maintaining and strengthening a conservative, pro-business Congress, which means, in over 90 percent of the contests, supporting Republicans in key races in which the outcome is up in the air. This network, combined with the extensive resources of the Republican party itself, encourages the use of money in elections to achieve broad partisan and ideological goals—ultimately majority control of Congress—and does not make its financial support contingent upon candidates making the kinds of specific promises that only incumbents are in a position to make to special-interest groups. At the same time, the Republican party structure is equipped both to cultivate and to direct supporters of the party, providing detailed assistance in the targeting of contributions to key, marginal races.

The Democratic party, in contrast to the Republican party, has become dependent upon a much more fragile rationale for financial support: incumbency. Both Democrats and Republicans in office can use their power and visibility to raise significant amounts of money. Part of the advantage of incumbency grows out of the automatic leverage held by members of the party in power. For twenty-six years, from 1955 to 1981, Democrats controlled both branches of Congress;

this control, in turn, forced the multitude of special interests whose economic success depended upon legislative decisions to support members of the party in power, no matter what the partisan inclinations of the special interest might, in unimpeded circumstances, be. This dependency of those interests seeking to influence legislation—the so-called special interests—was compounded by the congressional reforms of the early and mid-1970s expanding the number of subcommittees and increasing their legislative authority.

The most effective device for an incumbent in the raising of money is to have power over legislation affecting major economic interests. As an illustration of this, the two most sought-after committee assignments in the House are to the Ways and Means Committee and to the Energy and Commerce Committee.[12] These committees are attractive to any politician who wants to be at the center of legislative action; but membership also confers a guaranteed ability to raise large amounts of money for reelection campaigns. A listing of just part of the jurisdiction held by the Energy and Commerce Committee demonstrates some of the economic clout of the panel: 1) interstate and foreign commerce, 2) national energy policy, and measures relating to the exploration, production, storage, supply, marketing, pricing, and regulation of energy resources . . . as power, 3) railroads, including railroad labor, railroad retirement, and unemployment, 4) health and facilities and biomedical research.[13] The expansion and strengthening of the subcommittee system in the early and mid-1970s gave junior members the ability to use their subcommittee assignments, and, in many cases, their chairmanships, as bases for the raising of campaign money. The resulting ability of Democrats in office to raise money on their own significantly lessened internal pressure to establish fundraising capacities within the Democratic party, fundraising capacities to match, or approach, those of the Republican party structure. Without a well-financed and relatively independent party structure, there is no central force channeling money to those key races in which the Democratic candidate, in need of money, is a challenger, and without the advantages of incumbency.

From a tactical point of view, dependence of the Democratic party on incumbency has enormously distorting consequences. When the financial resources of all Democratic candidates are compared, the dependence on incumbency skews the flow of cash toward those who are not in danger of defeat and do not need the money, and away from those candidates for whom money could make the difference between victory and defeat. In 1982, forty-two Democrats won their elections by at least 80 percent of the vote but nonetheless raised in excess of $100,000 for their reelection drives. In contrast, only seven Republicans winning by similar margins raised more than $100,000 each. Dan Rostenkowski, Democrat of Illinois and chairman of the Ways and Means Committee, won with 83.4 percent of the vote in a Chicago district where a Republican stands no chance at all of victory; he raised $519,438. Wilbert Joseph "Billy" Tauzin and Charles E. "Buddy" Roemer, both Democrats of Louisiana, ran for reelection unopposed but raised, respectively, $415,797 and $480,173.

In contrast, in the absence of a highly effective, party-controlled fundraising apparatus, such as that available to Republican challengers, Democratic challengers attempting to defeat potentially vulnerable Republicans have access to no consistent base of financial support other than that provided by organized labor. Support from organized labor, however, can be an elective liability in many sections of the country, including the South and parts of the West and Midwest, where trade unions are viewed with deep suspicion by many voters. For Republican challengers, when the opportunity to defeat a Democratic incumbent, particularly a prominent and/or liberal incumbent, looks plausible, there is a large reservoir of party-directed cash to be tapped, just as there is in the case of an open seat. As a consequence, the Republican party is far better equipped financially than the Democratic party to capitalize on a period of weakness in the opposition.

The only political benefit to the Democratic party of dependence upon incumbency has been the party's ability to protect those incumbents who are in trouble. After the unexpected defeat in 1980 of such prominent House Democrats as Ways and Means Committee chairman Al Ullman, House Democratic whip John Brademas, senior Ways and Means Committee liberal James Corman, and Public Works Committee chairman Harold Johnson, incumbent Democrats demonstrated that they would not be caught unprepared again in the near future. In 1982 there were fifteen contests in which Democratic incumbents were in trouble, winning by 10 percentage points (55–45) or less in fourteen of the contests and losing the fifteenth. Unlike 1980, ten of the fifteen Democrats were able to outspend their Republican challengers; and in all fifteen cases, the incumbent Democrats were adequately financed, raising an average of $364,466 each, compared to an average of $315,133 raised by the Republican challeners.[14]

The inability of the Democratic party to capitalize on Republican vulnerability was most glaring in 1982. That year, a year when the state of the economy suggested the potential loss of forty-five or more House Republican seats,[15] the tactically effective distribution of money among Republican candidates was unquestionably a factor in keeping the losses to twenty-six seats. In Alabama's second district, for example, Republican Representative William L. Dickinson held onto his seat by the slim margin of 1,386 votes, winning by 83,290 to Democratic challenger Billy Joe Camp's 81,904; Dickinson raised $300,183 compared to Camp's $136,475. In a race of high symbolic importance, Democratic challenger Richard C. Bodine came within 3,912 votes of defeating John Hiler, the Republican congressman who had two years earlier defeated House Democratic whip John Brademas in Indiana's third district; Bodine, with 83,047 votes, raised $114,439 compared to Hiler, who won with 86,968 votes and $345,045. In the contest with the most national visibility, Democratic challenger G. Douglas Stephens won 48.4 percent of the vote in Illinois's eighteenth district, almost ending the twenty-six-year career of Robert H. Michel, the House minority leader. Stephens, who got 91,281 votes, raised a total of $174,556 compared to Michel, who got 97,406 votes, just 6,124 more than Stephens, while receiving contributions of $697,648, or $523,092 more than Stephens.[16]

In long-range terms, these partisan differences in contribution patterns suggest that whatever incremental gains and losses occur in open seats and in challenges to incumbents, they will be disproportionately favorable to the GOP, insofar as campaign money is the determining factor. Democrats, in effect, can raise money to protect the status quo, while Republicans can raise money to change it.

The more subtle, complex, and ideologically significant elements of campaign finance begin to emerge, however, when Democratic and Republican candidates are examined in terms of the sources of their support. Democrats and Republicans receive roughly the same total amount from political action committees. In 1982, House Democratic candidates averaged a total of $73,718 from PACs of all kinds, while House Republican candidates received an average of $64,630 from all PACs. In the Senate, Democratic candidates averaged $325,996 from PACs of all kinds, while Republican candidates averaged $329,876.[17] The overall pattern of partisan PAC receipts is shown in Table 2.4.

Table 2.4   DISTRIBUTION OF POLITICAL ACTION COMMITTEE MONEY IN HOUSE AND SENATE RACES IN THE 1981–82 ELECTION CYCLE BY PARTY[18]

Type of PAC	Total	Democrat	Republican
Corporate	$ 27,371,892	$ 9,384,166	$ 17,987,726
Associations	21,713,435	9,264,333	12,449,102
Labor	20,156,497	19,064,623	1,091,874

These figures suggest that for the candidates running for House and Senate seats, the differences between the two parties do *not* lie only in the total amount each receives. Rather, the differences center, first, on the incentives created by the differing sources of campaign contributions; and, secondly, on the distribution or allocation of money among incumbent and challenging candidates. In the case of Republican candidates for the House and Senate, money functions to encourage the development of a politically coherent conservative stance on matters of both economic and social policy. The ratio of corporate money to labor money going to Republicans is almost 18 to 1. This ratio increases when the money from trade and professional association PACs, most of which have a strong conservative bias, is factored in. The trade associations include the highly conservative organizations of independent oilmen; the National Association of Realtors; the Associated General Contractors; the American Medical Association; and the American Bankers Association. When the association PACs are added to the corporate side of the equation, the ratio of generally conservative PAC money to labor money going to Republicans becomes 30 to 1. When the money from conservative ideological groups is added to these figures, the financial strength of the right to the left, in terms of the sources of money going to Republican candidates, approaches 33 to 1.[19]

In direct contrast, the money going to Democratic House and Senate candidates encourages, indeed guarantees, ideological conflict. The ratio of labor money to corporate money going to Democratic candidates is just over two to one. But when the trade and professional association money going to Democrats is factored in on the corporate side, the Democratic party, in terms of the source of PAC contributions to its candidates, is split evenly right down the middle. The recent emergence of such liberal ideological PACs as the Fund for a Democratic Majority and Independent Action, Inc., which have contributed almost exclusively to Democrats, has tilted the Democratic balance slightly to the left, but only to a ratio of about 4 to 3 (Democratic candidates receiving $23.5 million from the labor/liberal side, and $18.6 million from the corporate/association side), compared to the 33 to 1 ratio of right to left in PAC campaign money among Republicans.

The ideological confusion within the Democratic party is, however, further compounded by the advantage the party has in receipts from two other smaller groups of PACs: cooperatives, and what are known as corporations "without stock," such as organizations of commodity dealers, law firms, and other incorporated professional groups. These PACs, from which Democrats running for Congress got $1.9 million in 1981–82, compared to $1.2 million for GOP candidates, are composed almost entirely of special-interest groups seeking specific legislative dispensation or protection, such as dairy organizations seeking continued, or raised, milk price supports, and commodity dealers who, during the 1981–82 election cycle, were fighting to preserve favorable tax treatment of commodity transactions.

From an ideological and economic point of view, then, campaign money for congressional races, insofar as it is reflected in PAC contributions, creates strikingly different incentives and pressures upon members of the two parties. For Republicans, the pressure is almost entirely from the economic and ideological right. A Republican candidate—with the exception of representatives of the remnants of what has been the Eastern establishment wing of the GOP, such as Senators Charles McC. Mathias, Jr., of Maryland and Robert Stafford of Vermont—has little or no chance of receiving significant support from labor or from liberal PACs. The kind of distribution of PAC contributions going to Republicans was reflected in part by the three leading recipients of PAC money in 1982, all of whom were Republicans: Pete Wilson of California, $1.2 million; David Durenberger of Minnesota, $1 million; and Orrin Hatch of Utah, $899,927. In each case, virtually all of their PAC money came from business, trade association, and health and conservative groups. Of the $3.1 million in PAC money raised by these three, they received from organized labor a combined total of just $38,842, or 1.2 percent, of their total PAC contributions.[20]

In contrast, for Democrats, particularly for Democratic senatorial candidates and senior House members, there are no clear or unambivalent pressures and incentives resulting from campaign support. The cases of the following Democrats, who in close battles in 1982 received significant amounts of money from both business and labor, are illustrative: based on reported receipts through October 12, 1982, George Mitchell of Maine received $161,997 from labor PACs and $107,850 from business PACs; John Melcher of Montana got $120,475 from labor and $122,050 from business; Quentin Burdick of North Dakota got $192,000 from labor and $111,827 from business; James Sasser of Tennessee received $199,350 from labor and $152,420 from business; Robert C. Byrd of West Virginia, got $213,500 from labor and $240,500 from business. For these senators, there are no conflict-free directives or incentives. In making a self-interested calculation on how to vote on a specific issue in committee or on the floor of the Senate, the only incentive created by campaign contributions is to avoid any issue that pits one major group or interest against another; in other words, for Democrats, campaign contributions constitute an incentive to inaction.

GOP Autonomy

The ability of the Republican party and of its candidates to raise money on the basis of coherent economic and ideological support, in contrast to much stronger dependence of the Democratic party and its candidates upon incumbency, has significant policy consequences. Since the Republican party is perceived in the corporate lobbying community as representing the broad interests of business as a class, as opposed to representing a collection of competing special interests, the Republican party has far more autonomy on specific legislative issues.

In 1982, for example, it was the Republican party in the Senate, not the House Democratic leadership, that took the initiative in enacting legislation raising and reforming taxes, particularly taxes on business, at a time when federal deficit projections reached new heights and when public anger at the mammoth tax breaks granted to the business community in 1981 was most intense. The Republican party was free to take these anti-business steps on lesser issues, without facing the prospect of retaliation in the form of withdrawn campaign contributions, because it has become the reliable representative of business on much larger issues, including passage of the 1981 tax cut bill, which lowered the effective tax rate on the profits from new investments to zero.

The fundamental depth of business loyalty to the GOP during the tax debate was demonstrated by the Associated General Contractors (AGC). On July 7, the regular newsletter of the AGC pointed out that the Senate Finance Committee had approved legislation restricting tax breaks in multi-year construction contracts by a vote of 13 to 7. The seven-member minority that had voted "for the Associated General Contractors' " position were all Democrats. The thirteen who voted "against [the] AGC position" included eleven Republicans. Two weeks later, however, the contractors association sent out a newsletter to members listing the ninety-four congressional candidates who had received money from the AGC during the week of July 14–20, of whom eighty-seven were Republicans. In other words, the contractor association's loyalty to the GOP far outweighed the organization's momentary anger at the partisan breakdown of the vote on a key tax issue. Similarly, during the debate over the 1981 tax cut, it was largely at the initiation of House Democrats that the chip in a bidding war between the Reagan administration and the Democratic leadership for the votes of conservative southern Democrats took the form of tax breaks for independent oil, ultimately producing tax reductions estimated in 1981 to be worth $11.8 billion over six years to the industry. The Democratic assistance to the industry did not, however, pay off, as, in terms of contributions, independent oil remained firmly in the GOP camp through the 1982 election. The Dallas Energy PAC, for example, gave $237,000 to GOP candidates and $7,000 to Democrats; the Louisiana Energy National PAC gave $228,500 to Republican candidates and $27,500 to Democrats; the Houston PAC gave Republicans $166,136 and Democrats $20,709.[21]

Party Strength

A key factor behind the ability of the GOP to make far better use of contributions to candidates is the emergence of a real Republican party structure, a structure vastly better financed than the Democratic party structure. Although the overall money going to candidates of both parties is relatively equal, there is an extraordinary disparity between the amount of money raised by the three major Republican party committees—the Republican National Committee (RNC), the Republican Senatorial Campaign Committee (RSCC), and the Republican Congressional Campaign Committee (RCCC)—and the money raised by their Democratic counterparts, the Democratic National, Congressional, and Senatorial committees (DNC, DCCC, DSCC). The consistent and growing disparity between money raised by the two parties themselves (as opposed to money raised by individual candidates) is shown in the following table.

Table 2.5 [22]   MONEY RAISED BY THE MAJOR COMMITTEES OF THE TWO
PARTIES—NOT INCLUDING MONEY RAISED BY INDIVIDUAL CANDIDATES FOR
OFFICE—OVER THREE ELECTION CYCLES

Election Cycle	Republican party fundraising	Democratic party fundraising	Democratic money as a percentage of GOP money
1977–78	$ 84.5 million	$25.4 million	30.1%
1979–80	169.5 million	37.2 million	21.9
1981–82	214.9 million	39.0 million	18.1

The ability to raise such large amounts of money has given the GOP the ability to guarantee both to Republican incumbents facing serious challenges and to all strong GOP challengers with a chance of victory the maximum party support allowed under law: $56,900 in the case of House candidates, and from $91,260 to $1.35 million in the case of Senate candidates, depending on the size and population of the state. Altogether, Republican candidates in 1982 received $19.8 million from the party committees, compared to $5.0 million received by Democratic candidates from their party committees.[23]

These figures, however, in no sense accurately reflect the full extent of the use of money by the Republican party. Taking just one of the Republican committees, the Republican National Committee, for 1981, an off-year when fundraising is generally at its lowest, extensive campaign expenditures were made. A total of $6 million went into political activities, providing campaign assistance to Republicans running for governorships, the Senate and the House, including $1 million for the successful New Jersey gubernatorial campaign of Thomas Kean. Another $1.32 million went to finance work at the state level on redistricting following the 1980 census—vital to Republican congressional interests—and, in California, to finance a petition drive to force a referendum on the majority Democratic party's redistricting plan. A total of $2.5 million was spent on a communications system, including a video satellite teleconference system permitting the party to hold meetings and seminars based in Washington but distributed throughout the country. The Republican National and Congressional Campaign committees joined forces to finance a $500,000 television advertising campaign in support of the 1981 tax cut and, later in 1981, spent $2.3 million for television commercials designed to give the GOP political credit for the tax cut. During this nonelection year, the RNC spent another $880,000 on national and state polling. In direct contrast, the Democratic National Committee in 1981 raised a total of $6.1 million —$27.4 million less than the GOP—and ended up $300,000 in the red. Of the $6.4 million spent by the Democratic committee, only $296,647 went to political activities, while $2.9 million was consumed by administrative expenses and $3.2 million was spent to pay the cost of fundraising. The enormous amount of money raised by the RNC permitted the Republican committee to spend $8.8 million on fundraising, more than the entire budget of the Democratic National Committee, and to significantly outspend the DNC on administration.[24]

The massive reservoirs of cash available to the GOP and its de facto alliance with a network of conservative and business groups have made it possible for the GOP to function with great effectiveness as a political party in the highly constricted terms of the present. The once-key role of the parties—the direct mobilization of voters—has all but disappeared. Gatherings on town squares and city commons, in political clubs and on whistle-stop tours have all become peripheral, important only insofar as they produce television coverage reaching mass audiences. The precinct lieutenant and the ward captain are no longer central or principal actors on election day. Instead, the political process, as far as the parties are concerned, is dominated by television and technology, which in turn means that the process is dominated by money. Money buys not only television and radio time but polls, newspaper clipping services, consultants, campaign managers, computers, computer lists, computerized mailings, the production of radio and television commercials, and the services of fundraisers to get more money.

The Republican party and its core base of supporters are equipped, well before candidates even get into a race, to conduct what amounts to constant surveillance and evaluation of each party's strengths and weaknesses in districts and states across the country. "There is a coordinated passing around of polling information between Republican committees, candidates, groups like ours and the corporate PACs," Paul Dietrich, chairman of the Fund for a Conservative Majority, said, in describing part of the process. In addition to the capacity to identify marginal districts and states, the huge financial advantage enjoyed by the Republican party permits it to assign full-time staff to the recruitment and training of new candidates, to set up computerized relations with every Republican candidate so that the office-seeker can be immediately informed on all specific legislation before Congress—how an opponent has voted minutes after a tally has been completed—and can receive on a daily basis speeches and press releases geared to events of the moment. The cash-laden RNC, RCCC, and RSCC permit these GOP committees to initiate television campaigns designed to be compatible with the party-determined general theme of a campaign year, such as "Vote Republican for a Change," the slogan of 1980; "Stay the Course," the slogan of 1982; and the highly effective television characterizations of House Speaker Thomas P. (Tip) O'Neill driving a car (symbolizing the federal government) until it ran out of gas.

Early Money

Three groups—the Republican party, the conservative PACs, and the entrepreneurs involved in the exploration for and production of independent oil—have been particularly aggressive in the recruitment of new congressional candidates and have been willing, in the case of good prospects, to guarantee early financial support. "If money talks," the Independent Petroleum Association has told independent oilmen, then "early money shouts." Beginning in 1978, and gaining strength in 1980, a network of a dozen independent oil PACs in the sunbelt and oil-rich states of Texas, Oklahoma, Louisiana, New Mexico, and Colorado began to seek out candidates running against incumbent Democrats and to provide them with the money to get their campaigns off the ground.

The scope of money available to a strong Republican challenge was demonstrated in the 1980 Senate campaign of Steven D. Symms, Republican of Idaho, against Senator Frank Church, the four-term, liberal Democratic incumbent. At the start of 1980, the Symms campaign had just $32,061 in the bank. During the next three months, the Symms campaign raised a total of $360,829. Of this, $154,000 was from Texas interests alone, almost all of it raised on a two-day swing through the state. During the first five months of 1982, well before most PACs get involved in elections, the Dallas Energy PAC, which is made up primarily of independent oilmen, had distributed $71,000, all of it to Republicans, and all in amounts of $2,000 to $5,000, the maximum a PAC can give to a candidate. In the critical early stages of elections, when technological costs (polling, consultant and fundraising fees, and preliminary television) require up-front cash, a prospective Republican candidate can receive the financial support not only of the party itself but of an allied set of business and conservative groups.[25]

Television

At the same time, the emergence of television as the central vehicle for campaigning and as a central force in the legislative process has in several ways proved far more advantageous to Republican interests than to Democratic interests. One of the greatest advantages to the Republican coalition has been the way in which television undermines the traditional political strategy of the Democratic party, a strategy of central importance to the Democrats since the formation of the New Deal coalition: the forging of a collection of minorities into an election-day majority. This kind of political strategy requires a candidate to direct campaign activities toward very different, and often conflicting, groups: blacks, conservative white southerners, environmentalists, Jews, the elderly, working women, the poor, courthouse politicians, liberal academics, housewives, suburban reformers, blue-collar homeowners seeking to control crime, and civil libertarians. Television campaigning directed specifically to any of these groups is difficult, since what is directed toward one group may be seen by all.

This universality of access to what have been traditionally sheltered or "hidden" communications makes every political message a potential political liability. Unlike pretelevision campaigning, when a politician could move from union hall to black church to nursing home to City Hall and adjust the content of his remarks to the group of the moment, television permits no such campaign targeting. For example, an attempt to appeal specifically to union members is likely to alienate as many votes among small-business owners and consumers worried about the wage-price spiral as it gains among card-carrying steel and auto workers. Television precludes the kind of campaign that emerges out of a collection of appeals to the various elements of the Democratic constituency, forcing, instead, a style of presentation appealing to an undifferentiated viewing audience.

There are additional ways in which television has functioned to push politics to the right. Such observers of the interrelationship between television news and public political perception as Austin Ranney and Michael J. Robinson[26] have argued on the basis of survey data that the brevity of television news—combined with its concentration on conflict between political personalities rather than on the substantive exploration of issues—has been a major factor in the growing public distrust of government. "Those who rely upon television in following politics are more confused and more cynical than those who do not. And those who rely totally upon television are the most confused and cynical of all," Robinson wrote.[27] This confusion and cynicism, however, is most heavily concentrated among the poor, the least educated, and those with the lowest-status jobs, just those voters upon whom the Democratic party depends for support and who are key to Democratic efforts to maintain public support for government intervention in the domestic economy. Taking this argument a step further, Ranney suggests that the cynicism and confusion generated by television have been contributing factors in both the declining level of confidence in government and in the decline in voter turnout.[28] If so, television has contributed to two trends both of which have been seriously damaging to the political left. The declining confidence in government has been a major basis for conservative attacks upon the federal government; and the decline in voter turnout has had a strong class bias in favor of the affluent.

Perhaps the most important political consequence of television, however, is the way in which it has shifted the dominant role of political parties to fundraising. The total cost of all House and Senate races grew by 74 percent in the four years from 1978 to 1982, from $197 million to $343 million. There have been no complete studies of precisely how this money has been spent, but the *National Journal,* in a sampling of 1982 races, found House members spending in the neighborhood of 25 to 30 percent of their budgets on advertising, and a far higher percentage, often in excess of 50 percent, being spent by Senate candidates. The *National Journal* estimated that the total cost for candidates at both the federal and local levels of television, radio and newspaper advertising, direct mail, and polling reached $285 million in 1982. For example, the 1982 reelection campaign of Richard Lugar, Republican of Indiana, cost $3.2 million through election day. The largest single expenditure, $1,593 million, was for advertising, of which 85 percent, or $1.35 million, went to television. In contrast, only $83,000 was spent on political meetings and campaign paraphernalia, the kind of expenditures associated with pretelevision campaigning. Similarly, Jerry Brown spent $3.9 million out of a total of $5.3 million on advertising, almost all of it on television, in his 1982 losing effort to become a senator from California, while the winner, Pete Wilson, spent $4 million on advertising, primarily on television, out of a $6.97 million campaign budget.[29]

The shift toward campaigns dominated by television and the parallel increase in the importance of fundraising have overshadowed the decline of the traditional political organization. Although present in both parties, clubs and machines were strongest in the cities, and consequently were most important to the urbanized Democratic party. In 1952, for example, the chairman of the Pittsburgh Republican Executive Committee, Thomas E. Whitten, told a congressional committee that Republican money could not stand up to Democratic political organizations: "Consistently over the years the Republican expenditures in Allegheny County [Pittsburgh] have been substantially greater than those of the Democrats, but to show you that money has had little effect . . . we lost the county in 1932 by about 37,000 [votes]; we lost in 1936 by 190,000; we lost in 1940 by 110,000; we lost in 1944 by about 105,000; and we lost in 1948 by slightly under 80,000. . . . Actually the amount of money spent in the past did not influence it."[30]

Urban Democratic organizations ranged from such well-known groups as Tammany Hall in New York to such smaller factions as the Stonewall Democratic Club in southwest Baltimore. In their day, these organizations wielded leverage at the polls within their jurisdiction that could not be challenged by candidates using, for example, radio or newspapers to win voter support for any office from city councilman to U.S. Senator. Combined with a union movement that grew steadily from 1932 to the mid-1950s, such organizations provided a consistent base of support for the Democratic party. By the 1950s and 1960s, the strength of city political organizations was on the wane, but their relative vitality was a major factor in the Democratic party's ability, until recently, to more than cope with what has been a consistent Republican fundraising advantage equal to or stronger than its advantage now.[31] Currently, such local clubs remain critically influential only in the most parochial of elections, for state legislature or city council, and in the large majority of cities even these offices are no longer under the firm control of locally based organizations.

The shift from traditional voter mobilization and from party organization work at the ward and precinct level toward fundraising and television-based campaigning has changed the terrain of battle for the two parties. People who contribute to political campaigns and to political parties are significantly richer than the average voter; the universe of contributors is, in terms of income, a top-heavy inversion of the Democratic party's general constituency, and far closer to the distribution of income among Republicans.

Table 2.6 [32]   DISTRIBUTION OF THE GENERAL POPULATION AMONG INCOME
GROUPS COMPARED TO THE DISTRIBUTION OF CAMPAIGN CONTRIBUTORS
AMONG INCOME GROUPS, 1972

Income	General population	Contributors
$0–4,999	16.6%	3.7%
$5,000–9,999	31.4	11.5
$10,000–14,999	26.1	11.5
$15,000–19,999	14.6	19.5
$20,000–24,999	4.3	23.4
$25,000 or more	7.0	36.8

In other words, the 11.3 percent in the highest income brackets make up more than three-fifths of all campaign contributors, 60.2 percent. These figures do not reflect the *amount* of money each income group gives; if those figures were available, they would unquestionably show even greater strength among the affluent, whose contributions are much larger than those of the middle class and poor, even with the restrictions of the 1974 campaign reforms.[33]

The chart also sheds some light on a claim made by the Republican party: that its average contributor in 1982 gave only $25 a year. The intent of this claim is to demonstrate that the party is not dominated by fat-cat or affluent contributors. While the average contributor to the GOP is not a rich industrialist attempting to buy a piece of a political party, those willing to give $25 a year to a political party come overwhelmingly from an economic elite. The development of a cadre of small Republican donors was started in 1962 through the acquisition of lists of the affluent: holders of Carte Blanche credit cards, who in 1962 formed a far more exclusive group than they do today; subscribers to the *Wall Street Journal,* McGraw-Hill business publications, and Standard & Poor; clients of investment and stockbrokerage firms.[34] While these men and women may have given only an average of $25, they are a natural Republican constituency. The elite characteristics of the population of campaign contributors are also suggested by a 1980 survey by the Center for Political Studies at the University of Michigan, finding that only 6.8 percent of the population reported making direct contributions to political candidates, and only 3.8 percent to political parties.[35]

Looking at the Republican party from another direction, not at the average contributor, but at the major donors to the Republican National Committee, those individuals who gave $500 or more, another part of the GOP mosaic begins to fall into place. For the first eighteen months of the 1981–82 election cycle, the Republican National Committee collected a total of $65 million, of which $8.43 million was from 3,798 individuals giving $500 or more, averaging $2,220 each. Among this elite group of contributors, fully $2.2 million, or 26 percent, came from three states, Texas, Louisiana, and Oklahoma. The population of these states is only 9.4 percent of the nation's total, but these three states contain the core of the nation's oil production.

The source of most of the money from oil-rich states has not been the major oil companies but the owners of independent oil companies, and the network of pipe suppliers, drill producers, industrial geologists, "mud" producers, bankers, lawyers, and truckers whose living depends on the industry. Unlike the major oil firms, independent oilmen are tied to domestic production and, in almost all cases, profit from only one stage of a process extending from discovery to retail sales, most often in drilling and production. The industry has a highly complex and ambivalent relationship with the federal government. It has bitterly fought price controls over oil and natural gas and has angrily denounced government intervention in the marketplace. At the same time, however, independent oilmen have struggled to obtain and to keep a network of special tax breaks, all of which have given the industry a government-created market advantage over its competitors, the major oil companies. The combination of dependence upon and anger at the federal government has made independent oil the most conservative industry in the nation. This conservatism has deep roots, dating from at least the Dixiecrat campaign of Strom Thurmond in 1948, financed in large part with oil money,[36] and to the anti-communist crusades of Senator Joseph R. McCarthy, Republican of Wisconsin, whom oilmen in the 1950s affectionately referred to as "Texas' third Senator."[37]

From the mid-1950s through the early 1970s, the domestic oil industry stagnated in the face of cheap imports from the Middle East, and its conservative influence on American politics was dormant. In 1973, however, OPEC-induced oil price hikes began to filter into the domestic market. The price of a barrel of oil rose from $3.89 in 1973, to $8.84 in 1976, to $14.27 in 1979, to a high of $33.76 in July 1981. With every one of these increases, the financial strength of oil-backed conservative organizations grew. In a sequence of steps, President Carter adopted energy policies that first enriched independent oil and ultimately converted the industry from a modestly ambitious adversary of the Democratic party into a powerful enemy bent on revenge. Initially, in 1979, Carter lifted oil price regulations, insuring a larger flow of cash to independent oil; in 1979, however, he successfully called for a windfall profit tax on a portion of these gains. The tax and the anti-oil rhetoric surrounding its enactment were to independent oil a classic federal intrusion on the industry's legitimate profits in a free market, an intrusion by a Democratic president seeking to shore up support on his liberal left.

It is impossible to determine precisely what this combination of sudden wealth, conservatism, and anger at the Democratic party translated into in terms of oil money in the 1980 election. A very cautious estimate would be at least $25.7 million channeled into Republican party coffers, the Reagan campaign, and the campaigns of nonoil state Republicans.[38] The amount of money given by independent oil to the Republican party and its candidates was larger than the amount raised by either the Democratic National, Senatorial, or Congressional committees. Acting as a conservative advance guard for the Republican party, independent oilmen provided the early financing to end twenty-five years of Democratic control of the Senate, and to send such prominent House members as John Brademas, the Democratic whip, and Al Ullman, chairman of the Ways and Means Committee, into electoral oblivion. In the Senate, oil money contributed significantly to the defeat of well-known, liberal Democratic Senators Frank Church of Idaho, John Culver of Iowa, Birch Bayh of Indiana, George S. McGovern of South Dakota, and Gaylord Nelson of Wisconsin.

Oil, more than any other source of money, has bridged the gap between the Republican party and its potentially conflicting constituent groups, particularly the sunbelt business community and the ideological right, providing what amounts to financial glue. When the financial elite of the GOP and the financial elite of the new right political organizations are compared, there is a striking overlap. Of the 915 contributions of $500 or more to the most prominent new right political organization, the National Conservative Political Action Committee (NCPAC) from the start of 1981 through September 1982, 363 of the contributions, or 39.7 percent, were from persons who had also given $500 or more to major Republican committees. A conservative estimate suggests that over one-third of the contributors to both the Republican party and the conservative groups are from the independent oil community.[39]

It is the convergence of the interests of the sunbelt business community and the ideological right-wing that has resulted in the sharpest growth for the Republican party, following the shift of the financial heartland of the GOP south from Wall Street and from downtown Chicago to Houston, Dallas, and Tulsa. The affluent frostbelt suburbs of Greenwich, Conn., Grosse Point, Mich., Wilmington, Del., and Haverford, Pa. remain significant sources of Republican money and, to a lesser extent, of Republican votes, but they are being eclipsed by such towns and cities as River Oak to the west of Houston, Beverly Hills, and Norman, Okla. Midland, Tex., has a population of only 84,300, but it ranked by 1081 among the top ten cities in the United States in terms of the number of contributors of $10,000 or more to the Republican National Committee.

The confluence of economic and ideological interests is reflected in the patterns of contributions by some of the major sunbelt donors. H. E. Eddie Chiles, owner of The Western Company, a Fort Worth supplier of oil equipment, achieved brief celebrity throughout the Southwest in the early 1980s for his "I'm Mad" commercials attacking the government and the liberal press. During 1981 and 1982, he and his wife, Frances, contributed $70,000 to candidates and committees registered with the Federal Election Commission. These included $10,000 to the National Conservative Political Action Committee, $14,000 to major Republican committees, and $45,400 to House and Senate candidates—all Republicans—spread through fourteen states. Roy Guffey, who began his career in oil as a roustabout in 1926 to later become president of the Roy Guffey Oil Company, believes that "a majority of the voters are a bunch of damn thieves," casting their ballots in an attempt to continue receiving some form of federal benefit, instead of recognizing the danger of a federal debt in excess of $1 trillion. In 1981 and 1982, Guffey and his wife gave $41,850 to candidates and committees, including $9,200 to Republican House and Senate candidates, $22,500 to such organizations as the National Conservative Political Action Committee ($17,000) and Senator Jesse Helms's National Congressional Club ($4,000), $8,650 to Republican committees, and $1,500 to the Dallas Energy PAC.[40]

Although independent oilmen make up the core of the large donors of the conservative wing of the Republican party, they are joined in force by such other sunbelt industrialists and businessmen as Roger Milliken, of Milliken and Company, in Spartansburg, S.C.; Joseph Coors, of the Coors Brewery; such early southern Californian backers of Ronald Reagan as Henry Salvatori, and Justin Dart, of Dart Industries. During 1981 and 1982, these four men and their wives gave a total of $266,350 to Republican party committees, to GOP candidates, and to conservative political action committees, including $58,250 to the National Conservative Political Action Committee, the Committee for the Survival of a Free Congress, and the National Congressional Club; $60,900 to Republican House and Senate candidates; and $129,200 to Republican party committees.

While the amount of money from these and a host of other sunbelt individuals and organizations is of major importance both to conservative politics and to the health of the Republican party, an equally significant function of these contributors has been the unifying effect

they have had upon business and the conservative ideological community. These men have personified the growing link between the business
community and the conservative right wing.

The defeat of Gerald Ford in 1976, the steady decline of the moderate
wing of the GOP in the Northeast and Midwest, the success of highly
conservative Republican candidates in the South, the steady movement
of the financial center of gravity of the GOP toward the sunbelt, the
expansion of the GOP's right wing in Congress from a dissident faction
into a strong voting block, and the increasing convergence of conservative ideologues and the business community behind the same set of
candidates have all functioned to ameliorate tensions within the Republican party. The result has been a far greater coherence of shared
ideological and economic interests within the GOP than within the
Democratic party.

In an additional manifestation of consolidation, the leadership of the
right wing has, in many ways, been integrated into the Republican
party. The Reagan administration has retained on the White House
staff, for example, specialists to deal with and attend to the concerns
of both the right-wing community and the business community. Before
the 1980 Reagan victory, Morton Blackwell, an employee of Richard
Viguerie, the right-wing fundraising specialist, conducted weekly sessions for representatives and staff of the conservative PAC community
in an attempt to formulate a common political strategy. After the
election, Blackwell continued to hold the sessions as a member of
President Reagan's Office of Public Liaison. Similarly, one of the
principal functions of Wayne Valis, who also worked in the public
liaison section of the White House, was not only to maintain the
support of the business community but to use the business community's
lobbying powers to win enactment of the administration's economic
program in Congress. The Republican National, Senatorial, and Congressional committees regularly hold strategy sessions with the conservative PACs, the business community, and the political specialists for the
trade associations. Although there is very little that is surprising about
a close working relationship between the GOP and business leaders, the

movement of the right wing from the status of outside critic of the GOP to partnership status within the GOP is a radical change from the recent past.

While the Chamber of Commerce, the National Conservative Political Action Committee, the National Congressional Club, the network of independent oil PACs, the American Medical Association, the Fluor Corporation's Public Affairs Committee, the Gun Owners of America, and the Realtors Political Action Committee may view each other with some suspicion, their mutual distrust is far outweighed by the fact that all have joined under the same tent—the Republican party. Although some of these organizations may place a higher priority on such social-legislative issues as abortion, tuition tax credits, busing, or school prayer, the financial elites of all these groups share a common conservative economic view. These organizations share an interest in the outcome of many of the same elections and, frequently, share the same contributors. Each claims to be nonpartisan, although each in fact channels from 75 percent to 95 percent of its financial support to Republicans and, in most cases, to the same set of Republicans in tight contests.

There is no such common ground underlying the diverse array of organizations within the Democratic camp. The United Steelworkers of America and the League of Conservation Voters each gave the overwhelming majority of its campaign money to Democrats in the 1981–82 election cycle, $719,807, compared to $450 to Republicans, for the steelworkers' union; and $123,302 to $14,648 to the GOP for the environmental group. These two groups, however, not only have few if any shared contributors, but their legislative agendas are often in direct conflict with one another over economic development, environmental protection, and industrial growth. The National Committee for an Effective Congress spent $366,443 in support of Democrats in 1982, and only $1,000 on Republicans, because it sought a more liberal, proconsumer Congress free of special-interest influence; the Agricultural & Dairy Educational Political Trust of the Mid-America Dairymen, Inc., favored Democrats by better than a 2–1 margin, $320,200 to $149,450, in order to maintain high dairy price supports, in direct conflict with consumer interests.

Policy Consequences

While revealing, the role of money in the two parties is just one aspect of the structure of political competition, which in turn sets much of the political framework for the formulation of economic policy. Changes in the structure of political competition over the past decade have been advantageous to the Republican party, providing the basis for significant elective victories, despite continued minority status. These advantages include, in summary, a class-skewed bias in voter turnout granting increased leverage to the affluent, among whom the Republican party is strongest; the shift in the central role of political parties from voter mobilization to fundraising, a shift again granting disproportionate strength to the affluent; and a pattern of campaign contributions that works to provide a clear mandate in favor of business and conservative interests, while encouraging legislative divisiveness and inaction within the Democratic party. Finally, the escalation of campaign costs at a rate far exceeding the rate of inflation functions to increase the leverage of the affluent, who make up a disproportionate percentage of campaign contributors.

The influence of these changes within the structure of political competition upon the balance of power between the two parties is less important, however, than the larger set of changing pressures on the formulation of economic policy. In terms of nominal voter allegiance, the Democratic party remains the majority party and the GOP the minority party, with both parties equipped to win the presidency and control of the Senate, while the House appears likely to retain a Democratic majority for the forseeable future.

In terms of economic policy, the political changes proving advantageous to the Republican party are part of a larger pattern of political transformations that are effectively pushing public policy initiatives and implementation toward the right. Television, as described above, has functioned to weaken support for government among those with the least education and the lowest income levels, a sector of the population essential to the Democratic party; there is, furthermore, a strong case to be made that television has contributed to the decline in voter turnout for reasons ranging from election-night projections to television-induced voter cynicism and apathy.

At the same time, the sharpest increase in partisan conflict in recent years has taken place in the South. This conflict has proven beneficial to the GOP, which in the South has gone from a 6–98 minority in the House of Representatives in 1960 to a 38–69 minority by 1980; and from a complete lack of southern Republican representation in the Senate in 1960 to the holding of ten out of twenty-two southern Senate seats in 1980. Just as important as these partisan changes is the fact that the partisan competition in the South is waged in conservative terms, and that the challenge from the GOP has functioned to force incumbent southern Democrats to protect their flanks by moving further to the right, insuring conservative votes in Congress, no matter which party wins a given election.

These political forces pushing economic policy toward the right are part of a much larger change in the distribution of power among basic institutions in American society, particularly in the balance between business and labor. The following chapters will explore some of these changes, including the rising power of the business community, the steady decline of organized labor, and a shift in voting patterns that has weakened the power of those in the bottom half of the income distribution. These political changes have been developing just when a cessation of growth in the economy has forced a shift away from economic policies seeking to correct inequities in the private sector through government intervention, and at a time of a simultaneous shift toward intensified competition between income and interest groups for the benefits of government, including the distribution of the tax burden, the distribution of subsidies, and the distribution of individual benefit programs, a competition that will be explored in the last chapter.

3

The Politicization of
the Business Community

DURING the 1970s, the political wing of the nation's corporate sector staged one of the most remarkable campaigns in the pursuit of political power in recent history. By the late 1970s and the early 1980s, business, and Washington's corporate lobbying community in particular, had gained a level of influence and leverage approaching that of the boom days of the 1920s. What made the acquisition of power in the 1970s remarkable was that business achieved its goals without any broad public-political mandate such as that of the 1920s, when probusiness values were affirmed in the elections of 1920, 1924, and 1928. Rather, business in the 1970s developed the ability to dominate the legislative process under adverse, if not hostile, circumstances. Corporate leaders had been closely associated with Watergate and its related scandals, and a reform-minded Democratic party with strong ties to the consumer and environmental movements had gained increasingly large majorities in Congress.

Despite these devastating odds, the political stature of business rose steadily from the early 1970s, one of its lowest points in the nation's history, until, by the end of the decade, the business community had achieved virtual dominance of the legislative process in Congress. The rise of the corporate sector is a case study in the ability of an economic elite to gain power by capitalizing on changes in the political system. In the case of the Democratic party, the shift in the balance of power toward the affluent, the erosion of the labor union movement, and the vastly increased importance of money in campaigns all combined to make Democratic politicians more vulnerable to pressures from the right. In the case of the Republican party, a de facto alliance has emerged between the GOP and much of the business community, a relationship paralleling the ties between the Democratic party and labor but lacking the inherent conflicts characteristic of that liaison. The political ascendancy of the business community, furthermore, has coincided with a sustained and largely successful attack upon organized labor, an attack conducted both in private-sector union representation fights and in legislative battles on Capitol Hill.

In 1978, in the midst of the corporate political revival, R. Heath Larry, president of the National Association of Manufacturers, contended that the single most important factor behind the resurgence of business was "the decline in the role of the party, yielding a new spirit of independence among congressmen—independent of each other, of the president, of the party caucus."[1] Larry's perception of the role of the decline in political parties in the revival of the stature of business was accurate, but his contention that this decline produced increased independence is wrong. In fact, the collapse of political parties and of traditional political organizations, especially those at the local level that formerly had the power to assure or to deny reelection, has been a key factor in a network of forces and developments undermining the independence of politicians and augmenting the strength of the business community.

Weakening of Parties

The decline of political organizations, rather than increasing independence, has eliminated a fundamental base of support for those elected to public office, functioning to intensify the elective anxieties of public officials, particularly members of the House and Senate. For

a member of Congress, a healthy local political organization traditionally both provided a secure source of backing at election time and
served as a conduit, transmitting to the congressman or senator spending
the majority of his or her time in Washington the assessment of the
local party leadership of public opinion—or the lack of it—on a
cross-section of issues. Without this source of information, and without
the security provided by the support of a strong local political organization, a House representative or senator becomes highly vulnerable,
not only to incessant reelection anxiety but to orchestrated public
pressure. Many of the toughest battles in Congress in recent years—
legislation to create a consumer protection agency; labor law reform;
regulation of used-car dealers and funeral directors; major tax legislation, including the $749 billion tax reduction in 1981, and the 1983
struggle over legislation mandating 10 percent withholding on interest
and dividend income—have been fought on this terrain: the organized
creation of seemingly spontaneous outpourings of public opinion for
or against specific legislative proposals, voiced through coordinated
letter writing, telegram, and telephone campaigns—all deluging members of Congress.

This form of lobbying, although highly centralized, is known as
"grass-roots lobbying" and has always been a weapon in the political
arsenal, becoming, during the late 1960s and early 1970s, an essential
mechanism in strategies to influence congressional decisions in the hands
of the environmental movements and of such organizations as Common Cause and Ralph Nader's Congress Watch, organizations that
coordinated citizens' grass-roots lobbying campaigns in the successful
pressuring of Congress to enact political reforms, health and safety
legislation, consumer protection legislation, and environmental conservation legislation. A similar but substantially different form of lobbying has characterized congressional procedures since the days of George
Washington: pressure on individual members from local contractors,
unions, bankers, chambers of commerce, and developers, to obtain
defense, road, dam, and other pork-barrel benefits from the federal
government. Pork-barrel lobbying and grass-roots lobbying differ,
however, in that pork-barrel lobbying traditionally seeks specific ben-

efits for a congressman's district or state—jobs, buildings, construction products, contract awards—while grass-roots lobbying is an attempt to seek to influence congressional votes on legislation of national importance, legislation that is seen or thought to transcend parochial boundaries.

In the mid-1970s, key leaders of the nation's corporate and trade association network perceived that their institutions and structures were far better suited to grass-roots lobbying than the liberal-reform groups that seemed to have a corner on these tactics. The interest of the constituencies of the liberal-reform organizations in the political process is fluid, rising when issues have high visibility—such as President Nixon's highly controversial Supreme Court nomination of G. Harrold Carswell, the southern judge with a segregationist background whose appointment was opposed by groups ranging from the American Bar Association to the NAACP; or the post-Watergate campaign to enact election reform—and falling when issues are no longer unambiguous.

In contrast, the nation's corporate and trade association communities have a sustained economic interest in the outcome of the legislative and elective process, day in and day out.[2] The basic function of Washington's corporate and trade association lobbying community, a network of well over 150,000 professionals, is not only the defeat or passage of major bills but, in a much more complex process, the shaping of the precise language of legislation and of the committee reports that accompany legislation. This process involves the addition, deletion, and alteration of individual words, paragraphs, and sections of bills as they wend their way from House committee, to House floor, to Senate Committee, to the full Senate and then to a House-Senate conference committee. One seemingly minor provision in the 1982 tax bill retroactively legalized corporate sales of investment tax credits from January 1, 1981, to October 20, 1981. This provision, which occupied nine lines out of a 465-page report, in fact sanctioned a controversial $20 million tax deal between Chris Craft Corp and International Harvester.

Economically driven, sustained interest in the legislative process does not stop with the passage or defeat of legislation. A battle lost on legislation to create a program can be partially redeemed when entirely separate legislation setting the dollar appropriation for the program is later taken up by Congress. An agency empowered to enforce workplace health and safety regulation, without money for an inspection staff, in effect has little or no power. Finally, the way in which a law mandating certain general health and safety requirements will be specifically applied on the production line and on the office floor is determined by the detailed rules and regulations written in the executive branch, and subject in turn to pressure and counterpressure from the White House, Congress, the industry, and the enforcing agency itself.

Just as important as the sustained interest of business in all aspects of the legislative process is the compatibility of the structure of corporations and trade associations with the mechanics of orchestrated grass-roots lobbying. Such diverse major United States companies as General Motors, American Express, Caterpillar Tractor, PepsiCo, Westinghouse Electric Corp., Standard Oil Co. of Ohio, U.S. Steel, Raytheon Company, Squibb Corp., American Airlines, and Allied Chemical Corp. each have networks of plants, suppliers, retailer outlets, subcontractors, salesmen, and distributors in every congressional district in the nation, as well as thousands of dispersed stockholders.

The scope of this leverage was demonstrated during the 1979 debate over legislation to provide federal loan guarantees to the Chrysler Corporation. In the attempt to convince conservative Congressman Elwood R. Hillis, Republican of the Fifth District of Indiana, to vote for the legislation, Chrysler produced for Hillis, as it did for all other members of Congress, a list of all Chrysler suppliers in his district. The list runs to three and a quarter single-spaced pages and includes the names of 436 companies in Hillis's district whose sales to Chrysler totaled $29.52 million, ranging from $5.67 million from the GTR Fiberglass Products Company in Marion to $90 from Leck's Radiator Repair Shop in Hillis's home town of Kokomo.

More recently, the Natural Gas Supply Association spent $1 million creating a "grass-roots" organization called the Alliance For Energy Security, which hired Matthew A. Reese, Jr., a Virginia public relations specialist, to organize a telephone and direct-mail campaign in behalf of full natural gas decontrol. This $1 million was spent primarily in just fifteen House districts represented by key members of the House Energy and Commerce Committee. As one organizer noted: "... even for $1 million, it can't be a nationwide effort. None of these grass-roots efforts comes cheaply. When you start mailing letters in any quantity, you run into a bundle." The Alliance sent out mailgrams to residents of the key districts, denouncing continued control of gas prices and asking the residents to volunteer to "become our personal representative in your neighborhood" by calling an 800 number for instructions on how to apply pressure on a member of Congress.[3] During tough legislative fights over such major weapons systems as the B-1 bomber and the MX missile, similar lists of all the major contractor and subcontractor plants, along with their suppliers, broken down by state and district, were prepared and distributed to wavering members of Congress, in behalf of corporations and industries standing to profit from the legislation.

Unlike other institutions, including both the liberal-reform organizations and labor unions, corporations are pyramid structures, with those on top empowered both to lobby on their own and to require parallel action by subordinates. A plant operator in Des Moines who receives a suggestion from company headquarters to encourage all management-level personnel to contact each member of the Iowa House and Senate delegations, in order to voice support for or opposition to legislation before Congress, is likely to interpret the suggestion in the strongest possible terms. A union member, in contrast, is just as likely to tell his shop steward to hire him a secretary as to write a union-suggested letter to his congressman.

The Corporate Mobilization

The revival of the political power of business began in 1973 and 1974, initiated in large part by a small group of Washington's most influential corporate lobbyists who began to meet privately to discuss the darkening storm clouds everywhere on the political horizon. Watergate had not only damaged the Republican party, but the taint of corruption had sharply altered the public perception of corporate

America. The secret financing for President Nixon's Committee to Re-elect the President in 1972; the cash for what was known as the "Townhouse Operation"; channeling unreported money to Republican House and Senate candidates in 1970; the bribes to foreign officials in charge of government contracts—all had come from business executives and from corporate treasuries. Furthermore, American corporations providing weaponry and material for the Vietnam War, ranging from Dow Chemical to the Raytheon Company, had been targeted with extensive and effective negative publicity by the anti-war movement. Public confidence in the chief executives of major corporations fell like a stone from the mid-1960s to the mid-1970s. The percentage of the public describing themselves as having a great deal of confidence in corporate leaders dropped from 51 percent in the 1966–67 period to an average of 20 percent in the 1974–76 period. The rate of decline in confidence was sharper than for any other major institution in the United States, public or private, including the executive branch, the press, organized labor, and educators—excepting only Congress, which fell from a favorability rating of 42 percent to 20 percent during the same period.[4]

At the same time, Watergate had revived the Democratic party, particularly that wing of the Democratic party supporting the environmental and consumer movements. After losing the 1972 presidential election under the leadership of George S. McGovern, by a 61–39 margin and by 17.9 million votes, the Democrats in 1974 would gain forty-nine House seats and five Senate seats. Before these Democratic gains, and despite the presence of a Republican in the White House, Congress by 1974 had already enacted into law the Environmental Protection Agency (1970), the Occupational Safety and Health Administration (1970), the Consumer Product Safety Commission (1972), the National Traffic Safety Commission (1970), the Mine Safety and Health Administration (1973), increased food stamp funding (1970), a 20 percent Social Security increase (1974), Supplemental Security Income (1972), and the Employee Retirement Income Security Act.

"The danger had suddenly escalated," Bryce Harlow, senior Washington representative for Procter & Gamble and one of the most respected members of the old-line corporate lobbying community, commented later. "We had to prevent business from being rolled up and put in the trash can by that Congress," he said, referring to the Ninety-fourth Congress elected in 1974.[5] The mobilization of business in this critical period, the early and mid-1970s, began at the top. Harlow worked most actively with the elite Washington lobbyists, men like William Whyte of the United States Steel Corporation; Albert D. Bourland, Jr., of General Motors; Don A. Goodall of American Cyanamid Company; and Wayne H. Smithey of Ford Motor Co. These men were an integral part of the Washington establishment, not only representing some of the largest American corporations but conducting their business in such exclusive downtown facilities as the Metropolitan and University clubs. Their roots, however, were in a style of lobbying that no longer worked on Capitol Hill—the cultivation, largely behind closed doors, of a few key holders of power: committee chairman who could determine with the tap of a gavel or a nod to the staff the content of legislation; cabinet secretaries who could be persuaded over lunch that their employees were pressing a regulatory mandate with too much vigor; and key White House aides whose political currency was the provision of favors for the influential.

By the mid-1970s, however, the decline of party loyalties, congressional reforms weakening the power of committee chairmen, and the diffusion of power to junior members of Congress forced a major alteration in lobbying strategies. "As long as you could go and get the cooperation of the committee chairman and the ranking members, and maybe a few others, you didn't have to have the vast network we are talking about now," Smithey noted.[6] Smithey's reference to a "vast network" describes both the development of grass-roots lobbying as a legislative tactic and a much more pervasive effort to set the terms of the legislative debate in the nation's capital. Not only have the targets of lobbyists changed over the past generation, but the technology of public opinion molding has undergone changes of unprecedented magnitude, producing computerized direct-mail communications in which much of the nation's adult population has been broken down into demographic and "psychographic" profiles. A group or institution seeking to mobilize support or opposition on any issue can seek out ready-made lists of allies in the general public from computer specialists who can then communicate almost instantaneously with any selected constituency via letters produced on high-speed laser printers. If lobbying during the 1950s, in the words of one of the most eminent Washington lobbyists, Charls E. Walker, consisted of personal access to four natives of Texas—President Dwight Eisenhower, House Speaker Sam Rayburn, Senate Majority Leader Lyndon Baines Johnson, and Treasury Secretary Robert Anderson—it currently involves minimally the ability to recognize the interests of 535 members of the House and Senate, an acute sensitivity to potential malleability in public opinion, the cultivation of both print and electronic media, the use of sophisticated technologies both to create and to convey an impression of public sentiment, and the marshaling on Capitol Hill and across the country of legions of newly enlisted corporate personnel.

The effort on the part of the business community to shape the legislative debate has taken place on a number of fronts, one of the most important of which has been the politicization of employees and stockholders. Atlantic Richfield (Arco), for example, spends about $1 million annually on a program in which 15,000 employees are members of politically active local committees. In addition, the nearly 80,000 Arco stockholders, suppliers, and distributors are on a mailing list for company newsletters and publications focusing on political and public policy issues. W. Dean Cannon, Jr., executive vice-president of the California Savings and Loan League, suggested in 1978 to savings and loan firms that they give employees "specific assignments to work in politics" and that an employee's raises "might well be tied directly to his involvement in the political assignment you have given him."[7] During the debate over the 1978 tax bill, officials of a single, mid-sized firm, the Barry Wright Corporation in Watertown, Mass., generated 3,800 letters from its stockholders to members of Congress in favor of a reduction in capital gains taxation.[8]

The politicization of management-level employees is a critical element in achieving effective grass-roots lobbying: an employee who sees a direct economic interest in the outcome of legislative battles will be a far more effective and persistent advocate than an employee who is acting in response only to orders or implied orders from superiors. Stockholders, in turn, represent an ideal target for political mobilization. Only 15 percent of American citizens hold stock, according to liberal estimates by the Securities Industry Association, and those who do are, on average, in the upper-income brackets. They have little or no direct interest in the expansion or maintenance of domestic spending programs, although they have considerable interest in lowering tax rates. In this sense, the economic interests of affluent individuals and of corporations are sharply intertwined. Both stockholders and corporations, for example, share a direct interest in either lowering the capital gains rate or shortening the minimum holding period to qualify for the more favorable capital gains rate.[9]

The scope and cost of politically directed corporate activity is extremely difficult to gauge. It is an integral part of a broader effort to shape public opinion, including the steadily increasing amount of corporate advertising that does not promote a product but a point of view. The issues can range from a highly detailed and specialized set of arguments on deregulation of natural gas directed at knowledgeable committee staff and at other technically sophisticated audiences, to W. R. Grace Co.'s televised commentary, designed for the general public, on the abstract principles of freedom and small government, presented as background to a film of windsurfers succeeding and failing to negotiate cresting waves, in a visual analogy to the vicissitudes of the free market. The cost of this kind of advertising for Mobil Oil Company alone has run to about $3.5 million a year. In 1978 a Congressional committee estimated that the total annual cost of this kind of corporate issue advertising amounts to $1 billion a year.[10] The figure is, at best, an educated guess.

The expenditure of large sums on corporate advertising has not, however, altered public opinion of business leaders, which, if anything, has become less favorable. After falling to 22 percent in the mid-1970s, the percentage of the public saying that it has a "great deal of confidence" in the leaders of major corporations has remained at an historic low, fluctuating between 16 and 27 percentage points, despite the steady erosion of the memory of Watergate and associated scandals.[11] Instead, the success of corporate advocacy advertising has probably been to cast public doubt on the solutions offered by adversaries of business. The most consistent theme of corporate advocacy and public-interest advertising has been a sustained attack on the use of government money and regulation to solve social problems.

An equally, if not more, effective use of business money in altering the terms of the policy debate has been in the total or partial financing of such private institutions engaged in research and scholarship as the American Enterprise Institute; the Heritage Foundation; the Hoover Institution on War, Revolution and Peace; the National Bureau of Economic Research; the Center for the Study of American Business at Washington University in St. Louis, and the American Council for Capital Formation. In a decade during which economic stagnation contributed to the undermining of the intellectual basis of traditional Democratic economic and political strategies, these organizations, among others, have functioned to lay the scholarly and theoretical groundwork for a major shift in public policy favoring business and the higher-bracket taxpayers.

Since the early 1970s and into the present, these organizations have prospered. Created in 1973, the Heritage Foundation in Washington has seen its budget grow by 40 percent per year: in the 1976–77 fiscal year, its budget was $1,008,557; by 1980–81, it had expanded to $5.2 million and by 1981–82 to $7.1 million. Major supporters of the Heritage Foundation include Joseph Coors, President of the Adolph Coors Company; Richard Mellon Scaife, heir to the Mellon banking, oil, and industrial fortune and the Sarah Mellon Scaife Foundation; the John M. Olin Fund, established by the chairman of the board of the Olin Mathieson Chemical Corporation, a foundation chaired by former Treasury Secretary William Simon; the Noble Foundation, established by Edward E. Noble, an Oklahoma oil and gas company president; the Reader's Digest Association, Inc.; Mobil Oil Corp.; Dow Chemical Co.; Fluor Corp.; Gulf Oil Corp.; Sears Roebuck; and Dart and Kraft.[12] Many of these corporate backers have become integral parts of that nexus of interests uniting a major segment of the business community, the ideological right wing, and the Republican party, described in chapter 2.

Perhaps the most prestigious of the institutions that have helped to push the economic debate to the right is the National Bureau of Economic Research (NBER) in Cambridge, Mass. A highly reputable, distinguished, and long-standing research institution established in 1920, NBER was run from 1977 to 1982 by Martin Feldstein, professor of economics at Harvard and appointed in 1982 as chairman of the Council of Economic Advisers to President Reagan. NBER is closely affiliated not only with the academic community but with the nation's business and corporate establishment. In 1983, its operating budget amounted to $5.8 million, of which 42 percent was in the form of government grants, 13 percent was from its own endowment, valued at about $50 million, and the remaining 45 percent, or $2.61 million, was from corporations and foundations, about equally split. Its major corporate donors are the same corporations that head the Fortune 500 list; the top ten of the Fortune 500 are all significant supporters, including IBM, Exxon, and AT&T.

The Hoover Institution, at Stanford University in Palo Alto, California, founded by Herbert Hoover in 1919, has a broad array of support from the corporate community, although from a more conservative wing of the business establishment. Its 1982 Board of Overseers includes at least three of the financial supporters of the Heritage Foundation, among them Joseph Coors; William Simon, of the John M. Olin Fund, identified by the Hoover Institution as chairman of Crescent Diverified Limited; and Richard Mellon Scaife, identified by the Hoover Institution as publisher of the Tribune Review Publishing Company. Other board members include John E. Swearingen, chairman of the board of the Standard Oil Company (Indiana) and John R. Grey, president of the Standard Oil Company of California. In 1982, the Hoover Institution had a budget of $8.4 million, of which 32 percent was provided by Stanford University, 4 percent came from the sale of publications, 24 percent from its endowment, and the remaining 40 percent from private donations from corporations, foundations, and individuals. Three highly conservative foundations have emerged as principal sources of money for the Hoover Institution. For the three years from 1979 to 1982, the Scaife Foundation; the John M. Olin Fund; and the J. Howard Pew Freedom Trust, created by the former chairman of the board of the Sun Oil Company, gave a total of $4.89 million to the Hoover Institution.[13] In just one year, 1981, the Scaife and Pew foundations gave the Hoover Institution a combined total of $1.9 million, the equivalent of nearly a quarter of the institution's entire 1982 budget.

The Center for the Study of American Business at Washington University, founded in 1975, is a far smaller operation, with an annual budget running below $750,000. The principal benefactors of the center were the John M. Olin Foundation and the late James S. McDonnell, Jr., chairman of the board of McDonnell-Douglas Corp., who together gave $793,000 from 1976 through 1979.[14] On a similarly small scale, the American Council for Capital Formation in Washington, D.C., was started in 1973, backed largely by George H. Weyerhaeuser, president of the Weyerhaeuser Company, a lumber and wood products company, and by the National Forest Products Association. By 1976, its budget reached $105,000, and by 1983, $768,000. It now has the backing of over 340 corporations and trade associations, each of which gives $500 to $10,000, many of them capital-intensive Fortune 500 companies, a strong contingent of oil and chemical companies, utilities, banks, and the nation's largest accounting firms. The strength of the American Council lies, however, in the extensive Washington connections of its chairman, Charls E. Walker, former deputy secretary of the Treasury under President Nixon, head of a lobbying firm carrying his name, and chairman of President-elect Reagan's Transition Task force on Tax Policy; and of the American Council's president, Robert Keith Gray, secretary to the cabinet under President Eisenhower, vice-chairman of the Washington public relations firm of Hill and Knowlton until 1980, director of communications for the Reagan-Bush campaign, chairman of the 1981 presidential inaugural committee, and now chairman of the public relations firm of Gray and Company.

The American Enterprise Institute (AEI), in 1970 a minor think tank with a budget of $879,000 and a staff of 19, by 1980 had grown into an organization with a staff of 135 and a budget of $10.4 million. The scope and sources of the funding of AEI are reflected in the membership of the executive committee of the board of trustees, which includes, in addition to William J. Baroody, Jr., AEI's president, Richard B. Madden, chairman of the board of the Potlatch Corporation; James G. Affleck, chairman of the board and chief executive officer of the American Cyanamid Company; Willard C. Butcher, chairman and chief executive officer of the Chase Manhattan Bank; and Paul F. Oreffice, president and chief executive officer of the Dow Chemical Company. A critical source of financing for AEI has been the J. Howard Pew Freedom Trust, which gave AEI a total of $5.85 million in the six-year period from 1976 through 1981.[15]

These figures do not suggest that corporate or conservative foundation money has been used to buy predetermined conclusions. Instead, the financial backing for these institutions reflects the astute use of philanthropy by the corporate and conservative foundation community to finance credible intellectual arguments produced by highly respected and independent but conservative economists and social scientists. In this light, the Scaife Foundation, for example, gave $650,000 to Public Broadcasting of Northwest Pennsylvania, WQLN in Erie, Pa., to finance the cost of conservative economist and Nobel laureate Milton Friedman's ten-part television series, "Free to Choose." National Affairs, Inc., the company publishing *The Public Interest,* a central disseminator of conservative economic and social views, received $770,000 from three conservative foundations between 1977 and 1982, including $380,000 from the Scaife Foundation. The scholarship and policy recommendations emanating from these and other institutions will be examined in the final chapter.

Mobilization of the Business Lobby

While the business community has financed an advertising agenda and a set of organizations helping to push the economic debate into a more favorable context, key business lobbying organizations were revitalized and new ones formed. A critical starting point in this process came in November 1972, when two business organizations whose main purpose was to restrict the influence and bargaining power of unions —the Construction Users Anti-Inflation Roundtable and the Labor Law Study Committee—merged to form the Business Roundtable. The original central purpose of the Roundtable continued to be curtailing the power of unions; in the middle of 1973, however, when Watergate and associated scandals were beginning to emerge, and with them growing signals that both the Republican party and the business community faced serious political challenges, the direction of the Roundtable began to change. In June of 1973, in part at the urging of Bryce Harlow of Procter & Gamble, the Roundtable merged with an informal organization of chief executive officers of major companies known as the March Group, retaining the Business Roundtable as its name. Key principals, in addition to Harlow, were W. B. Murphy, former chief executive officer of Campbell Soup Co.; Roger M. Blough, former U.S. Steel Board chairman; Fred J. Borch, chief executive officer of General Electric Co.; and John D. Harper, chairman of the board of Alcoa.[16]

The merger with the March Group marked a substantial change both in the membership of the Roundtable and in its purpose. From a diffuse collection of mid-sized and large companies, the Roundtable shifted to its new status as an elite organization, composed largely of members of the Fortune 500; it became, in effect, the political arm of big business. In terms of its goals, it shifted from concern with the details of specific labor-management contracts in the field to the entire spectrum of public policy issues in Washington. Labor law remained a central issue but by no means the exclusive issue. Broad questions of taxation, anti-trust, regulation, banking, and employment became part of the Roundtable's self-imposed mandate.

In addition to changes in the composition and goals of the Roundtable, the organization adopted a lobbying strategy requiring the direct participation of the chief executive officers of member corporations. Men like Irving Shapiro of Du Pont, Reginald Jones of General Electric, and Robert S. Hatfield of Continental Can Company began to make personal visits to individual members of Congress, senior and junior. These visits by CEOs were targeted particularly toward those members of Congress whose districts contained plants and facilities belonging to the corporations in question. This kind of targeting was most graphically laid out in a strategy session held by the paid staff of the Business Roundtable during the 1977 House debate on legislation to create a consumer protection agency. The staff went down a list of uncommitted and wavering members of the House, carefully attempting to link these congressmen with the chief executive officers and lobbyists of corporations employing significant numbers of persons in the congressmen's home districts. The following conversations by Roundtable staff were recorded verbatim in *Fortune* Magazine on March 27, 1978, p. 53:

"Henry Gonzalez [a Texas Democrat] of San Antonio . . . should we use Sears? We have problems with Jake Pickle [another Texas Democrat] on this. I'm not sure we can get him . . . OK, let's ask Sears about Gonzalez.

"Delaney [James J. Delaney, a New York Democrat] of Long Island . . . well, Delaney's a character, but he can be helpful as chairman of the Rules Committee . . . Bristol-Myers is close to Delaney, let Bill Grief handle that.

"Steed [Tom Steed, Democrat] of Oklahoma . . . He hasn't committed himself, Phillips should call him . . . ask the Chamber of Commerce.

"Gaydos (Joseph M. Gaydos, Democrat) of Pennsylvania . . . Ask Alcoa if they'll do it, John Harper was very enthusiastic about this one . . . Hatfield of Continental could do it, but I hate to ask him.

"Marks (Marc L. Marks, Republican), Pennsylvania . . . Ask Ferguson of General Foods to call Kirby of Westinghouse about Marks.

"Gore (Albert Gore, Democrat) of Tennessee . . . Carrier Corp and TRW . . . Do we really have a chance with Gore? We really think we do? Ask Lloyd Hand of TRW."

Although the Roundtable portrays itself as a kind of executive grass-roots uprising, with the highest-paid and most powerful men in American industry rolling up their sleeves and sitting down as equals at the political bargaining table, the organization has hired a cross-section of Washington's most influential Republican and Democratic law firms and lobbying firms, including Patton, Boggs and Blow; Williams and Connolly; Wilmer and Pickering; and Charls E. Walker Associates.

A second critical development in the mobilization of the business community was the revitalization of the Chamber of Commerce, in which many of the principals in the formation of the Roundtable participated. At the start of the 1970s, the Chamber of Commerce was an almost moribund organization; its total membership was large, about 50,000 corporations, local chambers, and trade associations, but it was stagnant, failing to grow over the years. And although headquartered across Lafayette Square from the White House, it had no muscle either in the executive branch or on Capitol Hill, where the Chamber was seen as a one-line organization—cut spending and taxes—with no program, and no power to back up its position. The Chamber, in effect, was on the far periphery of the national debate, dismissed as a collection of unrealistic fiscal conservatives who were still fighting causes that had been lost in the 1930s and 1940s, unequipped to participate in the highly complex contemporary battles involving the relationship between consumer and producer, labor and management, and between the federal government and almost every facet of industry and commerce. When, however, such key leaders of the business community as Bryce Harlow and Lewis Powell (now a member of the Supreme Court) recognized the growing political threat to business in the early 1970s, it was to the Chamber that they turned. "The Chamber was a sleeping giant," Jeffrey H. Joseph, who has subsequently become the organization's vice-president for domestic policy, said. "It was a sleeping giant waiting to be woken up." During the latter half of the 1970s, the Chamber woke up with a vengeance, with its membership increasing at a rate of 30 percent a year. From a budget of $20 million and 50,000 members, it has grown to an organization with a $65 million budget in 1983, 215,000 members, and a staff of 1,000.

The revitalization of the Chamber did not involve a significant strengthening of its policy-making abilities. To this day, the Chamber remains relatively irrelevant to the detailed decision making on Capitol Hill and has failed to become a major participant in the working out of the specifics of legislation or in the setting of new, highly specialized agendas. Instead, the rebirth of the Chamber has centered on the conversion of the organization into the political arm, or club, of business. The network of 2,800 state and local Chambers of Commerce in cities and small towns across the country, the 210,000 corporations that are members, and the 1,400 professional and trade associations[17] provide an ideal base for grass-roots lobbying, particularly when the issue before Congress is perceived as a threat by the business community, as in the case of labor law reform or legislation setting up a consumer protection agency. When an issue touches the heart of the business community, as in such cases, or, on the positive side, in the case of the 1981 tax cut, the number of telephone calls, letters, and mailgrams that the U.S. Chamber can generate to members of Congress is extraordinarily impressive as a political weapon, numbering well into the tens of thousands.

The Chamber has computerized its grass-roots lobbying mechanisms so that it is not only able to generate massive outpourings when major bills are before the full House or Senate but can also target pressures from congressional districts to small subgroups of congressmen—to committees, subcommittees, and even to the wavering members of a subcommittee. In addition, the Chamber's computers have broken down corporate and trade association members into subsets, so that, for example, in seeking out corporate members in favor of increased U.S. support of the International Monetary Fund (IMF), the Chamber can send out special "issue alerts" to only multinational corporate members who have a direct profit-based interest in beefing up the IMF, while leaving off the communication list small-business owners, many of whom would be opposed to federal aid to the international banking system. Similarly, in the initial phases of the Chamber's efforts to defeat 1982 legislation mandating 10 percent withholding on interest and dividend income, the first group of corporate members to receive issue alerts was made up of those financial institutions that had the most direct interest in stopping the bill.

The political emergence of the Chamber has been critical to the renewed political vitality of the business community. Working in tandem with another organization specializing in the representation of small businesses, the National Federation of Independent Business (NFIB), the Chamber gave traditional Washington-based business lobbyists and the CEOs of the Roundtable the credibility and numerical strength of the voting small-business owners. While the Chamber orchestrated grass-roots lobbying to apply pressure to Congress, the NFIB has developed a second tactic, conducting regular surveys of members on issues before Congress. As a floor vote approaches, the NFIB can take this survey data, including the names of individual small-business owners for or against certain bills and amendments, to each member of Congress so that he or she is informed as to the specific views of named and often locally influential constituents.

While small business has provided the muscle within congressional districts for this corporate alliance, the record of legislative victories and defeats suggests that the larger corporations have gained far more from the partnership than have the smaller companies. On such issues as labor law reform and consumer protection, where the interests of all business organizations have coincided, the alliance has been remarkably successful in winning key votes in Congress. During the Senate's consideration of the Labor Law Reform bill in 1978, for example, those representatives of big business who were lobbying Senator Lawton Chiles, Democrat of Florida, heard him complain that most of the pressure he had received had come from large corporations. Almost immediately, the large corporations switched tactics, abandoning the attempt to directly lobby Chiles, and instead used their corporate jets to fly small-business owners from Florida to Washington to take over the job of convincing Chiles. "I can't remember when we last experienced a lobbying effort like this," a Chiles aide commented. "It is so well-structured, so well-organized, and I don't think they missed a single possible opponent of that bill in our state."[18]

When, however, Congress took up legislation raising the minimum wage, the results were quite different. The legislation was opposed most intensely by small businesses, which had the most to lose, while the major corporations, many of which have pay scales above the minimum wage, were only lukewarm in their opposition. The legislation passed.

When big and small business were on opposite sides of the fence, as in the case of the fight over the distribution of tax breaks in 1978, big business won. "The bigs lobbied against us and squashed us," James (Mike) McKevitt, head of the National Federation of Independent Business, complained after enactment of the 1978 tax bill.[19] In 1981, when the business lobby in Congress and in the administration was so strong that it wrote the business tax cut enacted by Congress and signed into law by President Reagan, the overwhelming majority of the tax reductions resulting from a new, accelerated depreciation schedule went to capital-intensive big businesses. Small-business organizations, including members of the NFIB and the Chamber, as part of their political commitment to the Business Roundtable and other organizations representing larger corporations, were locked into a commitment to support the administration bill. As a consequence, small business was left out in the cold, unable to bargain, when a competition for votes between the administration and House Democrats resulted in a bidding war upon which other special interests ranging from independent oilmen to savings and loan associations capitalized to force approval of enlarged tax breaks in their own behalf.

The Chamber, in addition to providing perhaps one of the best grass-roots lobbying operations in America, performs two other basic political functions. The first has been to recommend to the business community at large which House and Senate races are close—in which, consequently, campaign contributions can make a difference—and which candidates in these contests are the more "probusiness." These recommendations go to corporations and businesspeople outside of Washington without the resources to learn where money might be used most effectively. Working in close contact with the political parties, particularly the GOP, the Chamber develops throughout the election process information identifying tight, competitive races. A number of probusiness organizations now do this, but the Chamber, with its network of 210,000 member companies and 1,400 member trade associations, has an extremely broad audience for such information. Chamber officials claim that their endorsement is worth $100,000 or more in additional contributions in a Senate contest, and proportionately less in a House contest, depending on the size, location, and competitiveness of the race. "We get lobbied morning, noon, and night" by politicians and their supporters seeking endorsements, Richard L. Breault, group vice-president for the Chamber, said.

Throughout an election year, the Chamber sends out updated lists of key races. The list of recommended candidates is in theory based on whichever candidate is more probusiness. In fact, this has translated into a strong Republican bias. In the 1982 election the Chamber backed 132 House and Senate candidates and actively opposed 6 others. Of the 132 endorsed candidates, 119 were Republicans, and all but two of the 13 Democratic endorsements were to support a conservative in a primary fight against another more liberal Democrat. All 6 of the candidates actively opposed by the Chamber were Democrats. In other words, in only 2 out of 138 selected races were Democrats endorsed against Republican opponents. Calculated in terms of the cost of newsletters and other mailings sent out by the Chamber in support of or in opposition to candidates, the Chamber spent $182,299 either in behalf of Republicans or opposed to Democrats and just $7,524 in support of Democrats, a ratio of 24 to 1.

Both the Democratic party and Democratic members of the Chamber complained about the growing ties of the Chamber to the GOP during the 1982 election, and the Chamber has modified its endorsement system to a limited extent. For 1984, the Chamber intends to endorse all members of Congress who have strongly probusiness voting records, a step that would increase the number of Chamber-endorsed Democrats, but the Chamber will continue past practices by placing in the lists of campaigns in their newsletters a highlighted star identifying those races it believes deserve special attention within the business community.

The third major political function of the Chamber of Commerce has been to act as a centralizing focus for increasing numbers of ad hoc coalitiions forming within the business community on specific issues. The Chamber's role in this process has been to provide staff, television studios, meeting space, and coordination for alliances of trade associations, corporate lobbyists, and other interests uniting in support of or opposition to legislation before Congress or before a regulatory agency.

The Chamber's role in this process of forming ad hoc coalitions has been, however, far less important than the proliferation of coalitions, some of which were organized by the Chamber, that began in the 1970s. This process of forming alliances has been a key element in the growing power of business in Washington. The formation of the Consumer Issues Working Group, an alliance of 400 separate organizations ranging from Procter & Gamble to the Grocery Manufacturers of America, under the leadership of Emmett Hines, chief lobbyist for Armstrong Cork, was critical to the defeat of the Consumer Protection Agency. A similar alliance of over 100 corporations and associations, the National Action Committee on Labor Law Reform run by Clarence Randall, chief lobbyist for the Associated Builders and Contracctors,[20] was the mechanism for one of the most intense legislative campaigns in the history of Congress, resulting in the defeat by filibuster in 1978 of Labor Law Reform legislation. These coalitions have formed around both large and small issues, including, for example, an alliance of bankers, oilmen, realtors, and cattlemen calling itself the Families Associated for Inalienable Rights (FAIR), which successfully won repeal of a provision in the estate tax in 1980 that would have significantly increased the tax liability of the top 2.6 percent of estates.

Class Incentives

While the record of victories of these kinds of business alliances over the past decade is impressive, more important has been the underlying shift in the political posture of business that has made the formation of such coalitions possible. During the 1970s, business refined its ability to act as a class, submerging competitive instincts in favor of joint, cooperative action in the legislative arena. Rather than individual companies seeking only special favor in the award of a contract, in the dropping of an antitrust case, or in State Department assistance in gaining exclusive franchising rights in a foreign country, the dominant theme in the political strategy of business became a shared interest in the defeat of such bills as consumer protection and labor law reform,

and in the enactment of favorable tax, regulatory, and antitrust legislation. Competitive lobbying, particularly among defense contractors
seeking to maintain congressional support for ships, aircraft, and weap-
ons systems, continues, and remains a major factor in very specific
decisions in Congress and within the executive branch. General Electric
and Pratt and Whitney, for example, have been engaged in a long and
bitter fight for control of the Pentagon market for jet engines. But the
willingness of a host of business interests, many of them competing for
the same markets in the private sector, to join together on larger issues
before Congress and before the regulatory agencies has significantly
altered the balance of power in Washington, providing, when such
unity emerges, a single, immensely powerful voice for the business
community.

A major source of pressure on the business and trade association
community to join forces and to act cooperatively has been created by
the threat in the early and mid-1970s of a federal government dominated by liberal Democrats. If the perceived threat of a Democratic
caucus guided by Ralph Nader and George Meany had been the driving
force behind the political coalescence of business in the 1970s, a second
incentive encouraging business to act as a class grew out of a different
source altogether: the campaign reforms enacted in 1971, and expanded
in 1974 in response to Watergate. The central goal of these campaign
reforms was to prevent any single political contributor from gaining
excessive influence over Congress or over a presidential administration.
The 1974 reforms, which proved critical to later political developments, were prompted by disclosures of massive secret contributions to
President Nixon's 1972 reelection campaign, which in turn resulted in
the conviction of eight business executives for using corporate money
in making contributions of $50,000 or more.

Under terms of the legislation seeking to reform such practices,
individuals were prohibited from giving more than $1,000 to any single
candidate for a specific election—primary, run-off, or general—and
from giving more than $5,000 in any year to any political action
committee. During a full year, the sum total of an individual's political
contributions to federal candidates and to federal committees may not

exceed $25,000. The existence of political action committees predated these reforms; previously, however, the use of PACs had been the province of organized labor, which had been using them to raise and contribute money since the 1940s. In large part as a response to pressure from organized labor, which thought it would continue to dominate this kind of fundraising, the campaign reforms of the early and mid-1970s gave specific legal authority to political action committees. Not only were PACs authorized, but the law was changed to explicitly permit the sponsoring organizations, unions, or corporations, to use money from corporate or union treasuries to pay the costs of forming a PAC, of staffing, and of soliciting contributors. Once established, PACs are prohibited from contributing more than $5,000 to any specific candidate for any given election, although there is no ceiling on the total amount that can be given.[21]

Just as orchestrated grass-roots lobbying had proved to be uniquely compatible with the pyramid structure of corporations, corporations proved to be almost perfectly suited to the creation and ongoing maintenance of political action committees. Once a chief executive officer and a board of directors approve creation of a PAC, contributions to the corporate PAC by management-level personnel become an integral part of company policy. Although no coercion may be involved, a middle-level executive choosing not to contribute has to consider whether his or her decision will be interpreted as a failure to endorse and support the goals of the corporation. Additionally, the corporation is already equipped with a payroll system permitting the direct collection of monies before they are paid out, as long as the employee has authorized automatic payroll deduction.

On just a single, but typical, payroll day, June 15, 1983, the Amoco Oil Co. PAC collected $2,788, in amounts ranging from $24.74 from E. J. Sullivan, an environmental control official in the Chicago offices of the company, to $127.26 from M. R. Waller, vice-president for research in Tulsa, Oklahoma.[22] The steady flow of money mounts up: the Amoco PAC raised a total of $455,589 from employees during the 1981–82 election cycle. In 1977 Clark MacGregor, senior vice-president of United Technologies, Inc., sent a letter to management level employees telling them the company had formed a PAC: "This is your opportunity to voluntarily contribute to the benefit of United Technologies' employees and shareholders in signing a check." By the 1981–82 election cycle, voluntary support for the United Technologies PAC produced a campaign chest of $245,560.[23]

The strongest evidence for the adaptability of the corporate structure to the creation of PACs is the growth of corporate PACs themselves. In 1974 there were 89 corporate PACs, in 1978 there were 784, and by the end of 1982 there were 1,467. During the same period, the number of what the Federal Election Commission classifies as Trade-Membership-Health PACs doubled from 318 to 628. This classification generally has close links to the business community and is dominated by such groups as the Realtors, the American Medical Association, the National Rifle Association, the National Association of Homebuilders, the American Bankers Association, and the Automobile and Truck Dealers Association. Labor PACs, in turn, grew only from 201 to 380 in the period from 1972 to 1982. In terms of the money spent by different classifications of PACs since 1972, the changing financial strength of these three different interests, corporations, trade associations, and labor unions is shown in table 3.1.

Table 3.1 [24] EXPENDITURES OF LABOR, CORPORATE, AND TRADE ASSOCIATION PACS IN MILLIONS OF DOLLARS

Type of PAC	1972	1978	1982
Labor	$8.5	$18.6	$35.0
Corporate	8.0	15.2	43.2
Trade association		23.8	41.7

The amount of money labor is channeling into federal campaigns has grown fourfold over the decade, from $8.5 million to $35 million, but the combined fiscal muscle of corporate and trade association PACs has grown tenfold, from $8 million to $84.9 million, or at more than twice the rate of labor. The effects of the growth of business and trade association contributions have been magnified by several other factors that have combined to encourage and indeed to force businesses to join together and to act as a class rather than as a series of individual, or competing, interests. These factors include the restrictions on the amount of money a single PAC can give to a candidate, and a substantial change in the kinds of issues and legislation brought before Congress during the past fifteen years.

The $5,000 restriction on the size of contributions any single PAC can give to an individual candidate in a primary or general election has forced separate business and trade association interests to band together in the course of major legislative battles. In a tough congressional contest pitting powerful forces against each other, a $5,000 contribution to a congressman whose total election costs are $350,000 is not going to guarantee a favorable vote. The $5,000 ceiling severely restricts the amount of leverage one company or one trade association can exert on Congress.[25]

The 1970s were, additionally, a period in which many legislative initiatives were not limited to specific industries. The earlier creation of such regulatory bodies as the Interstate Commerce Commission, the Federal Aviation Administration, the Atomic Energy Commission, the Securities and Exchange Commission, and the Federal Communications Commission all involved industry-wide regulation—trucking, radio and television, the airlines, stockbrokers, etc.—and it was possible for a specific industry and even for specific companies to gain leverage over both the legislative and regulatory processes. The more recent initiatives, however, have involved the creation of such agencies as the Environmental Protection Agency and the Occupational Health and Safety Administration, whose mandates cut across all industry lines. Other initatives have involved proposals to create a consumer protection agency or to strengthen the bargaining power of unions seeking to organize company employees. These were issues that affected the entire business community and required cooperative action.

At the same time, for corporate PACs attempting to influence the legislative process through campaign contributions, there were not only the $5,000 limits on individual contributions but also internal constraints: the vast majority of corporate PACs raise less than $100,000 in each election cycle, making it impossible for a single PAC to alter the course of legislation significantly. During the 1979–80 election cycle, the average corporate PAC contributed a total of only $19,583 to federal candidates, and in 1981–82 this grew to only $22,344.[26] In other words, the average corporate PAC in 1981–82 could only hand out a maximum of four $5,000 contributions, with a remaining $2,344 to spread out for good will. Without cooperative efforts, then, individual corporate PACs would remain minor-league figures, without significant impact on the content of legislation.

Cooperative action among corporate PACs has emerged through two interrelated strategies: the channeling of money to incumbent Democrats, whose votes provide the margin of victory or defeat on major issues, particularly in the House, where the Democratic majority remains firm; and the channeling of money to Republicans who are both incumbents and challengers but whose votes and overall philosophy of government are far more reliably favorable to business than the votes and philosophy of their Democratic counterparts. Table 3.2 breaks down the partisan distribution of corporate PAC money between House and Senate candidates.

Table 3.2 [27] THE DISTRIBUTION OF CORPORATE PAC MONEY IN THE 1981–82
ELECTION CYCLE

| | Democrats: | | Republicans: | |
HOUSE	Total contributions	% of total	Total contributions	% of total
Incumbents	$ 6,182,364	86.7	$ 8,540,516	70.0
Challengers	296,344	4.1	1,745,790	14.3
Open seats	653,653	9.2	1,922,539	15.7
Total	7,132,361	100	12,208,845	100
SENATE				
Incumbents	$ 2,604,400	89.0	$ 4,220,891	60.6
Challengers	198,900	6.8	1,517,975	21.8
Open seats	123,491	4.2	1,225,877	17.7
Total	2,926,791	100	6,964,743	100

This pattern of contributions is a key element of the financial support that provides vitality to the Republican party, as described in chapter 2, the practice, within the business community, the conservative community, and the Republican party, of channeling money to those GOP candidates most in need of cash. From the vantage point of the business community, this pattern of contributions functions to maintain working relations with incumbent members of both parties, while, in competitive election contests, financing the more conservative of the two parties, the GOP. Of the total of $7.6 million in corporate PAC money going to all challengers and open-seat candidates in 1981–82—and these are the contests that, more than any others, determine partisan shifts in Congress—$6.4 million, or 84.2 percent, went to Republicans. In the case of incumbents, corporate PACs are using money to protect their direct interests in legislative decisions by contributing to incumbent members of both parties. In the case of incumbents, the partisan disparity favoring Republicans among business PACs was only 59%–41% in 1981–82, or $12.8 million going to incumbent Republicans and $8.8 million to incumbent Democrats. The long-range interests of business, involving a shift in the partisan balance of power in the House and Senate, were reflected in a much stronger bias in favor of non-incumbent Republican candidates, 84%–16%, or $6.4 million to $1.2 million.

One effect of this contribution pattern was demonstrated earlier in 1977 when the House unexpectedly defeated common situs picketing legislation. This measure, which had passed Congress in 1975, only to be vetoed by President Gerald Ford, would have allowed one striking construction union to picket all entry points to a construction site. Existing law prohibits a specific union from picketing at sites where it has not been actively working prior to striking. Expansion of the picketing jurisdiction forces other unions either to honor the strike or to violate a basic rule of organized labor by crossing a picket line. Democratic strength in the House in 1977 was equal to its strength in 1975; and with a newly elected Democratic president committed to sign the legislation, the common situs bill appeared assured of enactment. On March 23, 1977, however, the House rejected the legislation by a margin of 205 to 217. A number of freshman Democrats were from nonunion suburban districts and voted against the bill, but the key votes were cast by eleven Democrats who had supported common situs legislation in 1975 only to oppose it in 1977.

The votes of these eleven Democrats were critical to the outcome of the bill: without their defection, the legislation would have passed 216 to 206. Labor had provided the eleven with strong support before the vote, giving them a total of $166,987 in the 1976 election. Voting against the bill threatened curtailment of this support, and labor implemented its threat, reducing contributions to the eleven by $69,167, giving only $97,820 in the 1978 election, reductions effected most sharply by those unions with the greatest stake in common situs: the building trades. Business and trade association PACs, however, more than made up for this loss. In 1976 the business and trade association PACs had given the eleven Democrats a total of $177,208; in 1978, after the votes in Congress against common situs, campaign contributions from business shot up to $346,293. In other words, voting against labor resulted in a net gain for the defecting Democrats: the loss of a total of $69,167 in labor contributions was more than made up for by an increase of $169,085 in business and trade association contributions, an improvement of $99,918. Harold E. Ford, Democrat of Tennessee, for example, saw his backing from labor drop from $28,750 in 1976 to $10,990 in 1978, a decline of $17,750; during the same period, however, his business and trade association contributions went from $4,100 in 1976 to $29,750 in 1978, an increase of $25,650, or a net gain of $7,900. Viewed strictly in terms of campaign contributions, the decision to vote against labor resulted in no penalty; instead, net contributions went up. Similarly, other Democrats among the eleven included James D. Santini of Nevada, whose labor backing fell by $14,417 but whose business and trade association support increased by $19,141, for a net increase of $4,727; John R. Breaux of Louisiana, who lost $6,170 in total labor contributions but saw business and trade association support increase by $19,750, for a net increase of $13,580; and Mike McCormack of Washington, who saw labor backing drop by $11,800 but business and trade association support increase by $24,300, for a net increase of $12,500.[28]

Coordination of Contributions

Coordination of campaign contributions, particularly when it involves a much larger attempt to change the ideological thrust of Congress, requires some central direction. The emergence of well over 1,500 corporate and trade association PACs, not to mention individual donors seeking direction in the distribution of their own campaign contributions, has produced a network of specialists in the effective use of campaign contributions. To a certain extent, these specialists perform a role analogous to that of the traditional boss in the days when local political organizations could control the outcome of an election. Just as the boss rewarded loyalty with promotion up the political ladder, new specialists in coordinating the distribution of campaign money are besieged by candidates for the House and Senate, who promise allegiance throughout their elective careers.

The proliferation of PACs and the more general attempt of business, environmental, reform, conservative, labor, and liberal groups to shape the content of legislative decisions have produced specialists in the channeling of campaign contributions working in behalf of each of these interests. Those who have been most effective and influential, however, are part of the nexus of shared political goals among business interests, many of the trade associations, the conservative groups, and the Republican party itself. While not a formal alliance, the shared interest of business, the ideologically conservative groups, many of the trade associations, and the Republican party in giving financial support to extensively overlapping slates of candidates has provided a basis for the sharing of information that gives these groups a strong advantage in the effective use of campaign money.

The key function of these new specialists in campaign finance is the acquisition of detailed and accurate information identifying the close House and Senate contests across the country. The most important periods during which to obtain this information are also the most difficult in which to do so: very early, a year or more before the general election, when money is hardest to raise but essential to getting a fledgling campaign off the ground; and very late, as last-minute swings of just 1 or 2 percentage points can signal where money to a favored candidate will be effective and where it will be wasted. This information is then passed on to networks of contributors seeking to make the most effective and timely use of their money.

The need for this information has been most intense within the business community, where the proliferation across the country of relatively small corporate PACs has created a host of contributors hungry for intelligent direction but lacking the resources of Washington at their fingertips. And it is this need that is directly met by business-supported specialists through the identification of key races and through the making of recommendations in each of these races. Among those who, in the late 1970s and early 1980s, have been filling this specialized role, directing campaign contributions for sectors of the business community, are: Bernadette Budde of the Business and Industry PAC; William C. Anderson, senior government relations representative for the Independent Petroleum Association of America; Richard Thaxton of the National Association of Realtors; Clyde A. Wheeler, Jr., vice-president for government relations of the Sun Co.; Peter Lauer of the American Medical Association; and John Kochevar and Neil Newhouse of the political division of the National Chamber of Commerce. The detailed newsletters issued by BIPAC and by the Chamber of Commerce summarize close races, recommend specific candidates, and attempt to signal where business money will make a difference, not only in the election outcome but in the resulting ideological tenor of Congress. Dealing with a smaller audience, but an audience with large amounts of money to hand out, William Anderson identifies what he calls "wildcat prospects," who are almost universally conservative Republican challengers to incumbent liberal-moderate Democrats.

One of the most important factors contributing to the effectiveness of the political coordinators of the campaign money of the Washington business community is the information provided by the Republican party. In seeking to influence the general pattern of contributions among a large constituency, such as the business community, the more accurate and timely the information, the stronger the credibility of the recommendations. The detailed polling available to the Republican party has no parallel either within the Democratic party or in the public surveys conducted by such institutions as the Gallup Poll; Louis Harris and Associates; Yankelovich, Skelly & White; the National Opinion Research Center; or by such newspapers and networks as the *New York Times,* the *Washington Post,* the *Los Angeles Times,* ABC, CBS, and NBC.

Republican polls provide data on trends within congressional districts across the nation, a very costly and detailed process in itself. Then, within each of those districts, where there is the potential for partisan political change, they identify specific census tracts and income, ethnic, religious, and other demographic groups whose patterns of voting can be influenced by the adoption of varying campaign strategies. The availability of this kind of data twelve to eighteen months before the general election is crucial to the organization and to the recruitment of the most effective candidates and the targeting of early money. In the closing weeks of campaigning, the Republican party's ability to conduct daily tracking polls permits the party, its candidates, and its supporters to identify exactly where a last-minute infusion of cash can put a candidate over the top, and where the battle has become a lost cause. In the final ten days of the 1980 election, for example, when the nearly unanimous view of most political analysts and reporters was that Democrats might lose four or five Senate seats but would retain majority control, the Republican Senatorial Campaign Committee had tracking polls signaling the devastating twelve-seat Democratic loss that in turn gave the GOP majority control of the Senate for the first time since 1955.[29]

Business and Economic Policy

The rising political power of business has been associated with the general increase in the number of political action committees and with the growing volume of money channeled through them. This line of thinking, in turn, has given rise to charges that Congress, overwhelmed by the flow of cash from the PACs, has become the puppet of special interests, a forum in which every organized group, from doctors to dairymen, can, in return for campaign contributions, receive special antitrust exemption from competition or from taxpayer-financed price supports, or special insulation from the federal regulatory process. The most vocal critic of the system has been Common Cause, the principal reform lobby. "Our system of representative government is under siege because of the destructive role that political action committees or PACs are now playing in our political process," Fred Wertheimer, president of Common Cause, declared in 1983. "We are not obtaining the best judgment of our elected representatives because they are not free to give it to us. PACs, through campaign contributions, are creating a higher obligation for our representatives, an obligation to serve PAC interests, first and foremost."[30] Along similar lines, Elizabeth Drew, Washington correspondent for the *New Yorker,* has written: "The acquisition of campaign funds has become an obsession on the part of nearly every candidate for public office. . . . The role of money has delivered us into the special interest state."[31]

These analyses, while both accurate and timely, fail to take into account a number of less frequently reported factors adding to the complexity and subtlety of the current political situation on Capitol Hill. For one, Common Cause and the press have become increasingly effective watchdogs over the legislative process, preventing many of the attempts by special-interest groups to slip through favorable legislation. More important, however, while these analyses, particularly Drew's detailed description of the overwhelming concern with fundraising in Congress, accurately portray an essential element of the political process, neither recognizes what has been a major ideological shift in Congress. Business has played a key role in this shift, using not just PAC contributions but increasingly sophisticated grass-roots lobbying mechanisms, the financing of a sympathetic intellectual community, and the expenditure of somewhere in the neighborhood of $1 billion annually on institutional advertising.

This ideological shift in the nation's capital has been pervasive, altering basic tax, spending, and regulatory policies and moving both political parties well to the right over the past decade. Of the various elites that have gained strength in recent years, business has been among the most effective. Not only has it gained from highly favorable tax treatment and from a major reduction in regulation, but government action has increased the bargaining leverage of management in its relations with organized labor. This increased leverage grows out of reductions in unemployment compensation and out of the elimination of the public service job programs, and through the appointment of promanagement officials at such key agencies as the Occupational Safety and Health Administration and at the National Labor Relations Board. The end result is a labor movement that has lost much of its clout at the negotiating table and in the polling booth. High on the list of losers in the new politics of inequality are the organized workers of this country. Their situation will be explored in the next chapter.

4

Labor Unions
and Political Power

For the past thirty years, the broadly representative power of organized labor in the United States has been on the wane. The trade union movement reached the height of its powers in the early 1950s, just before the nation's two largest labor federations, the Congress of Industrial Organizations and the American Federation of Labor, merged to become the AFL-CIO. Since then, the proportion of the workforce represented by labor unions has steadily declined. This decline, however, reached critical levels during the last decade. Through two decades of prosperity, the 1950s and 1960s, organized labor had developed a deceptively cooperative alliance with big business. When, in the mid-1970s, the business community adopted an intensely adversarial posture, both in the private marketplace and in the legislative arena, labor was caught not only unprepared but politically weakened through the erosion both of its ties to the Democratic party and of its ties to many of the organizations making up the liberal-left.

These two interrelated developments—declining workforce representation and increasing hostility from management—are the primary factors in a web of forces that have undermined the basic social, political, and economic functions of organized labor in America. At a time when legislative and political conflicts are falling increasingly along income lines, when the business community is making a concerted effort to define the terms of the economic debate, and when the Democratic party is ill equipped to represent its own consituencies, organized labor remains the major institution in theory most capable of pressing the interests of the working and lower-middle classes. The potential scope of this representation goes far beyond the demand for higher wages, extending to participation in the formulation of government policies concerning taxation, the distribution of wealth and income, health care, disability compensation, employment safety, education, vocational training—the list covers the entire spectrum of possible government activity. In advanced Western democracies both on this continent and in Europe there is a direct and demonstrable correlation between government commitment to domestic social spending and the strength of the trade union movement. There exists in no Western democracy any other major organization cutting across racial and ethnic lines that can defend progressive distributional policies of both taxation and spending.

In this context, the decline of organized labor in the United States takes on new and significant meaning for the formulation of economic policy. At the end of the Second World War, 35.5 percent of the workforce, exluding agricultural workers, were members of unions. Unionization remained close to that level for the next ten years, with the second highest level of representation, at 34.7 percent, occurring in 1954, the year before the AFL and the CIO merged. Since then, however, there has been a steady decline, with union membership falling to 31.4 percent in 1960, to 27.3 percent in 1970, to 25.5 percent in 1975, and to 23.6 percent in 1978, the year for which the most recent statistics are available.[1] This translates into a decline of just under a half a percentage point a year.

The shift away from union membership has had grave consequences for the Democratic party. In the nine states where the decline in union strength has been most precipitous—California, Colorado, Idaho, Nevada, Oregon, South Carolina, Texas, Utah, and Virginia—the number of Democratic senators fell from a majority of ten out of eighteen in 1970 to a minority of four out of eighteen in 1983.

One of the most direct repercussions of the declining strength of organized labor has been the freezing of a major wing of the labor movement into a defensive posture, both on internal issues of union jurisdiction and on broader questions of politics and public policy. For such cornerstone unions as the United Automobile Workers (UAW) and the U.S. Steelworkers, the dominant concerns are the seeking of government protection from foreign competition, through tariffs, import restrictions, or other legislative mechanisms mandating a share of the market to American companies. For a number of other unions representing declining trades and skills, particularly those in manufacturing and transportation, there is little or no incentive either to expand or to develop political power. Automation and changing industrial practices are eliminating the job base; there is no new generation of activists joining the union membership; and the major concern of the remaining membership is the protection of retirement benefits and the winning of lucrative buy-out contracts as workers are replaced by machines. Membership in the Glass, Pottery, Plastics, and Allied Workers Union fell from 92,395 in 1980 to 82,603 in 1981 to 76,879 in 1982, a 16.8 percent decline in two years; over the same period, membership in the Railway Carmen fell from 54,609 to 42,761, a 21.7 percent decline; membership in the Woodworkers of America fell from 44,384 members in 1980 to 35,019 in 1982, a 21.1 percent drop. The driving objective for the leadership of these dying unions, in addition to the protection of the retirement benefits of the remaining members, is the guarantee of secure union funds to finance pensions for the union leadership, and perhaps a successful merger with another union. Insofar as high-technology and information processing and transmitting industries have created new jobs, these industries have proven resistant to unionization. An additional difficulty facing trade unions, and one that is hard to overestimate, has been the farming out of enormous numbers of previously American-held, semiskilled manufacturing jobs to so-called export platforms—assembly plants in low-wage, third world countries established by multinational corporations—where workers are paid far less than the American minimum wage and where they are beyond the reach of the American trade union movement.

Throughout the past decade, the lack of vitality in much of the trade union movement has to some degree strained relations between organized labor and the Democratic party. In 1981, when the Democratic party lost control of both the Senate and the White House in its worst defeat since 1952, a number of key Democratic elected officials treated the leadership of the AFL-CIO with disdain, not as the central representative of working men and women with a history of casting majorities for Democratic candidates.

On May 4, 1981, Lane Kirkland, president of the AFL-CIO, went before the House Budget Committee to testify not only as the spokesman for the nation's central labor federation, representing ninety-six unions with a total membership of 13.5 million workers, but also as a spokesman for an ad hoc alliance of organizations representing the core of what remained of the Democratic coalition: the NAACP, the National Council of Senior Citizens, the National Women's Political Caucus, Americans for Democratic Action, and the Environmental Policy Center. Kirkland encountered a display of hostility and disregard from Democratic members of the committee, an antagonistic reception by members of the major party of the left for the nation's most important labor leader, an antagonism that would have been inconceivable in any other Western democracy.

Representative James R. Jones of Oklahoma, the Democratic Budget Committee chairman elected to the post by the full caucus of House Democrats, told Kirkland: "I am troubled by the overall context of your testimony. It is basically 180 degrees from what others have recommended to this committee. . . . I think that is an overwhelming feeling among my colleagues." Along the same lines, Representative Leon E. Panetta, Democrat of California and perhaps the most influential member of the Budget Committee, said: "Mr. Kirkland, I think your testimony has obviously some weaknesses. . . . We came through a November election in which the issue of growth in government, tax burden, and deficits were major issues. I think it is generally accepted that President Reagan won the victory he did largely based on the frustrations of the people with a lot of what government has been doing over the years. Your proposals generally endorse doing more of the same."[2]

It was Kirkland's 1981 testimony, in fact, that presaged what would become Democratic campaign rhetoric a year later. "The administration is gambling with the well-being of those who can ill afford to gamble in order to provide a sure winner for the wealthy who are not asked to take any of the risk," Kirkland had told the committee. "Tax cuts loaded on the side of the rich ignore the evidence of history that such cuts do not produce the type of investment society needs most and do not trickle surely down to enhance the general welfare." The sharp differences between Kirkland and the committee Democrats, however, reflect the weak base of support both within the United States and within the Democratic party for domestic government spending, for policies that maintain high employment as opposed to lower rates of inflation, and for tax policies that have progressive distributional results. In what amounts to a vicious circle in the strained relations between organized labor and Democratic elected officials, and a major factor behind the weakness of the Democratic commitment to social spending and progressive tax distribution, is the weakness of the labor movement itself.

In this respect, it is difficult to underestimate the importance of the labor movement to the Democratic party and to the network of programs that the party has enacted since the start of the New Deal. The necessity of organized labor to the maintenance of support for Democratic social and economic policies is best demonstrated through international comparisons, both of the political strength of organized labor in advanced, capitalist countries, including the United States, and of the relationship of the strength of organized labor to economic policy. Some of the most detailed work in this field has been done by David R. Cameron of Yale University. Cameron has devised a three-part formula to determine the relative strength of labor in each of eighteen advanced countries.[3] The first variable in his formula is the percentage of the workforce represented by unions. The second is a rating that estimates the degree to which unions in a given country are

Table 4.1   CORRELATION OF UNION STRENGTH WITH ECONOMIC POLICIES

	Strong union countries	Moderate union countries	Weak union countries
Unemployment rate, 1980–81	4.9%	5.7%	7.4%
Average unemployment, 1965–81[4]	2.8%	3.3%	4.6%
Total tax revenue as a percentage of gross domestic product, 1980[5]	44.0%	36.4%	31.5%
Percentage of GNP spent on social security and welfare programs[6]	21.3%	15.5%	13.7%
Income inequity: the higher the number, the larger the disparity in income between the top 20 percent, the rich, and the bottom 20 percent of the population, the poor[7]	28.3	36.0	38.8

fragmented or unified, both in terms of participation in central federations along the lines of the AFL–CIO and in terms of large, industry-
wide unions, as distinguished from more numerous, but smaller, labor

organizations. The third factor in Cameron's formula is a rating of the power of the central labor federation over the collective bargaining negotiations of individual unions: does the central federation have the power to veto settlements; does it control strike funds, in effect determining whether an individual union can exercise the strike weapon; does the central labor federation have the power to order member unions to honor each others' picket lines? The application of Cameron's formula results in the following breakdown:

Countries with strong union
                    movements: Sweden, Norway, Austria, Denmark,
                                      Belgium, and Finland

Countries with moderately
                strong unions: Netherlands, West Germany, Britain,
                                      Ireland, Australia, and Switzerland

Countries with weak unions: Italy, Canada, United States, Japan,
                                      France, and Spain

Taking these three classifications, it is then possible to compare in table 4.1 the strength of labor unions with key economic policies and practices.

By every measure—unemployment rates, taxation, social spending, and income distribution—those countries with strong labor union movements have in place policies of taxation, employment, and social spending advantageous to the working class. Further evidence of the use of government policies aimed at helping the majority of the population dependent upon wage and salary income in countries with strong unions is shown in the use of taxes on wealth. Five of the six strong union countries have an annually collected tax on wealth, while three of the six moderately strong union countries, and only one of the six weak union countries, use such taxes.[8]

The United States is a weak union country,[9] and, as table 4.1 shows, the welfare state here is smaller than in most other advanced countries. Organized labor has played, however, a key role in the development of the network of programs in the United States designed to provide support, protection, and benefits to the poor and working classes. During the critical early years of the administration of Franklin Delano Roosevelt, the mobilization of labor was an essential part of the creation of the New Deal Democratic coalition, which, in turn, formed the basis for a public consensus in favor of a large-scale federal intervention in the economy. In 1933, the first year in which Roosevelt held office, organized labor represented only 11.3 percent of the nonagricultural workforce. By the start of Roosevelt's second term in office, 1937, that percentage had doubled to 22.6, and two years later, in 1939, it had grown to 28.6. In terms of people, the number of unionized workers grew from 2.69 million in 1933 to 8.76 million in 1939, an increase of 226 percent, by far the fastest rate of growth for union membership in the past 50 years.[10]

To touch briefly on some of the key pieces of legislation that labor helped first to enact, secondly to expand during favorable administrations, and thirdly to protect during hostile administrations, there are: the Social Security Administration, with a 1982 budget of $156 billion; Medicare and Medicaid, with a combined 1982 cost of $64 billion; federal aid to elementary, secondary, and vocational education, at a 1982 cost of $6.8 billion; unemployment compensation, $23.6 billion in 1982; the Occupational Safety and Health Administration, with a 1982 budget of $194 million; the Mine Safety and Health Administration, with a budget of $139 million; the Black Lung Disability Fund, $884 million; the Employment Standards Administration, $912 million; the National Labor Relations Board, $119 million; and federal minimum wage legislation. Labor has not been the only force behind the enactment of this legislation, nor has it been the principal force in every case. It has been, however, an essential base of support, not only for these programs but in the drive to enact the civil rights legislation of the 1960s and in the passage of all tax legislation from 1935 through 1976 aimed at maintaining the progressivity of the individual income tax system.

In the 1970s, however, the capacity of organized labor to provide political support for programs and policies beneficial to the working class swiftly began to deteriorate. In 1975 unions began to lose a majority of their attempts to organize nonunion plants and other facilities; for the first time since the passage of the National Labor Relations Act and the creation of the National Labor Relations Board in 1935, the victory rate in representation elections—that is, elections in which the employees of any individual workplace vote on whether or not to have union representation—fell below 50 percent. In 1976, the percentage of the workforce represented by unions fell below 25 percent, the lowest level since 1938.[11] At the same time, there was no mobilization of a new block of support for the Democratic party, such as that mobilized by the civil rights movement in the 1960s, or the mobilization of urban, ethnic support of the 1930s. Rather, Democratic congressional strength survived through the mid-1970s largely as a result of Watergate, a historical anomaly that provided no long-term base of constituent support or of growth for the Democratic party.

Well before federal election results began to show a significant shift to the right and toward the Republican party—that is, well before 1978 —the union movement had begun to lose its leverage in Congress. Elected officials, acutely aware of the strengths and weaknesses of the organizations seeking their votes, began to distance themselves from labor unions in the middle of the 1970s. In the 1976 election, Democrats won the presidency for the first time in eight years and maintained their strong margins in both the House (292–143) and Senate (62–38); but the labor agenda collapsed. Common situs picketing was rejected in the House. Labor law reform, legislation strengthening the hand of labor in collective bargaining, which had appeared assured of enactment in 1977 at the start of the Ninety-fifth Congress, was defeated by Senate filibuster. Even with the federal government in the hands of Democrats, organized labor proved weaker than a revived business lobby.

By 1978, when the short-term boost to the Democrats from Watergate had run its course, the stage was set for the onset of a major shift in the political balance of power, in terms of the determination of economic policy. This shift in power first manifested itself in the 1978 tax bill. As originally proposed by President Carter, the bill was to have been continuous with previous Democratic tax policy: it included the elimination of many tax breaks beneficial to the affluent; individual tax cuts were skewed toward the poor, the working class, and the lower-middle class, as part of a Democratic tradition of increasing the progressivity of the income tax system; and the rate of taxation on capital gains—income from the sale of such assets as stock, real estate, and bonds, most of which goes to the rich—was to have been raised. By the time a solidly Democratic House and a solidly Democratic Senate completed action on the legislation, however, it was the first major tax bill since the 1930s that did not skew benefits toward those at the bottom and middle of the income spectrum. The capital gains rate, furthermore, was lowered. In effect, the legislation marked a complete reversal of Democratic tax policy, and it was a reversal conducted in direct defiance of organized labor. By the time an even sharper reversal of tax policy was achieved with the passage of the Reagan administration's 1981 tax bill, labor had been relegated to the far periphery of the political and economic debate, a once-powerful lobby that no longer had leverage over the content of legislation.

The decline of labor's influence over legislatively determined economic policy is only one aspect of recent political and economic change, but it is an essential aspect. In many regards, the decline of labor went largely unnoticed, particularly in the media. As the power of organized labor in the United States fell, the interest of the press shifted elsewhere. In a direct reflection of the importance attached to the trade union movement, the assignment to cover labor—the labor beat—on many newspapers, which had been a high-status assignment in the heyday of labor's prestige, serving both as a valued specialty, as in the case of A. H. Raskin of the *New York Times,* who won national recognition for his work, or as a stepping stone up the journalistic ladder to political assignments or editorial work, has been relegated to much lower status, and in many cases has been eliminated altogether. A consequence of this abandonment of media interest in organized labor has been a failure to recognize the impact of a weakened labor movement upon the determination of basic employment, taxation, and social spending policies.[12]

While the public and the media may have failed to recognize the broad significance of the decline of organized labor, many key labor leaders have dismissed the failure of organized labor to grow as an irrelevant issue. "Why should we worry about organizing groups of people who do not want to be organized? If they prefer to have others speak for them and make the decisions which affect their lives without effective participation on their part, that is their right," George Meany commented in early 1972. "Frankly, I used to worry about the membership, about the size of the membership. But quite a few years ago, I just stopped worrying about it, because to me it doesn't make any difference. It's the organized voice that counts—and it's not just in legislation, it's any place. The organized fellow is the fellow that counts."[13]

Attack on Labor

The business community, however, did not make the same error in judgment. A concerted effort by corporate leadership to weaken the labor movement began somewhat cautiously in the late 1960s but reached unprecedented intensity in the period from 1970 to 1980. In the 1970s, American industry abandoned the cooperative tenor that had dominated much of labor-management relations in favor of a tough, adversarial stance. The strongest evidence for this change has been in the willingness of business to violate provisions of the National Labor Relations Act when fighting unions in representation elections. Since 1970, the total number of representation elections in the United States has remained relatively constant: 8,074 in 1970 and 8,198 in 1980, an increase of just 5.4 percent. During the same period, however, the number of workers reinstated to their jobs on orders of the National Labor Relations Board after having been illegally fired rose from 2,723 in 1970 to 8,592 in 1980, an increase of 216 percent. Under federal labor law, an employer found to have illegally discharged an employee for union activity is required to offer reinstatement and back wages, less whatever income the employee has earned while fired. During the past decade, companies seeking either to keep unions out of their plants and shops or to decertify representation rights held by unions have clearly found these penalties worth the cost. Table 4.2 demonstrates the

willingness of companies to violate the National Labor Relations
Act.

Table 4.2 [14]   GROWTH IN WORKER REINSTATEMENTS, AWARDS OF BACK PAY,
AMOUNT OF BACK PAY, CHARGES OF UNFAIR LABOR PRACTICES, AND
REPRESENTATION ELECTIONS, 1970–80

	1970	1980	% increase, 1970–80
Number of workers reinstated	2,723	8,592	216
Number of workers awarded back pay	6,828	15,566	128
Amount of back pay awarded to workers	$2.7 million	$31.1 million	1,052
Number of charges of unfair labor practices filed against employers	13,601	31,281	130
Number of representation elections	8,074	8,198	2

The clear implication of these figures is that an increasing number
of businesses have found the sanctions imposed for fighting unions
through illegal tactics worth the price. Richard B. Freeman, in a paper
for the National Bureau of Economic Research, supports this assessment concluding that intensified management opposition, both legal
and illegal, has sharply reduced labor's ability to increase its membership through collective bargaining elections: between 1960 and 1980,
the "number of all employer unfair practices charges rose fourfold; the
number of charges involving a firing for union activity rose threefold;
and the number of workers awarded back pay or ordered reinstated to
their jobs rose fivefold. . . . If one divided the number of persons fired
for union activity in 1980 by the number of persons who voted for a
union in elections to obtain an indication of the risk faced by workers
desiring a union, one gets a remarkable result: one in twenty workers
who favored the union got fired."[15] In elections where unions are

seeking the right to represent workers at the collective bargaining table with management, the percentage won by unions has steadily declined.

During the 1960s, the union victory rate in collective bargaining elections remained constant, with labor winning 58 percent of the contests during the first five years, 1960 to 1964, and 59.1 percent in the second five-year period, 1965 to 1969. At the start of the 1970s, the rate began to drop sharply, falling to an average victory rate of 52.7 percent in the period from 1970 to 1974, and then down to 48.6 percent in the last five years of the decade. In 1980, the victory rate for unions was 48.1 percent, and in 1981, 45.4 percent.[16]

These figures, however, mask another trend that compounds the problems of organized labor: not only are unions now losing a majority of collective bargaining elections, but the losses are concentrated in the larger factories, plants, and other facilities. In 1980 and 1981, for example, there were on the average fifty people in the bargaining units where unions won representation rights, while there were eighty people in the units where management won. During this two-year period, unions won 46.8 percent of the elections, but since the unit size of the union victories was smaller, organized labor won the right to represent only 36.5 percent of the total number of workers involved in representation elections, 147,353 out of 403,387.

In other words, when the record of organized labor in collective bargaining elections is calculated in terms of the percentage of *workers* won or lost, the record is far worse than it appears to be from the win-loss rate for elections. The number of people won or lost as union members in the elections is by far the more important figure, because it reflects both success in winning new dues-paying members and the strength of labor in the workforce itself. That the number of management victories in those contests involving larger units has grown over the years—in the early 1950s, unions won in the larger units and lost in the smaller units—suggests that it is in the larger companies where the willingness to counter union organizing efforts through both legal and illegal means—that is, unfair labor practices—has grown.

Labor also no longer has, in the private sector, such major organizing opportunities as the Ford Motor Company, Bethlehem Steel, or the railroads. Instead, the average size of the bargaining unit that unions have sought to represent through NLRB elections has steadily declined. At the height of union organizing, from 1936 through 1945, the average bargaining unit in representation elections contained 356 persons. By the first half of the 1960s, this declined to an average size of 73 workers, and by the second half of the 1970s, it fell to 63 persons. The costs of attempting to unionize small units is far greater per employee than in large units, but the amount of money in real inflation-adjusted dollars that unions have been spending on organizing has remained steady over the years.[17]

Management, in addition to putting up much tougher fights in representation elections, has intensified the conflict with organized labor through decertification elections: campaigns to persuade a majority of employees to vote to get rid of existing union representation. Throughout the 1960s, the number of decertification elections remained basically constant, averaging 241 in the years from 1960 to 1964 and 237 from 1965 through 1969. In the 1970s, however, the number shot up, first to an annual average of 419 in the first five years of the decade and then to an annual average of 712 during the second half of the 1970s. In 1980 there were 902 decertification elections, and in 1981 there were 856. Labor has a consistently poor record in decertification elections, which can only occur when there is significant employee dissatisfaction with the union and, in most cases, when management presses an anti-union drive—and management has won about 70 percent of these elections over the years, although in recent years this margin of victory has gotten closer to 75 percent.[18]

The number of employees involved in decertification elections is far smaller than the number involved in representation elections, 45,406 to 403,837 in 1981, but the proportion is growing. In the second half of the 1960s, 76,000 persons were involved in decertification elections, or 2.6 percent of the 2.85 million persons involved in collective bargaining elections; by the second half of the 1970s, there were 174,000 workers involved in decertification elections, or 7 percent of the 2.49 million people involved in collective bargaining contests.[19]

More recently firms including Continental Airlines, Eastern Airlines, and the Wilson Foods Corporation have been exploring the use of bankruptcy as a means of abrogating union contracts, a practice that the Supreme Court signaled it will uphold, in a February 1984 decision. The use of bankruptcy is particularly threatening to organized labor because trade unions are strongest among the nation's financially weak, capital intensive industries, just those industries that are most likely to take advantage of the legal maneuvering that Chapter Eleven bankruptcy reorganizations permit.

The apparently sudden abandonment by business of a cooperative relationship with organized labor caught the leaders of organized labor largely by surprise, and they were ill equipped to counter the offensive. In 1970, AFL-CIO President George Meany, lulled by a decade of continuing economic growth during which management agreed to higher and higher pay scales for members of the prestige unions (the construction trades, steelworkers, auto workers), foresaw what amounted to an end to hostile labor-management relations: "We wouldn't want to give it [the strike] up as a weapon, but I can say to you quite frankly that more and more people in the trade union movement—I mean at the highest levels—are thinking of other ways to advance without the use of the strike method. . . . Voluntary arbitration, for instance," he told a press conference on August 25, 1970. "Where you have a well-established industry and a well-established union, you are getting to the point where a strike doesn't make sense. . . . When you have an area where an employer doesn't want to have anything to do with a union, or listen, then of course you have to strike. But those areas are certainly not as numerous as they were some years ago."[20] Just as management was beginning to gear up for a major battle aimed at undermining the base of organized labor, Meany was under the impression that labor's relationship to management in the future would be so cooperative that conflicts could be resolved through voluntary negotiations conducted under the auspices of the American Arbitration Society.

This cooperative posture remained labor's stance through most of the 1970s, as Meany and the secretary-treasurer of the AFL-CIO at that time, Lane Kirkland, joined together with the chief executive officers of America's largest corporations, including Irving S. Shapiro of du Pont and Reginald H. Jones of General Electric, to form the Labor-Management Group in 1976, theoretically an organization providing labor and management with a vehicle by which to jointly address such issues as productivity, trade, tax, and energy. Labor did not recognize the adversarial posture of business until 1978, when its supposed allies in big business, particularly the members of the Business Roundtable, turned on the union movement in the congressional battle over the Labor Law Reform bill, pulling out the stops to defeat the legislation.[21] Both Shapiro and Jones served as chairmen of the Business Roundtable. As A. H. Raskin later wrote: "What galled labor beyond measure, oddly enough, was not the treason of politicians who had taken labor's shilling at election time. It was the defection to the anti-union camp of a raft of chief executives from the Fortune 500—men whom the unions had come to think of almost as allies. As many labor leaders see it, that crucial battle marked the end of a thirty-year entente cordiale. During this era of good feelings, many big companies had come to depend on the unions as a primary force for stabilization, both in equalizing basic labor costs within each major industry and in maintaining uninterrupted production for the life of the contract. In return, management became the principal recruiting agent for a labor movement that had run out of steam. The operation of union shop contracts automatically delivered over tens of thousands of new employees, the ultimate in push-button unionism."[22]

Meany and Kirkland found partial expression for their anger at business by withdrawing in 1978 from the Labor-Management Group, but two years later, in the summer of 1980, Jones and Shapiro, along with Thomas A. Murphy of General Motors and Walter B. Wriston of Citicorp, persuaded Kirkland, who had by then succeeded Meany as president of the AFL-CIO, to rejoin the organization. Kirkland and Clifton C. Garvin, chairman of Exxon and head, at that time, of the Business Roundtable, became co-chairmen. That same year, Exxon began a multi-billion-dollar Rocky Mountain oil shale project using nonunion labor; and du Pont continued to reduce the percentage of its $600 million to $1 billion annual construction budget that went to union contractors, from 100 percent in 1970 to 50 percent or less by the start of the 1980s.[23]

The intensity of the conflict between labor and management was exacerbated by the unanticipated consequences of a major change in the content of many union contracts in the late 1960s and early 1970s. These contracts provided for automatic cost of living salary increases pegged to increases in the Consumer Price Index (CPI). The CPI is heavily weighted toward oil and mortgage interest rates, which in the eyes of many economists made it a flawed price index in the 1970s, giving labor a 6 to 8 percentage point wage hike above settlements consonant with actual increases in the cost of living. The result was, just at a time of increased overseas competition, an inadvertant CPI-pegged wage hike that functioned to push U.S. wage rates up, in international terms, to noncompetitive levels, levels that were, in the view of at least management, economically not sustainable.

To a certain extent, then, the forcing of union wages downward in the late 1970s and early 1980s was an adjustment to the fortuitous cost-of-living-induced wage excesses negotiated ten to fifteen years earlier. In many cases, however, management drives have gone past efforts to reduce the union/nonunion wage differential and have become successful efforts to break unions altogether. Once a union is broken, there is no longer any union/nonunion differential. There is no union.

Just as labor entered the 1970s unprepared for the attack by business, and not fully politically cognizant of the long-term consequences of cost-of-living provisions, it also began that decade caught in a severely debilitating political posture, enmeshed in a bitter conflict with the Democratic party. Under Meany, the AFL-CIO maintained strong support for the war in Vietnam and, at a time of growing détente with the Soviet Union, retained a strong commitment to the cold war. In 1968, these policies, together with the growing personal and policy schisms between Meany and Walter Reuther, president of the United Auto Workers, resulted in the withdrawal of the UAW from the AFL-CIO, which in turn meant the loss of $1 million and 1.3 million members from the nation's central labor federation. (The UAW would not rejoin the AFL-CIO until 1981, well after the decline of labor became an established fact.)

By the start of the 1970s, as opponents of the Vietnam War became increasingly strong within the Democratic party, Meany contended that the Democratic party had "become the party of the extremists. . . . As they take it over and as they move more and more to the left —and I mean away over to the left—I think, more and more, the Democrats are going to lose the support of our members. Our members are basically Americans. They basically believe in the American system. And maybe they have a greater stake in the system now then they had 15 or 20 years ago, because under the system and under our trade union policy, they have become 'middle class.' They have a greater stake."[24] In 1972 Meany, adamantly opposed to the liberal-reform wing of the Democratic party that won the presidential nomination for George S. McGovern, led a successful effort to prevent the AFL-CIO from endorsing the Democratic nominee, the first time this had happened since the AFL-CIO was formed in 1955.

Meany, in an assessment of the results of the Democratic party reforms that had been set for the party by the McGovern-Fraser commissions, contended that the reforms had created a "convention of the elite." Meany pointed out that the McGovern delegation from California was made up of "53 college students, 18 white-collar miscellaneous, 45 managerial representatives, plus professors from colleges, plus an additional group of 37 teachers, 35 people from the poverty program staff, 20 political office holders, 24 owners of small businesses, 19 retired people and 9 trade union officials. Nine—3.2 percent of that delegation was made up of trade union officials, and this is the convention of the party which, history shows, from the Roosevelt days up to now, had its bone and sinew furnished by the American trade union movement."[25]

Meany's characterization of the unionized workforce as middle-class is accurate, however, for only one segment of this workforce: in 1977, according to a study by the Department of Labor, there were 16.58 million full-time wage and salary workers who were members of labor organizations. Of those, 1.77 million, or 10.7 percent, were earning

$350 or more a week, the highest wage range covered in the study, which translates to an annual income of $18,200 or more. At the same time, a slightly *larger* block of union workers, 1.84 million, or 11.1 percent, reported making less than $150 a week, or $7,800, at a time when the poverty line for a family of four was $6,157. In fact, while a number of union members experienced significant wage increases pushing them into the middle class, and even into upper-middle-income status—particularly members of the United Automobile Workers, the U.S. Steelworkers, the Teamsters, and the United Mine Workers, whose average gross income exceeded that of college professors by 1978—these select highly paid workers mask what is a significant disparity of income within the union movement. While, for example, 37.1 percent of all unionized construction workers and 16.5 percent of all automobile workers in 1977 reported weekly earnings in excess of $350, 63.3 of all unionized apparel workers and 30.2 percent of all unionized textile workers reported incomes of less than $150 a week.[26]

At the same time, however, Meany's hostility toward the reform of the Democratic presidential nominating system and toward the party's 1972 nominee, McGovern, reflected accurately the views of a substantial portion of the working class, particularly of the white working class. McGovern's margin of support among white working-class voters was lower than that of any Democratic presidential nominee since such statistics were first gathered, in 1944, and significantly lower than the level of support received by Jimmy Carter in both the 1976 and 1980 elections.[27] This conflict between the working class and the McGovern wing of the Democratic party did not, however, result in an erosion of support among union workers for the Democratic party itself. Even with McGovern at the top of the ticket, Democrats, with continued union support, held their own in the congressional elections of 1972, gaining two seats in the Senate and losing only thirteen in the House, despite Richard Nixon's overwhelming defeat of McGovern by a margin of 47 million to 29 million votes. Analysis of the allegiance of union members to the Democratic party shows that their 5–2 ratio of support for the Democratic party over the Republican party remained firm from the 1950s through the McGovern election and throughout the rest of the 1970s.[28]

The conflict between labor and the McGovern liberal-left wing of the Democratic party came at a critical juncture, not only for the party and for organized labor but also in the formation of economic policy. This schism occurred at the beginning of a decade during which the business community would intensify efforts to weaken the strength of unions, during which conservatives would increase their political muscle, and during which economic deterioration would place severe stresses on both the Democratic party and on the union movement. To be riddled with internal conflict was, for both labor and the Democratic party, a dangerous position. In effect, the political conflict between the left wing of the Democratic party and organized labor resulted in a deterioration of the liberal lobby on Capitol Hill, making the base of support for domestic spending programs, and for tax legislation skewed toward the working and lower-middle classes, highly vulnerable.

From the vantage point of labor, George Meany's assumption, shared by many others, that the trade union movement had become middle class—a part of the establishment and no longer a part of the vanguard for economic and social change—may have accurately reflected the views of many of the more affluent union members, but such an assumption constituted a complete failure to anticipate the beleagured and defensive posture of organized labor a decade later, at the start of the 1980s. By the beginning of the Reagan administration, organized labor was forced to rèverse tactics completely. The September 19, 1981, Solidarity Day protest organized by the AFL-CIO, which brought well over 250,000 union members and supporters to Washington to denounce Reagan administration policies, was the act of a labor movement under siege, not of a labor movement proclaiming its entry into the comfort of the suburbs and into successful cooperation with corporate employers. After the 1972 convention, Meany had complained: "We heard from the abortionists, and we heard from people who look like Jacks, acted like Jills, and had the odor of johns about them."[29] The political director of the AFL-CIO's Committee on Political Education at the time, Alexander E. Barkan, described the membership of the

Democratic National Committee as a collection of "kooks, crazies, queers, and feminists." In a reflection of the scope of the forced reversal of strategy, ten years later, Lane Kirkland would lead the Solidarity Day march down Constitution Avenue with Eleanor Smeal, president of the nation's largest feminist organization, the National Organization for Women, to his right; and, in the kind of irony that springs from coalition politics, organized labor would be the single largest supporter of the Democratic National Committee, which in turn had developed formal political ties to the gay political community.

At the same time, those unions that were most affluent and middle class were the ones to face the severest repercussions from the effort on the part of business to weaken organized labor, and from the recession of 1981 and 1982. From 1979 to 1982, the unions that lost the largest numbers of members included the Teamsters, one of the most affluent and conservative of unions, losing 400,000 members from 1977 to 1983; the United Auto Workers, which in just one year, from 1981 to 1982, lost 8.8 percent of its membership, dropping from 1,107,576 to 1,010,595; and the United Steelworkers of America, in which the drop has been even more precipitous, with membership falling 25 percent in two years, from 927,869 in 1980 to 692,897 in 1982. In a demonstration of the fragile strength of the labor union movement, President Reagan was able in 1981 to replace striking air controllers with military personnel, destroying the Professional Air Traffic Controllers, an organization with 14,500 members whose annual incomes had averaged above $30,-000. Reagan's hard-line stand against the air traffic controllers was seen by both labor and management as an event triggering the resurgence of strike-breaking during the Reagan administration, leading to far tougher negotiating positions on the part of corporate executives and far more aggressive corporate techniques in riding out strikes.

The split between labor and the Democratic party's McGovern wing in the early 1970s cracked the base of the liberal coalition that had largely set the Democratic agenda during the 1950s and 1960s. The overlap between many of the core groups of the liberal coalition—Americans for Democratic Action, the National Committee for an Effective Congress, the NAACP, the Democratic Study Group, Public

Citizen, the American Civil Liberties Union, the Urban League—and the opponents of the Vietnam War made many of these groups suspicious of working with organized labor, which, in the main, had supported the war.[30] The result was a cessation of labor's central role in the lobbying process in behalf of the Democratic agenda. The Democratic-liberal agenda of the 1950s and 1960s—civil rights, housing, programs to alleviate hunger and malnutrition, federal aid to education, health coverage for the elderly and the poor, welfare assistance, job programs to counter recessions—was initiated by a wide range of forces. The one consistent element in all of these legislative battles, however, was labor's active presence in each of the lobbying coalitions. In the case of the battle to win approval of Medicare, a battle that was conducted over fifteen years, labor did more than any other group to organize and finance the creation of golden age and senior citizen clubs, many of which joined together to become the politically skillful National Council of Senior Citizens.[31]

The wounds of the Democratic party dating from the early 1970s, and the breach between labor and the McGovern wing of the party, were aggravated again in the mid-1970s, although in far more subdued fashion, by a parallel split between labor and the ascendant reform wing of the congressional Democratic party. This reform wing of the party was made up of new, junior Democrats elected to the House in 1974 and 1976. Victors in large part because of the public's anti-Republican reaction to Watergate, many of these new members came from largely suburban, previously Republican districts with few, if any, union voters. As a result, they saw organized labor both as a liability and as a benefactor. Once the Chamber of Commerce, the Business Roundtable, and other business organizations began in 1976 and 1977 to mobilize grass-roots lobbying in these districts, corporate strength far outweighed union leverage.

The loss by labor of its centrality on Capitol Hill and within the Democratic party resulted from a number of complex forces, including labor's own intransigence within the Democratic party, the sustained attack from business, labor's failure to devote money and energy toward the organizing of unorganized workers, the creation of a set of rules by the Democratic party that weakened labor's influence over the presidential nomination process, and finally, the steady decline in union membership. The loss of labor's centrality has altered the political equation in Washington, and one of the first consequences was labor's inability to produce congressional victories for legislation at the top of its own agenda.

On a larger scale, however, the decline of the political power of labor, and the conflicts between labor and other constituencies within the Democratic party, resulted in an inability to provide a solid foundation of political support for the network of protective social legislation and regulation enacted into law in the fifty years since the New Deal. How vulnerable this foundation was became apparent as protective social legislation first came under attack in the latter half of the Carter administration, when balancing the budget gained the highest priority. This vulnerability became even more strikingly apparent two years later, when President Reagan sought substantial reductions in social spending during the Ninety-seventh Congress.

Labor's growing weakness in the legislative process coincided with a sequence of three presidential elections in which the leadership of organized labor first withdrew, refusing to endorse altogether in the 1972 election when McGovern was the nominee, and then remained on the periphery in 1976 and 1980, no longer a key force in selecting the Democratic nominee. Jimmy Carter became the presidential nominee in 1976 by defeating a series of candidates who had varying degrees of union backing, particularly Senator Henry M. Jackson. In a head-on contest against Jackson, who was strongly backed by labor, in heavily unionized Pennsylvania, where 36 percent of the workforce was organized in 1976, Carter beat Jackson by 12 percentage points. In the 1980 election, labor itself was split between Carter and his Democratic challenger, Senator Edward M. Kennedy of Massachusetts. In the general election, labor poured money and whatever manpower it could muster into the Carter campaign, but Carter failed to generate support among union members, carrying the votes of union-member households by only 4 percentage points over Reagan, according to the *New York Times* poll, and by 7 points, according to the Gallup poll.[32]

The 1980 election was, in many respects, as much a defeat for labor as for the Democratic party. Not only were labor union officials unable to persuade their members to cast strong majorities for the Democratic presidential candidate—with one major union, the Teamsters, endorsing Reagan—but the results in Senate races gutted the power of labor in Congress. Such defeated senators as John Culver, Democrat of Iowa; Jacob K. Javits, Republican of New York; Birch Bayh, Democrat of Indiana; Frank Church, Democrat of Idaho; Warren G. Magnuson, Democrat of Washington; and Gaylord Nelson, Democrat of Wisconsin had helped form the nucleus of labor support in Congress.

In the years since the 1980 election, organized labor, both under the direction of Lane Kirkland and within individual unions, has taken a series of steps to regain political and policy-making leverage. It is difficult at this time to determine the success or failure of the adoption of new tactics by labor. One of the first steps has been a restoration of full participation in the Democratic party, and what amounts to an abandonment of past claims of nonpartisanship. Fifteen of the twenty-five at-large seats on the Democratic National Committee were granted to union officials in 1981, along with four of the party's thirty-five-member executive committee seats. Labor has become a financial mainstay of the Democratic party itself, providing in 1983 about $2.5 million, or just over one-third, of the Democratic National Committee's operating budget of $7 million.

In the 1982 election, labor unions were critical sources of financial support in almost all of the races where Democratic House candidates either won close elections or came close to winning. In a break with practices of the 1970s, labor began in the early 1980s to function in large part as a surrogate Democratic party, channeling money in far larger amounts and with far better targeting than the Democratic National, Congressional, and Senatorial committees. The pattern of recent effective strategic use of money by labor is clear from an examination of the distribution of contributions in eighty-seven close House races in 1982, in which the winning margin was no more than 10 percentage points (55–45). In every one of these contests, labor provided vital support for the Democratic candidate, except in certain southern districts, where the acceptance of money from labor unions constitutes a political liability. In the eighty-seven close House contests, labor provided an average amount of $58,200 to each Democratic candidate. In contrast, the Democratic committees provided an average of $9,900. This disparity between the levels of support from labor and from the party itself largely results from the fact that the Democratic party is substantially poorer than organized labor; even taking this difference into account, however, labor consistently provided support to Democratic candidates in close, marginal elections, while the Democratic party's contributions were inconsistent, as the party channeled as much as $46,000 into some close races, while missing others altogether.[33]

The discrepancy in the strategic use of money by labor and by the Democratic party is most apparent in the twenty-nine close races in which Democrats challenged, and barely lost to, incumbent Republicans: these were contests in which Democrats were outspent by an average of $198,000 to $382,000, or just under a 2 to 1 ratio, and in which a relatively slight boost in campaign contributions, particularly early in the race, might have made a significant difference. There were, for example, two contests with high symbolic potential, one in Indiana, the other in Oregon. In Indiana's Third Congressional District, the GOP had scored a major coup in 1980 when John Hiler, the Republican nominee, defeated John Brademas, the House Democratic whip. In 1982, however, the Democrats had a chance to take back the seat as the recession severely crippled the economy in this midwestern center of the recreational vehicle industry. In the contest where he was outspent $114,439 to $345,239, Richard C. Bodine, the Democratic nominee, barely lost, 49–51. The Democratic party, however, failed to recognize the potential of the Bodine candidacy, giving him a total of $460, less than one-half of 1 percent of his total campaign fund. In contrast, labor gave Bodine $38,175, one-third of his total receipts.

Similarly, in Oregon's Fifth Congressional District, Denny Smith, the Republican incumbent, had received extensive publicity in 1980 when he defeated Al Ullman, the Democratic chairman of the Ways and Means Committee. By 1982, the recession, which produced heavy unemployment in the district's lumber mills and forests, made Smith vulnerable. In a pattern almost identical to the Hiler–Bodine contest, Smith beat his Democratic challenger, Ruth McFarland, by a slim 51–49 margin, raising over twice as much money as his Democratic opponent, $491,122 to $205,062. Labor provided McFarland with $55,-788, just over 25 percent of her total receipts, while the Democratic party gave her a total of $1,440, 0.7 percent of her campaign contributions.[34]

While labor has become increasingly astute in the use of campaign contributions, it is also attempting to build up its grass-roots lobbying capacity in an attempt to match the influence of business in the orchestrated creation of district and state pressures on members of the House and Senate. Perhaps the most sophisticated of these efforts has been developed by the National Education Association (NEA), a labor organization with a highly articulate constituency, schoolteachers. The NEA has set up what it calls legislative "contact teams" in every congressional district that can be quickly mobilized as specific legislative issues arise in Congress. These teams carry special leverage because they also perform the function of deciding which candidates will be endorsed and will receive campaign contributions. In what is perhaps its most sophisticated tactic, the NEA maintains a list of 100,000 teachers who have given advance permission for the organization to send telegrams over their names to members of Congress on such key issues as tuition tax credits and aid to education.[35] In addition, the number of members of public employee unions has been growing at a significant rate, from 915,000 in 1956 to 3,626,000 in 1978, providing a potentially strong base of increased political activism within the labor movement. Unions that are growing and have the potential to emerge as influential political and lobbying forces include the Communications Workers of America, which by 1982 had grown to 583,096 members; the American Federation of State, County and Municipal Employees (AFSCME), which had 955,992 members in 1982; the United Food and Commercial Workers (UFCW), which had just over 1 million members in 1982; and the Service Employees' International Union, which had a membership of 625,000 in 1979.[36] Each of these unions is attempting to build up grass-roots organizations to apply pressure to members of Congress, and each has become increasingly sophisticated in the use of campaign money targeted to key, marginal races. Some of the AFSCME locals, particularly the union network in New York City and New York State, have become powerful political tools in the absence of local Democratic parties, with, for example, Norman Adler, political director of New York AFSCME, effectively running the successful 1982 gubernatorial campaign of Mario Cuomo.

At the same time, the AFL–CIO, in a move to strengthen its political power, is using computers so that all 13.5 million members of affiliate unions will be broken down by congressional district, ward, precinct, party registration, past political activity, sex, and race. Such lists are difficult to maintain with a high degree of accuracy, however, and privately labor activists acknowledge that existing computer lists are frequently "dirty"; that is, as many as 40 to 50 percent of the names, addresses, and ward and precinct numbers are inaccurate or no longer current. In a move paralleled by many of the affiliate unions, the AFL–CIO has raised its dues from nineteen cents a month per member in 1981 to twenty-seven cents in 1983, largely to finance expanded political, organizing, and promotional activity, a step that will increase the federation's revenues by $12 million annually. In terms of total contributions to 1982 House and Senate candidates, labor's political action committees remained behind both corporation and trade association political action committees. Stepped-up fundraising through intensified pressure on union members to contribute, however, and requests for support from retired members, have resulted in a faster rate of growth for the labor PACs from 1980 to 1982 than for either business or trade association PACs—the first time that labor's growth rate has outpaced its competitors' since the FEC began compiling statistics in 1974.

For labor, contributions to candidates went from $13.2 million in the 1979–80 cycle to $20.2 million in 1981–82, an increase of 52 percent; corporate PAC contributions went from $19.2 million to $27.4 million, an increase of 42 percent; and trade association contributions went from $15.8 million to $21.7 million, an increase of 37 percent.[37] Just as labor leaders are accepting key posts within the Democratic National Committee, the overwhelming proportion of money from labor PACs goes to Democrats. In the 1981–82 election cycle, labor gave $19.1 million, or 94.6 percent of its contributions, to Democrats, and $1.2 million, or 5.4 percent, to Republicans. This campaign contribution strategy, far more partisan than that of the business PACs, effectively rules out attempts to gain any kind of significant GOP support on controversial legislation. Labor has, however, been careful to provide campaign support to two key moderate Republicans, Senators Lowell P. Weicker, Jr., of Connecticut, and Robert T. Stafford of Vermont, both of whom sit on the Labor and Human Resources Committee. Both a result and a cause of this support is that, despite a 9–7 GOP majority, labor has been able to protect its interests with the backing of all seven committee Democrats along with Weicker and Stafford.

The AFL-CIO, working with twenty-nine member unions, put together $1 million for the first major organizing drive in nearly a generation, the Houston Project. Houston, Texas, by southern standards, has a relatively strong labor movement; at the time it was selected as a target for organizing in 1980, it was a booming city, where the job market was expanding, providing organized labor with an opportunity to strengthen its jurisdiction. Since them, however, Houston has experienced a sharp economic downturn, sending unemployment rates to unprecedented levels exceeding 9 percent and creating a labor surplus —including a large pool of low-wage illegal aliens—which in turn has made union organizing increasingly difficult. During its initial years of operation, the Houston Project has met with only mixed success. "We're swimming against the tide, that's for sure," Charles McDonald, of the AFL-CIO's organizing office, commented.[38]

In 1982 the AFL-CIO set up the Labor Institute of Public Affairs with an annual budget of $2 million, which in 1983 began producing prolabor television programs. These are designed, in part, to counter the proliferation of business-financed shows on public television that promote conservative economic views, although at this writing the labor effort has just begun, and it is difficult to gauge its success. On a parallel front, at least twenty unions have experimented with more aggressive public relations, polling, and direct-mail tactics, by hiring a new labor consulting organization, the Kamber Group, run by Victor Kamber, a former aide to Meany and to Robert A. Georgine, president of the AFL-CIO's Building and Construction Trades Department, and, briefly, advisor to Alan Cranston's 1984 presidential campaign. Kamber, one of labor's sharpest critics, contends that unions have largely failed to recognize the necessity of developing new organizing tactics using polls and direct mail, and that the failure of unions to promote their own case publicly in labor-management conflicts has resulted in a perception that a strike is "not only against the employer, but against society," and that labor has not "learned how to convert political success into legislative success." A central claim of the Kamber Group is that for a fee it will help to correct these failings.

In a highly risky gamble, the AFL-CIO attempted to force its way back into the center of the Democratic presidential selection process by endorsing Walter Mondale for the Democratic nomination in October 1983, well before the caucus and primary season began. This unprecedented tactic offered a number of possible advantages: if Mondale were the winner in 1984, labor would be able to claim major credit. In addition, with the goal of winning Democratic approval of a specific candidate, such an endorsement left labor union members far better equipped to compete to become convention delegates from both primary and caucus states. In effect, in the delegate selection process, the idea was for labor to be at least on reasonably equal footing with other Democratic activists who are most often tied to specific presidential candidates. On the other side of the coin, such an early endorsement tactic had the potential to create a severe political setback for organized labor in the event of a failure of the Mondale campaign either at the preconvention stage or in the November election, particularly if that failure were linked to the unpopularity of organized labor. Defending the early endorsement decision, Lane Kirkland contended, "There is only one risk that concerns me. That is the great risk of doing nothing and letting other people run your life."

While labor may during the coming years regain some political muscle, the magnitude of its losses in recent years suggests that the prospects for regaining centrality in the legislative debate and for setting and enforcing the Democratic agenda are far from good. In hard numbers, the elections of 1978, 1980, and 1982 resulted in a net loss for labor of sixteen votes in the Senate.[39] The loss of these supporters, combined with the political reality that new Democratic senators elected in 1984 are by no means guaranteed labor votes, indicates that labor has little or no chance of winning approval of legislation opposed by business before 1987 at the earliest, and even that would require a major ideological shift both in the electorate and in Congress.

Much worse for labor, however, will be the long-term effects of the 1981–82 recession on the private sector (as opposed to government employee) unions. Viewed in terms of its consequences for labor-management relations, the recession was a major victory for mangement. Meeting in Hot Springs, Virginia, over the weekend of May 14–15, 1983, just as the recession was lifting, members of the Business Council, an organization of major corporations similar to the Business Roundtable, declared that very few of the men and women laid off during the downturn would be rehired in the recovery. James H. Evans, chairman of the Union Pacific Corporation, noted that his transportation company had laid off 6,000 of 44,000 employees. "Will they come back?" Evans asked rhetorically. "The answer is probably not. We're running 40 percent more freight tonnage than we did 20 years ago, with half as many employees. If we had the same number of employees we had then, we would have priced ourselves out of the market. How have we done it? Automation." Along similar lines, Edward G. Jefferson, chairman of E. I. du Pont de Nemours & Company, said that 7 percent of du Pont's worldwide workforce of 174,000 had been laid off, and even if the economy were to boom, only "a few" would be hired back.[40]

While companies used the recession to reduce their workforces—one of the reasons for the sharp boost in the stock market from the summer of 1982 through the summer of 1983—the recession resulted in a sharp acceleration in the rate of decline in the membership of private sector unions. From 1980 to 1982, unions affiliated with the AFL-CIO lost a total of 986,794 members.[41] Adding in the losses from such unions as the Teamsters and the United Mine Workers, which are not affiliated with the AFL-CIO, the total decline is well in excess of 1.5 million workers. As one aspect of the Reagan administration budget cutbacks, the Department of Labor no longer calculates the percentage of the workforce that is organized, but figures supplied by the unions themselves suggest that union representation has fallen by close to one worker out of every six persons in the workforce.

The steady decline of private sector unions has forced these unions into a defensive legislative posture, just the kind of posture that drives off potential allies. The major goal of the largest private sector unions is the seeking out of government protection, or insulation, from competition, most often in the form of legislation seen by a wide segment of the public as anti-consumer. Through the Ninety-seventh Congress and well into the Ninety-eighth Congress, for example, the Auto Workers have been pressing for enactment of "domestic content" legislation requiring that an increasing percentage of all cars sold in the United States be made with American-produced parts. The Steelworkers have been seeking import and tariff restrictions on foreign steel. The Teamsters have fought to restore past protective regulation and have been adamantly opposed to further deregulation of their industry. The leading priority of the construction trade unions has been the preservation of the Davis-Bacon Act, effectively requiring all federal contractors to pay union scale wages, whether or not they are unionized. As an example of the tide against which proponents of the Davis-Bacon Act are swimming, union contractors in the Maryland, Va., and Washington, D.C., area controlled better than half the construction work as recently as 1974. By 1983, however, nine out of ten construction projects were being built by nonunion labor.[42] While these issues are complex, the union position in every case is likely either to maintain high costs or to force up consumer prices by restricting cheaper foreign imports.

The result is that labor's power and its role in the legislative process are diminishing at an accelerating rate. As labor declines, the more protectionist it becomes, the more it is perceived as a special-interest group, and the less it is seen as an institution with the potential to represent a broad core of the Democratic coalition. Stephen Stark, who served as Jimmy Carter's issues director in the 1976 campaign, warned in 1983 that labor's plan to endorse early in the 1984 presidential nomination process "is a curse, not a blessing. . . . The labor endorsement is going to end up sinking the candidate who gets it because most voters don't like labor leaders."[43] A lengthy article in the June 1983 issue of *Harper's* Magazine, a traditionally liberal publication, argued that labor unions in the United States represent only a small elite of the workforce using work rules and collective bargaining procedures that discourage economic growth and create a distorted wage system hurting the majority of unorganized workers.[44] The *Washington Monthly,* a self-described neo-liberal magazine with a strong reformist bent, early in 1983 severely criticized House Speaker Thomas P. (Tip) O'Neill for attempting to strengthen ties between the House Democratic leadership and organized labor. "What's sad is that the Democratic party needn't be so imprisoned. The Democrat beholden to no interests can respond to the larger interests of everyone. . . . It means overpaid union members, the un-needy elderly, and all the other Democratic constituencies symbolized by Tip O'Neill must be convinced to give up some of what they've got."[45] This deep disdain for organized labor and for its leaders is very similar to the views of such Democrats as Representative James Jones and Leon Panetta, described earlier in this chapter.

At the same time, public confidence in labor leaders has fallen to even lower depths from the already very low levels of the mid-1960s. In the mid-1960s, the percentage of the public saying that it had "a great deal of confidence" in the leaders of organized labor was only 21 percent, the lowest favorable level of confidence of any of the leaders of ten major American institutions. In polls taken from March 1978 to November 1980, the level of confidence in labor fell to an average of 13 percent, and in September 1981, to 12 percent. The public has continued to voice majority support for the basic concept of trade unionism, but the percentage who voice this support has been steadily declining. Asked, "In general, do you approve or disapprove of labor unions?," the percentage of the public voicing approval remained in the upper 60s and low 70s from 1936, when the Gallup Organization first began asking the question, all the way into the late 1960s. In the 1970s, however, the percentage voicing approval began to fall sharply, reaching 55 percent in both 1979 and 1981.[46]

A central factor in the lack of public confidence in the labor movement has been the series of highly publicized disclosures of corruption, illegal activity, and the abuse of union funds over a period of thirty years on the part of labor leaders. These disclosures have run a wide gamut—from practices violating the basic tenets of trade unionism, to illegal profiteering, to the commission of crimes of violence—and include the defrauding of union pension funds; payoffs by management to labor leaders for keeping union wages low; salaries for some union leaders now exceeding $400,000 annually; ties between key major unions and organized crime; the 1969 murder of Jock Yablonski, his wife, and his daughter by men hired by Tony Boyle, president of the United Mine Workers; and the mysterious disappearance of Jimmy Hoffa.

Disclosures of this kind date from the 1948 investigations of racketeering in the waterfront unions by Malcolm Johnson of the *New York Sun,* giving rise to the commercially successful movie *On the Waterfront;* and from the investigations between 1957 and 1959 of the Senate Select Committee on Labor and Management, chaired by Senator John L. McClellan.

The McClellan Committee provided the basis for the conviction of Maurice Hutcheson, president of the Carpenters Union, and for the convictions of two of the presidents of the International Brotherhood of Teamsters: David Beck, on charges of income tax evasion, and Jimmy Hoffa, on a series of charges including mail fraud, jury tampering, and fraud in connection with $20 million in loans from the Teamsters' Central States Pension Fund. Throughout the history of union corruption, the Teamsters have played a central role. Of the last five presidents, three—Beck, Hoffa, and Roy Williams—have been convicted of union-related crimes; the current president, Jackie Presser, whose annual salary is $540,000, is presently under investigation by federal authorities. The scope of union corruption is far broader than even this, however, as, in 1979, six officials of the International Longshoremen's Association were found guilty of charges of labor racketeering, extortion, and conspiracy, including Anthony Scotto, president of International Longshoremen's Association Local 1814 in New York, who was sentenced to five years in jail on charges of racketeering and filing false income tax returns. During the two-year period from 1981 through 1982, 105 union officials from across the country were convicted of federal labor racketeering crimes, and more than half were from just two unions, the Laborers International Union, with 28 convictions, and the Teamsters, with 31.[47]

While labor leaders complain that the history of corruption within certain unions does not reflect the more general commitment of organized labor to honest representation of the workforce, the record of the Teamsters and of some other unions has weakened organizing drives in geographic areas with no tradition of trade unionism, damaged the confidence of the rank and file in union leadership, alienated middle-class, liberal allies, and severely eroded confidence in organized labor among the general population. A December 1976 poll found that 64 percent of the public believed that "Many union leaders have known ties with racketeers and organized crime" and that 59 percent of the public believed that "Many union leaders have abused union pension funds."[48]

For an institution attempting to regain centrality in the legislative debate, liabilities such as low public esteem, rank and file disillusionment, sustained high unemployment levels, and overall declining workforce representation are extremely serious, if not fatal. Through astute use of money, and through stepped-up efforts to politically mobilize the membership, labor does appear assured of regaining some of its lost leverage in the Democratic presidential nomination process, and it has increased its muscle significantly within the Democratic National Committee. But there is no chance that Democratic elected officials in the foreseeable future will permit a declining labor movement with little public support to regain the influence and stature it had in Congress in the mid-1960s.

This disparity—moderately growing political strength within the Democratic party for labor, and continued weakened legislative power

—results in part from the fact that the political wing of the party, particularly the Democratic National Committee, is very different from the legislative wing of the party, those Democrats elected to the House and Senate. The DNC is in desperate need of money, and labor has stepped in to fill much of that vacuum. Without loans and direct infusions of cash from labor in 1981, there were moments when the DNC would not have been able to meet its own payroll. Similarly, the decline of local political party structures has made it far easier for well-financed active groups to gain leverage in the presidential nomination process, with labor taking advantage of this access to attempt to achieve power through the early endorsement of Mondale and through concentrated efforts to have union members and leaders win election as convention delegates.

In contrast, incumbent Democratic members of Congress are not desperate for money.[49] Once in office, it is not difficult for a Democrat to raise adequate funds for reelection; labor in many cases provides incumbent Democrats substantial support, but it is not, so to speak, lifeblood support, in the same way that labor money is to the DNC. In addition, the decline of local party structures has functioned to make incumbent Democrats vulnerable to a host of district and Washington-based pressures, creating a network of forces seeking to influence the votes of members of the House and Senate, in which labor is only one of many competing interests. Finally, union strength tends to be concentrated in the urban areas of northern states, creating severe geographic restrictions on labor's influence over members of Congress, a restriction that is growing as union membership declines. The huge geographic differences in union strength, ranging from 6.5 percent of the workforce in North Carolina to 39.2 percent in New York State, reflect one of the major differences between business and labor when lobbying Congress: business is present as a major force in every state. There are at present eighteen states, however, in which the percentage of the nonagricultural workforce represented by trade unions is below 15 percent and continuing to decline rapidly. In these states, which elected 10 of the 46 Democratic senators in 1983, and 76 of the 267 Democratic House members, both support from unions and votes cast in favor of union positions can become elective liabilities.

In other words, the Democratic National Committee and Democratic officeholders in Congress are distinct and separate constituencies. Unions can, and are, filling a major need within the Democratic National Committee. But among those Democrats in Congress whose votes define substantive policy, the need for organized labor is far smaller, and highly fragmented geographically. Translating institutional political success—that is, success in providing assistance to the DNC—into legislative strength has proven very difficult: after the 1982 congressional elections, which were a significant, if modest, victory for a Democratic party reunited at the political level with labor, the Ninety-eighth Congress was unable to alter the distributional outcomes of the Regan tax program, a central theme in many 1982 political campaigns; and was unable as well to rescind the 1981 cuts in food stamps, in welfare payments, in health programs, in child and maternal nutritional grants, and in public service jobs programs.

The loss of labor's centrality to the setting of the Democratic-liberal agenda has, however, far greater long-range consequences than the difficulty of the Democratic party in regaining its voice in 1983. In the late 1970s and early 1980s, when inflation and the failure of the economy to grow created intense pressure to adopt new political and policy strategies, the collapse of labor's legislative power facilitated the adoption of a set of economic policies highly beneficial to the corporate sector and to the affluent. The 1978 and 1981 tax bills marked the end of a history of tax cuts designed to increase the progressivity of the tax system, signaling instead the restoration of a belief that economic growth will emerge from a reduction of the tax burden borne by the owners of capital; and that economic growth will be best achieved through the elimination of taxes on corporate profits resulting from new investments. The 1981–82 recession, created in part by federal monetary policy, forced a reduction in union strength and permitted management to win significant concessions in the workplace. In the aftermath of the recession the 8 percent of the population that hold significant blocks of stock saw the value of their holdings increase by 52 percent from August 1982 to June 1983, while organized labor not only saw its ranks thinned by permanent layoffs but saw as well projections for an unemployment rate staying well above 7 percent through the end of 1985, despite the economic recovery.

Even as the economy improved in late 1983 and early 1984, with inflation lowered and business spending beginning to increase, the setbacks for labor placed it in a weak position to capitalize on renewed economic vigor and to press for wage hikes. Instead, labor entered the middle of the 1980s with diminished vitality, vulnerable to continued attacks both in the immediate present and in any future downturn. In the economic recovery, there is every indication that organized labor will receive a disproportionately small share of the general benefits, and in the next recession, labor is unprepared to protect its constituents when management seeks to place the largest burden of restraint on the workforce.

Without a strong labor movement, there is no broad-based institution in American society equipped to represent the interests of those in the working and lower-middle classes in the formulation of economic policy. This power vacuum has been apparent throughout the late 1970s and early 1980s, and the continued lack of institutional representation for the 48 percent of the population with family incomes below $20,000 will be critically important during the rest of this decade. The country faces the choice of accepting deficits now projected in the $180 billion to $200 billion range for the foreseeable future or of adopting taxation and spending programs designed to reduce the deficit. These choices will have major consequences both in the distribution of the tax burden among income groups and in the distribution of government benefits. Similarly, the debate over the adoption of a national economic or industrial policy, if such a policy becomes a seriously considered alternative, will involve fundamental questions concerning the relationship of government to new and old industries, to the workers in new and old industries, to defense- versus nondefense-related industries, to automation and robotics, to the unemployed, to the creation of new jobs, and to the training of new workers entering the marketplace.

The existence of a declining labor union movement, mistrusted by the public and to some degree by its own rank and file, with a history of seeking protectionist government legislation, points to the prospect of a poorly represented working class as these debates develop. This weak representation has been compounded by an additional trend, the decline in voter turnout, which is the subject of the next chapter.

5

Voting Patterns

THE single most important characteristic of voting in the United States is the economic bias of turnout patterns. In every survey of voter participation, those at the top end of the income scale turn out in far larger numbers than those at the bottom end. Within political circles, this disparity is an accepted fact of life. In terms of the making of economic policy, however, trends and patterns of turnout coincide with recent fundamental shifts in government tax and spending practices. There is a substantial debate as to whether the low and class-skewed voting turnout patterns in the United States significantly affect the outcome of elections. There is, however, little doubt that politicians are responsive to those who vote: voters determine who is elected; nonvoters do not.

In this context, there are two political policy-making forces in turnout patterns. The first is the relative strength of demographic groups, and particularly, when the issue is tax and spending policies, the relative strength of income groups. On this score, the voting strength of the affluent far outweighs their numbers, while the poor are disproportionately underrepresented. The second force, however, is the trend in voting patterns: is the disparity in turnout between rich and poor increasing or decreasing? For a politician who represents a politically competitive district and who is faced with specific legislative

choices in Congress, the turnout trends in his or her constituency are
of vital importance: a relatively small increase or decrease in voting by
a specific demographic group—the rich, the poor, blacks, whites, union
members, Hispanics, Protestants, etc.—can determine the success or
failure of a bid for reelection. At a time when voting appears likely
to be structured increasingly along income and racial lines, these trends
become all the more important. As they become more important, they
will echo into the legislative decisions of Congress.

The sharply contrasting voting patterns of different income groups
can be seen in the following table based on census data for 1980.* The
first vertical column of the table divides the full population into income
categories. The second column describes the percentage of the total
population made up of persons within each of these income categories;
for example, persons with family income of $5,000 to $9,999 in 1980
made up 15.5 percent of the population. The third column describes the
percentage of each income group that reported to the census that it has
registered to vote; for example, 58.4 percent of those making $5,000
to $9,999 said in 1980 that they had registered. The fourth column
describes the percentage of each income group that reported actually
voting in 1980; for example, 44.8 percent of those making $5,000 to
$9,999 reported voting in 1980. The fifth and final column describes
the distribution of each income group among actual voters; thus, those
making $5,000 to $9,999 make up 15.5 percent of the total population,

---

*There is an extensive debate in academic circles concerning almost all voter turnout
data, including those developed through the census. A number of critics have noted
that census data tend to overestimate the percentage of nonvoters, because the data
compare the number of persons who reported voting to the number of persons in the
entire population. The entire population, however, includes a number of persons who
are not eligible to vote—such as illegal aliens—and, consequently, the measure exag-
gerates nonvoting. Conversely, the census consistently overestimates voter turnout,
because it is based on interviews, and varying percentages of respondents, generally
estimated to be in the range of 6 to 11 percent, report that they have voted when in
fact they have not. To a certain extent, these two statistical factors tend to cancel each
other out. More important, in this book, census voting statistics are used primarily to
point out the class bias in voter turnout. In this respect, census figures are probably
conservative in reporting the degree of class bias: poor persons, more than middle-class
persons, report voting when in fact they have not; as a result, the actual voter turnout
among poor persons is lower than that reported by the census.

but, because of their low turnout rate, make up only 12.4 percent of all voters. Conversely, those making $25,000 or more make up 29 percent of the population, but, since their turnout rate is high, they make up 35.1 percent of the voters.

Table 5.1 [1]   VOTER PARTICIPATION BY FAMILY INCOME CATEGORY

1980 Income Categories	% population	% registered	% voted	% voters
Under $5,000	7.0	50.4	39.4	4.5
$5,000–$9,999	15.5	58.4	48.8	12.4
$10,000–$14,999	17.8	63.6	54.8	16.0
$15,000–$19,999	15.0	66.8	60.3	14.8
$20,000–$24,999	15.7	73.5	67.2	17.2
$25,000 and over	29.0	79.2	73.8	35.1

Americans as a whole, then, have become relatively rich—almost three-fifths of the population and two-thirds of all voters reported family incomes at or above $15,000—but the very poor, those with incomes below $5,000 a year, have about two-thirds the representation among voters that their numbers would suggest. Conversely, those in the upper brackets, with incomes of $25,000 or more, are 21 percent stronger among voters than they are in the total population. Looked at another way, the 40.3 percent of the population with incomes below $15,000 cast fewer votes, 24.5 million, than the 29 percent of the population with incomes of $25,000 or more, who cast 26.1 million votes. These figures, additionally, are likely to underrepresent the scope of the disparity in turnout between rich and poor. The census figures are based on interviews in which people are asked whether or not they voted. In 1976, for example, 59.2 percent of all those interviewed reported that they had voted, but election returns show that only 53.6 percent voted; in 1980, 59.2 percent again reported voting, but the turnout rate was in fact only 52.6 percent. The census figures, however, probably understate the voting disparity between rich and poor, because the nonvoting poor tend to claim more often that they have voted than do nonvoters from other income groups.[2]

The same class skewing of the vote can be seen when the voting population of 1980 is broken down according to occupation:

Table 5.2[3]   VOTER PARTICIPATION BY OCCUPATION

Occupation	% of population	% registered	% voted	% of voters
White Collar	52.0	76.5	70.9	60.8
Professional, technical, and kindred	16.3	82.4	77.7	20.9
Managers and administrators	11.2	77.9	71.8	13.3
Sales workers	6.1	73.9	68.6	6.8
Clerical and kindred	18.5	71.3	65.0	19.8
Blue Collar	32.9	56.6	48.0	26.1
Craft and kindred	13.1	61.8	53.8	11.6
Operatives, machine, and transport	15.3	53.5	44.7	11.3
Laborers	4.5	51.9	42.1	3.1
Service Workers	12.5	59.4	51.7	10.6
Household workers	1.0	56.0	47.0	0.7
All other service workers	11.5	59.6	51.7	9.9
Farm Workers	2.6	68.0	59.9	2.5
Farmers and managers	1.4	82.0	74.8	1.8
Farm laborers and foremen	1.1	49.7	40.2	0.7

Table 5.2 parallels the findings of voting turnout by income group. Just as the average reported turnout for those making less than $15,000 was 49.8 percent, compared to 73.8 percent for those making $25,000

or more, a difference of 24 percentage points, the difference in turnout between white-collar voting strength, 70.9 percent, and blue-collar voting strength, 48 percent, is 22.9 percentage points. For any politician calculating the economic interests of his or her constituents, these figures of relative voting strength are of key importance. If a politician makes a legislative choice based purely on the calculation of the balance of economic interests among voters in a state or district, then the affluent will receive disproportionately strong representation and the poor will receive disproportionately weak representation.

These tables and figures portray only the situation in 1980. Over the past two decades there has been a steady decline in voter turnout that remained consistent until the 1982 congressional elections (about which there will be more detail later in this chapter). In the six presidential elections from 1960 to 1980, the turnout as a percentage of the total voting age population fell from 63.1 percent in 1960, to 61.8 percent in 1964, to 60.7 percent in 1968, to 55.1 percent in 1972, to 53.6 percent in 1976, to 52.6 percent in 1980. Similarly, in the five off-year congressional elections from 1962 to 1978, the turnout went from 43.6 percent in 1962, to 45.4 percent in 1966, to 43.8 percent in 1970, to 35.7 percent in 1974, and to 34.5 percent in 1978.[4] These declines were not equal among all income groups; rather, the voting rate among the poor, working, and lower-middle classes fell off much more sharply than among the affluent.

Just as a politician making a legislative decision weighs the relative voting strength of all of the demographic groups within his or her constituency, including income groups, a second major concern of the incumbent politician is the prospective trend in future turnout patterns. The dominant concern of all politicians planning to stay in office is the next election, not the past result, and consequently changes in the prospective electorate are central to the calculation of legislative decisions. In this respect, analysis of the census voting studies over the past twenty years, dating from the first such analysis in 1964, shows a progressive intensification of the class bias of voting patterns.

In the presidential elections of 1964 and 1968, the reported turnout among white-collar workers averaged 81.3 percent, and among blue-collar workers, 62.8 percent, a difference of 18.5 percentage points in favor of white-collar workers. In the subsequent three presidential elections, the reported turnout among white-collar workers has averaged 73.1 percent, while for blue-collar workers it has averaged 50.7 percent, a difference of 22.4 percentage points. In statistical terms, the disparity between white- and blue-collar workers has grown in fifteen years by just over one-fifth, from 18.5 to 22.4 percentage points.[5]

This growing division within the electorate is more striking when the group with the highest turnout rate, white-collar professional, technical, and kindred workers, is compared to two major blue-collar groups—laborers and operators of machinery and transportation equipment. The census did not begin to make these finer demographic breakdowns in presidential election years until 1968. Table 5.3, derived from those more highly detailed demographic breakdowns, traces the reported turnout rates for each of these occupational groups for the years from 1968 to 1980. Table 5.3a shows the difference in voting turnout rates between the high-turnout white-collar group and the two blue-collar groups.

Table 5.3[6]   VOTER TURNOUT RATE BY OCCUPATIONAL CATEGORY

	% voting in 1968	% voting in 1972	% voting in 1976	% voting in 1980
White-collar professional, technical, and kindred	83.1	82.3	78.4	77.7
Blue-collar machine and transport equipment operators	58.9	49.8	46.1	44.7
Laborers	54.8	48.6	43.7	42.1

Table 5.3a   COMPARISON OF TURNOUT BETWEEN WHITE-COLLAR
PROFESSIONALS AND BLUE-COLLAR EQUIPMENT OPERATORS; AND BETWEEN
WHITE-COLLAR PROFESSIONALS AND BLUE-COLLAR LABORORERS

	1968	1972	1976	1980
Percentage point difference in turnout rate between white-collar professionals and blue-collar operators	24.2	32.5	32.3	33.0
Percentage point difference in turnout rate between white-collar professionals and laborers	28.3	33.7	34.7	35.6

As Table 5.3a demonstrates, the voting disparity between blue- and white-collar workers increased significantly in the twelve years from 1968 to 1980. For white-collar professionals and skilled blue-collar equipment operators, the disparity grew from 24.2 percentage points to 33 percentage points, an increase of 8.8 percentage points; for white-collar professionals and blue-collar laborers, the disparity grew from 28.3 percentage points to 35.5 percentage points, a 7.3 percentage point increase. Overall, the change in voting patterns has functioned to alter the balance of elective power between different kinds of workers, accelerating and distorting the political consequences of basic changes that have been taking place in employment patterns. From 1968 to 1980, the percentage of white-collar workers among all workers has grown from 48 to 52 percent, while blue-collar workers have declined from 36 percent to 32.9 of the workforce. In terms of actual voting strength, however, white-collar workers have gone from 54 percent of all voters in 1968 to 60.8 percent in 1980, while blue-collar workers have fallen from 31.6 percent to 26.1 percent of all voters.

Taken all together, the class disparity in voting and the growth of this disparity in recent years have had significant consequences in the making of economic policy. For elected officials, these turnout patterns have meant that decisions are made within two universes or constituencies. The first is the general population, which, regardless of whether or not individual members vote, finds its economic status enhanced or diminished by tax, spending, and monetary policies set by the government. The second constituency, a subset of the first, is made up of those voters who will decide whether the elected officials who formulated and enacted those policies will continue in office. This second constituency, the one on which elected officials depend for survival, is far more affluent than the first. In 1976, for example, the average family income for all voters was $13,485; for nonvoters, $9,807; and for the two combined, $11,983. In other words, the income of voters was 37.5 percent higher, or $3,678 more, than that of nonvoters; and 12.5 percent higher, or $1,502 more, than that of the entire population.[7]

As a result, legislative decisions by politicians planning to seek reelection are made with the knowledge that the general constituency differs significantly from the voting constituency. A South Baltimore neighborhood of 10,000 blue-collar workers translates, in the mind of the astute politician, into 4,800 votes, while a white-collar community in North Baltimore of 10,000 people translates into 7,100 votes. Or, to use actual figures, a senator from New York recognizes that the overwhelmingly black and Puerto Rican Eighteenth Congressional District in the South Bronx, the poorest congressional district in the United States, produced 58,000 votes in 1982; while the affluent and 91-percent white Twenty-first District in the lower Hudson River valley produced 156,000 votes, or nearly three times as many, in 1982.[8]

It follows, then, that not only does the politician making a choice, for example, on alternative tax rate schedules that determine the progressivity of the income tax system—or on the allocation of spending cuts between domestic and defense programs—make the decision based on a voting constituency distorted in favor of the affluent; but the trends in voting patterns from 1964 to 1980 have functioned as well to enlarge this distortion. Arranging the census data from 1964 through 1980 in two tables, one for presidential elections in the text, the other for off-year congressional elections in footnote 9, it is possible to trace this trend of voter turnout biased toward white-collar workers. In each table, the reported turnout percentages for white-collar workers and blue-collar workers are given. The bottom line describes the percentage advantage in voting turnout of the white-collar voters over the blue-collar voters. For example, in 1964, 82.7 percent of white-collar workers reported voting, while 66.3 percent of blue-collar workers reported voting. In statistical terms, this means that white-collar voters turned out at a rate 25 percent higher than blue-collar workers.*

Table 5.4 [9]   VOTER TURNOUT ADVANTAGE OF WHITE-COLLAR OVER BLUE-COLLAR WORKERS

Presidential election years

Occupation	1964	1968	1972	1976	1980
White Collar	82.7%	79.8%	76.4%	72.1%	70.9%
Blue Collar	66.3	62.3	54.2	49.8	48.0
White-collar advantage or bias*	25	28	40	45	48

In both presidential and congressional elections, there was a sharp increase over the years from 1964 to 1980 in the bias favoring the white-collar voter over the blue-collar voter, the white-collar bias growing by 23 percentage points in the case of presidential elections and by 24 percentage points in the case of off-year elections. A second set of data supports this pattern: reported voter turnout rates in a series of surveys conducted by the Center for Political Studies in Ann Arbor, Michigan, covering a longer period of time, from 1952 to 1976. Table 5.5 shows the trend in the degree of income or class bias in voting patterns over seven presidential elections, from 1952 to 1976. In each of the elections, the general population has been divided equally into

*In order to derive the white-collar bias for this table and for the table in note 9, the steps taken are as follows: in the first vertical column, for the year 1964, 66.3 percent of blue-collar workers turned out to vote; 82.7 percent of white-collar workers turned out to vote. Subtracting 66.3 from 82.7 gives a 16.4 percentage point difference. The 16.4 percentage point difference is 25 percent of 66.3. In other words, the white-collar workers have a 25 percent voting advantage over blue-collar workers.

three income groups, the highest-income third, the middle-income third, and the lowest-income third. The class or income bias figure here is the turnout rate of the top third compared to that of the bottom third. In 1952, for example, the top third turned out at a rate 41 percent higher than did the bottom third.

Table 5.5 [10]   TURNOUT AMONG INCOME GROUPS IN PRESIDENTIAL ELECTIONS
FROM 1952 TO 1976

Family income	1952	1956	1960	1964	1968	1972	1976
Highest third	86%	84%	87%	86%	88%	87%	82%
Middle third	76	76	81	79	79	70	71
Lowest third	61	59	68	68	63	61	60
Income bias	41	42	26	26	40	43	37

In addition to tracing the pattern of income bias in voting, table 5.5 has far broader implications. While not constituting proof of any direct causal relationship, the table suggests a correlation between the pattern in the class bias of the vote in an election and the subsequent substance of enacted legislation. The Eisenhower years, a period when no major domestic spending programs were initiated, are marked by a high upper-income class bias in voter turnout, with the bias figure averaging 41.5 percent for 1952 and 1958. In contrast, the legislative period from 1961 to 1969, under the Kennedy and Johnson administrations, was governed by the elections of 1960 and 1964 and produced, among other domestic benefit programs, Medicare, Medicaid, federal aid to education, the Civil Rights Act of 1964, and the Voting Rights Act of 1965. This legislative phase, the most active period in terms of social spending initiatives for the federal government since the Roosevelt administration, was marked by a significant reduction of the upper-income class bias in the popular vote, with the bias figure falling to an average of 26 percent, 15.5 percentage points below the bias figure of the 1950s.

In the presidential elections of 1968, 1972, and 1976, the upper-income class bias in voter turnout returned to levels approaching that of the 1950s, with the bias figure averaging 40 percent. During those years, the willingness of Congress to initiate new domestic programs declined sharply. Census data on the white-collar and blue-collar turnout trends suggest that the upper-income class bias intensified further at the time of the 1980 selection, after which economic, social spending, and foreign policy initiatives shifted sharply to the right, with the administration of Ronald Reagan proposing, and Congress enacting, tax legislation providing more benefits to the rich than to the working and lower-middle classes, and reducing dramatically the level of spending for programs targeted largely toward the poor and toward those employed in marginal jobs.

The coinciding in the 1960s of high voter turnout with legislatively enacted liberal social policies and the coinciding by 1980 of a sharp legislative turn to the right with a decline in voter turnout have been reinforced by demographic shifts. Perhaps the single most important development in the 1960s in the determination of the electorate was the 1962 Supreme Court decision requiring one-man, one-vote apportionment in state legislative districts. This ruling shifted political power within states to urban areas, particularly to previously underrepresented black sections, and meant that congressional districts would be drawn by increasingly urban state legislators. The consequence was to increase the political power of just those groups benefiting most from the subsequent enactment in the mid-1960s of social programs.

Since then, however, demographically determined electoral strength has grown largely in the increasingly conservative, and increasingly Republican, southern, southwestern, and western sections of the country. From 1960 to 1980, the states losing the most population, and consequently losing the largest number of House seats, have been New York, losing seven seats; Pennsylvania, losing four; and Ohio, losing three; while the major winners have been California, gaining seven; Florida, gaining seven; and Texas, gaining four. More significantly, losses of House seats have been from highly Democratic urban areas in the North; and the gains in population, and in House seats, have been in increasingly suburban sections of the sunbelt, such as the community of Arlington, Texas, blossoming between Dallas and Fort Worth, and growing between 1950 and 1980 from a town of 8,000 into a city of 160,000. This national demographic shift has been echoed within the boundaries of many major states, as cities such as Chicago, Pittsburgh, Baltimore, Detroit, and New York lose population and congressional representation to their neighboring suburban counties.

Partisan Consequences

Just as turnout patterns are a major factor in the formulation of economic and social policy, they are also of major consequence for the balance of power between the two political parties. Using indicators of income, race, and education, those groups with the lowest turnout rates are the most Democratic, while those with the highest turnout rates provide the strongest Republican margins. Among those with family incomes below $10,000 in 1982 and 1983, the percentage of Democrats was more than twice that of Republicans: 46.7 percent to 17.1 percent. In contrast, among those with incomes of $50,000 and more, 44 percent described themselves as Republicans while 23.6 percent described themselves as Democrats.[11]

In the case of race, blacks reported Democratic over Republican allegiance by a margin of 70.7 percent to 2.8 percent, with the remaining blacks describing themselves as independent. The census reported a 50.5 percent voting rate in 1980 for blacks, who, when they cast ballots, have supported Democratic candidates by margins ranging from 5-1 to 18-1. Whites, who reported voting at a rate more' than 10 percentage points higher than that of blacks—60.9 percent in 1980 —have been far more evenly divided between the two parties, 36.5 percent declaring allegiance in 1982–83 to the Democratic party and 26.4 percent to the Republican party. In actual voting, whites, in both 1976 and 1980, favored the Republican presidential candidate by margins of 4 and 20 percentage points, respectively,[12] while in the 1982 congressional elections, whites reported casting a slight majority of their votes in favor of the Democratic candidates.[13] Similarly, voters with high-school educations or less were Democratic by better than a 2–1 margin, 44.4 percent voting Democratic to 20.2 perrcent voting Republican, with the remainder independent. This group of voters reported voting at a rate of 52.6 percent in 1980, fully 27.3 percentage points below the 79.9 rate for those who have completed college. Those with college educations or more identified themselves as Republicans over Democrats by a margin of 33.1 to 30.6.[14]

Not only has the steadily upward increase in the class bias of voter turnout from 1964 to 1980 been inherently damaging to Democratic elective prospects, but the effects of this trend have been compounded by parallel shifts in the composition of the body of voters within each party. As described in greater detail in chapter 2, there has been a growing class bias in the make-up of both the Democratic and Republican parties, with the Republican party increasingly dependent on upper-income voters for the core of its support and the Democratic party becoming a more bottom-heavy party, with its strongest pluralities among voters in the bottom third of the income distribution.[15]

The Reversal of Trends in 1982

After the liberalizing effects of the one-man, one-vote decision had become ingrained in the electoral system, subsequent voter turnout trends from the late 1960s to 1980 have functioned to shift power away from those in the bottom third of the income distribution to those in the top third, from blue-collar workers to white-collar workers, and from predominately Democratic groups to groups that lean toward the GOP. The trend toward increasingly class-skewed voting patterns from 1964 to 1980 was, however, reversed in 1982. The combination of the recession, the failure of the Reagan administration's budget and tax policies to produce the immediate economic revival that had been promised, growing public discontent with the perceived inequities of the administration's tax legislation and spending reductions, and voter registration drives significantly altered the nature of the participating electorate. Those who have been consistent voters in past elections shifted marginally toward the Democratic party and its candidates, and the voting population itself grew, primarily among those on the bottom half of the income distribution. This increase, in turn, translated into the addition of Democratic voters.

Calculated in terms of the disparity between white-collar and blue-collar-voters—the occupational bias of the vote, which had reached 59 percent in 1978, the previous off-year congressional election (see table in note 9)—fell by 11 percentage points to 48 percent. In other words, while white-collar voters turned out at a rate 59 percent better than did blue-collar voters in 1978, in 1982 they turned out at a rate only 48 percent better. Similarly, the disparity between black and white voter turnout fell sharply. In the four off-year congressional elections from 1966 to 1978, whites turned out at rates ranging from 27 to 37 percent higher than blacks, averaging 32.5 percent higher reported white turnout rates. In 1982, the white advantage fell to 16 percent, a drop of 16.5 percentage points. A third gauge of the class and income bias of the vote—the difference between the reported turnout rates of the employed and the unemployed—shows an even sharper reversal of past trends. In 1966 the employed reported turning out at a rate 45 percent better than the unemployed. In 1970 the disparity fell to 39 percent, but in 1974 and 1978 the difference between the two grew sharply, to 66 percent and 70 percent, respectively. In 1982, however, the disparity fell by 29 percentage points, to only a 31 percent turnout advantage for the employed.[16]

The clearest results of the changed voting trends in 1982 were in the partisan shift in the House of Representatives, where Democrats gained twenty-six seats, and in state races, where Democrats gained seven governorships and increased their control of state legislative chambers from sixty-three to seventy-one. In Texas, the Democratic ticket, in a strategy organized by Democratic Senator Lloyd Bentsen, pooled $1 million for a voter registration and turnout campaign directed toward strongly Democratic voting groups: union members, blacks, Hispanics, renters, farm workers, and the poor. The results were a sharp increase in turnout, from 42 percent of registered voters in 1978 to 50 percent in 1982, and an across-the-board sweep for all state wide Democratic candidates, including the underdog gubernatorial candidate, Mark White, who defeated William P. Clements, Jr., the first Republican

governor in the state's history. Clements, who had won the governorship in 1978, defeating John Hill by 1.18 million votes to 1.17 million
votes, lost to White in 1982, by 1.47 million votes to 1.70 million votes,
as the total number of votes increased by 821,327 in the four-year
period. Although Texas may have been the most dramatic case, a similar
pattern emerged in districts across the country. In Alabama's Sixth
Congressional District, which includes Birmingham and its surround-
ings, the 1982 turnout in key black sections rose by 58 percent when
compared to the 1978 vote, and the ballots were cast for the Democratic
candidate by a margin of better than 93 to 7.[17] The result was that
Representative Albert Lee Smith, Jr., an arch-conservative, freshman
Republican, was defeated by the Democratic nominee, Ben Erdreich,
88,029 votes to 76,726 votes.

The Contrast of 1974 to 1982

The 1982 election marked an increase in voting among those demographic groups with strong Democratic loyalties and produced significant gains for the Democratic party in the House of Representatives.
In this context, there are striking differences between the elections of
1982 and 1974, the latter being the last in which Democrats made
substantial gains with a Republican president in the White House,
achieving in that year even larger gains in the House: forty-nine seats.
Between the two off-year congressional elections of 1970 and 1974,
however, the relative strength of Democratic voting groups took a
nosedive. The disparity in voting strength between white-collar and
blue-collar voters, between the employed and the unemployed, rich and
poor, and white and black, increased across the board during this
period.

The Democratic election success in 1974 was heavily dependent upon
the public reaction to Watergate and the overwhelming association of
Republican elected officials with the scandal. Watergate, in effect,
created a distortion in voting results when compared to longer-term
demographic turnout trends: Democratic congressional victories in
1974 emerged at a time when voting patterns pointed toward increased
Republican strength. The census figures strongly suggest that the rise

in Democratic strength in the House and, to a lesser extent, in the Senate in the mid-1970s was largely the result of a switch of affluent voters from support for Republican candidates to support for Democratic candidates, a point developed in more detail in chapter 1.[18] In terms of the formation of economic and social legislative policies, this meant that a briefly ascendant Democratic party in the mid-1970s was dependent upon a largely ephemeral base of support, voters with little or no permanent allegiance to the Democratic party, whose class and income characteristics were far more well-to-do than the bottom-heavy core constituency of the Democratic party.

In direct contrast to the election of 1974, the growth in voter participation in 1982 occurred among those voters forming the traditional core of support for the Democratic party. The Democratic gain of twenty-six seats in the House coincided with the addition to the electorate of voters who fit the general pattern of a party weighted toward the lower half of the income distribution: blacks, blue-collar workers, and the unemployed, along with a relatively new addition, as a block, to the Democratic constituency: women. The long-range consequence for economic policy of the voter turnout increase of 1982 depends, however, both on the permanence of the commitment of these new voters and on continued further expansion of the electorate among those on the bottom half of the economic spectrum.

The economic policies of the Reagan administration have solidified the economic-partisan divisions among voters,[19] and a network of Democratic-oriented organizations has begun to attempt to capitalize upon the abundance of potential voters in heavily Democratic racial, ethnic, and income groups. The NAACP has been conducting a "Breadbox-Ballotbox Voter Drive," targeting unregistered voters among those waiting in line to receive free, surplus government cheese; the Southwest Registration Voter Drive has attempted to build up the voting strength of Hispanics; a network of trade unions and civic organizations in New England, New York, and New Jersey began organizing almost immediately after the 1982 election to register voters for the 1984 election; the Reverend Jesse Jackson, of Operation PUSH, entered the contest for the 1984 Democratic presidential nomination, in large part to add significant numbers of blacks to the rolls of registered voters, particularly in southern states where the black vote has the potential for switching federal, state, and local representation from conservative to liberal and moderate.

Much of the success of these voter registration drives has depended, however, on three motivating forces: first, the potential for blacks and Hispanics to elect blacks and Hispanics to higher office, as in the case of the election in 1983 of Harold Washington and Wilson Goode as the mayors of Chicago and Philadelphia; secondly, the recession, along with the prospect of a two-tier recovery, with sharp improvement in economic status for the well-to-do, coinciding with unusually high unemployment for those at lower income levels; and thirdly, a widespread and emotionally charged animosity toward the administration of Ronald Reagan. In direct contrast to the voting surge that took place in the 1930s, the Democratic party itself has not become a central, positive force in motivating increased participation in elections. Instead, the Democratic party has been the beneficiary of voter hostility and anger toward economic developments and policies associated with the Republican party.

At the same time, there is strong evidence that the growing allegiance of women to the Democratic party is based in large part on issues of domestic economic policy as well as on issues of militarism and foreign policy. Women, much more than men, have been opposed to cuts in domestic federal spending and to the increases in defense spending, and they have voiced much stronger opposition to the perceived inequities of the Reagan administration's redistributive economic policies.[20] The allegiance of women to the Democratic party appears to be currently based as much (if not more) upon opposition to the policies of the Reagan administration and of the Republican party—and perhaps as well on the absence of an effort by the GOP to establish a few policy initiatives favorable to women—as on positive support for the policies of the Democratic party. In the long run, the growing partisanship of women and the growing turnout among already deeply partisan blacks could significantly alter both economic policy and the policy-making vitality of the Democratic party, but for the moment, Democratic gains from these two groups of voters do not parallel the growth of the Democratic party that occurred in the 1930s, during the depths of the depression.

In the 1930s, the Democratic party was the agent and locus of a major mobilization of nonvoters and of a large-scale conversion of previously Republican voters. In McDowell County, in the heart of West Virginia's coalfields, the percentage of voters registered with the Democratic party rose from 29.5 to 58 percent in the two years from 1932 to 1934. In Pennsylvania's Allegheny County, which includes Pittsburgh, Democratic registration rose from 7 percent in 1930 to 58 percent in 1938. Not only in that decade did voters from New York to California switch to the Democratic party, but they turned out in much larger numbers than they had in the past. From 1932 to 1936, the turnout in Cook County (Chicago), Illinois, grew by 345,000; in New York City, by 146,000; and in Philadelphia, by 286,000. During this period of Democratic growth, total turnout grew from 49.2 percent in 1920 and 48.9 percent in 1924, to 61 percent in 1936, and to 62.4 percent in 1940, an increase of more than 12 percentage points.[21] At the same time, the Democratic party of the 1930s functioned as a traditional political party, using control of the government in order to provide benefits to its strongest supporters. The elderly got Social Security; those out of work got the Works Project Administration and a host of other job-creating programs; organized labor got the National Labor Relations Act; and, in terms of broad distributional policy, the Roosevelt administration won enactment of tax legislation creating a system of highly progressive tax rates—low for the working class and high for the wealthy.

The Democratic party in the 1980s is in no way prepared to replicate the willingness of the party fifty years earlier to target the benefits of government toward those demographic groups with the strongest Democratic loyalties. Instead, the party remains severely torn not just between its liberal and conservative wings—the traditional split between southern and northern Democrats that characterized the 1950s and 1960s—and not just between those Democrats who favor increased military spending and a hawkish defense posture, and their foreign policy adversaries, the doves—but also between the fiscal moderates largely elected as freshmen in the mid-1970s and the older generation of elected officials whose roots are to a greater degree in what remains of the New Deal coalition. In fact, it has been the Republican party, particularly the Republican party under President Reagan, that has been able to function as an effective political party, rewarding its core constituency through its tax and deregulatory policies and punishing its Democratic adversaries through a variety of means: through reductions in social programs; through cutting welfare, food stamp, and unemployment benefits, all of which are traditionally directed toward largely Democratic constituencies; and through elimination of jobs for the heavily Democratic employees who staff and run domestic spending programs.

The low and class-skewed voter turnout patterns prevalent in this country are by no means inherent in a democratic system of government. Voter turnout in the United States in the second half of the last century was far higher than it has been recently. From 1848 to 1896 the turnout among eligible voters averaged 76.7 percent, whereas by 1980 it had fallen to 52.6 percent.[22] In terms of contemporary international patterns, an analysis by G. Bingham Powell, Jr., of voting patterns in thirty democracies on every continent ranks the United States twenty-seventh in voter turnout. In analyzing the international data, Powell found a significant correlation between high voter turnout and the presence of political parties representing clearly defined strata of society—that is, parties strongly tied to specific income classes, religious groups, or language groups. In the United States, Ireland, Japan, and India, where the relationship between income groups and political parties is, by international standards, relatively low, voter turnout is low. In countries where voters are closely aligned by class, as they are in Finland and Sweden, voter turnout is considerably higher.[23]

Although the Democratic party in the United States has never been clearly or overtly tied to a specific social or economic class, the interrelationship between class, party, and voter turnout surfaced, to a limited extent, in the 1930s and early 1940s. At that time, under the pressures of widespread economic crisis, the class divisions between the Republican and Democratic parties became sharper than they had been historically, just when voter turnout increased sharply. In 1940 the Democratic party had a 66 to 34 advantage among voters in the bottom third of the income distribution, while the GOP had an almost mirror-image advantage among the top third of the income distribution, 64 to 36.[24] During the 1930s, when these class allegiances to the two parties were formed, voter turnout rose by 7.4 percent over the turnout rate for the 1920s. In the 1930s, voters in the bottom third of the income distribution had an incentive to vote, and the Democratic party had a major interest in making sure that its constituents went to the polls and cast their ballots.[25]

In the United States, political parties, particularly the Democratic party, have in the past substituted patronage for class representation in seeking to increase voter turnout. City jobs, along with many of the jobs with firms doing contract work for the city and state, were passed out on the basis of the loyalty of a largely working-class and immigrant population to the Democratic party. Control over the distribution of jobs, in turn, was central to the power of those who ran the machines and the political clubs. Just as patronage has partially substituted as a kind of party glue for the class representation characteristic of democracies in Europe and in other advanced industrial countries, it also appears to have increased working-class voter participation in elections. In a study comparing high patronage (or "machine") states within the United States with an equal number of states where reformers have largely eliminated patronage, political scientists Raymond E. Wolfinger and Steven J. Rosenstone found that government employees in the high patronage states—such as New York and Massachusetts—turned out to vote in significantly larger numbers than did those in "reform" states—such as Oregon and Minnesota.[26] The turnout differential was particularly strong among government employees with relatively little education: those government employees in patronage states with a grammar-school education or less turned out at a rate 13 percentage points higher than similar workers in the reform states; and those with a high-school education or less turned out at a rate 10 percentage points higher than did their counterparts in reform states. Similarly, among *all voters* in patronage states, not only government employees, those with high-school degrees or less turned out at a rate 6 percent higher than similarly educated voters in reform states, when the governorship, the key state office in the distribution of jobs, was at stake in the election.

Paradoxically, then, one of the main thrusts of reform has been to eliminate the patronage function of government, in effect eliminating a direct tie between the discretionary powers of elected officials and the working class—that is, jobs. The changing character of politics at the local level, when traditional, patronage-based political organizations are replaced by reform clubs, is reflected in part by the results of two surveys of political leaders. The first group studied was made up of politicians and political organization leaders in eight patrtonage-style New Jersey counties. The second group was made up of district captains and other leaders of the Greenwich Village Independent Democrats, a reform group that in the 1960s took over control of the Manhattan election district from political boss Carmine DeSapio. Both groups were asked the same set of questions, attempting to identify how often they provided specific "services" to constituents. The results were as follows:

Table 5.6 [27]   SERVICES TO CONSTITUENTS BY LEADERS OF PATRONAGE AND NONPATRONAGE POLITICAL ORGANIZATIONS

Service performed	Percentage of old-style New Jersey politicians performing service often	Percentage of Greenwich Village reformers performing service often
Helping deserving persons get public jobs	72	0
Showing people how to get Social Security, welfare, unemployment, or other benefits	54	5
Helping citizens who are in trouble with the law	62	5

The erosion in the United States of the patronage and constituent service links between the Democratic party, on one side, and the poor, the working class, and the lower middle class, on the other, has not been replaced by any broader form of representation designed to strengthen the ties between the party and its bases of support. In contrast to the four decades between 1932 and the mid-1970s, during which the Democratic party effectively set the national legislative agenda, winning enactment of a broad range of social programs and maintaining the progressivity of the income tax system, the Democratic party during the past ten years has come increasingly to depend upon its status as an alternative to the Republican party, rather than building a vigorous party able to compel reliable support on its own merits.

The elective gains of the Democratic party in 1982, both in terms of the twenty-six seats won in the House of Representatives and in terms of increased voter turnout, have their origins far more firmly in a degree of popular protest against the social and economic policies of the Reagan administration and in the hardship generated by the 1981–82 recession than in a solid and well-crafted Democratic appeal. The Democratic party remains trammeled by a set of party rules that increases the leverage of affluent elites in primary and caucus elections, and the party remains to some extent immobilized by the dependence of incumbent Democrats in the House and in the Senate on nearly equal amounts of campaign support from labor, business, and special-interest sources, constituencies with often directly conflicting legislative objectives. The decline in strength of organized labor, in turn, has severely weakened the ability of unions to speak for and to represent the interests of a major segment of society, those on the bottom half of the income distribution.

On the other side of the coin, the Republican party has gained increasing economic coherence as the affluent form a growing percentage of the GOP's membership. In addition, the GOP and its candidates have developed a base of campaign financing that, rather than encouraging internal conflict, works with the development by the party of a set of consistent economic policies beneficial to the affluent plurality of its own constituency. At the same time, while the power of organized labor has declined, the political strength, coordination, and activism of business interests has grown. Altogether, in combination with a sharp increase in the class bias of voter turnout patterns, there has been over the past decade a growing inability of the political system to represent, in the highly complex process of developing economic policy, the interests of the bottom three-fifths of society. The stakes involved in the struggle over the formulation of economic policy have become, in turn, increasingly high, and it is these high stakes, and the economic policies which set them, that are the subject of the next and last chapter of this book.

6

Consequences in Economic Policy

The Wages of Inequality

IN THE late 1970s, a set of political and intellectual forces began to converge and to gain momentum, joining together in a direction that substantially altered economic policy in the United States. While the forces involved were by no means in agreement as to the specific goals to be achieved, they shared an interest in seeking to change the basic assumptions that have dominated taxation and spending policies in the United States. For nearly fifty years, since the administration of Franklin Delano Roosevelt, two dominant themes of taxation and spending policy have been equity and the moderate redistribution of income.[1] The forces gaining ascendancy in the late 1970s sought to replace such liberal goals with a drive to slow the rate of growth in federal spending in order to incresae the availability of money for private capital formation; with a reduction of corporate and individual tax rates, particuarly of those rates in the top brackets, in order to provide predicted incentives for work, savings, and investment; and with the paring down of government regulation to facilitate a more productive marketplace. In short, the goal became to influence government policy so as to supplant, in an economic sense, equity with efficiency.

The inherent contradictions between equity, efficiency, redistribution, and investment go to the heart of the conflict in developing economic policy in advanced capitalist democracies. The political resolution of such contradictions determines the balance between competing claims on government: that is, whether government is granted the authority to intervene in the private marketplace in order to correct or to modify inequities inherent in the market system, through a progressive tax rate schedule and through the payment of benefits to the poor; whether it is the role of government to subsidize, encourage, and direct marketplace forces with tax incentives and loan subsidies targeted toward specific industries; or whether government should reduce to a minimum its role in the economy, remaining as remote from and as disengaged as possible from the private sector.

The period from 1977 through the first months of 1982, however, marked a rare moment in American history, when the disparate forces supporting the conservative coalition on these basic economic questions all simultaneously became politically ascendant. Forces coalescing on the political right included a politcally revitalized business community; increasing sophistication and centrality among leaders of the ideological new right; the sudden explosion of wealth in the domestic oil community following the 1973 OPEC embargo; the emergence within the academic community and within the major economic research institutions of proponents of tax cuts and of sharp reductions in the tax rate on capital income; a Republican party whose financial resources were exponentially increased by computerized direct-mail and other new political technologies, providing often decisive access to television, to polling, and to highly sophisticated voter targeting tactics; and the rise of politically conservative evangelical Christian organizations. The emergence of these forces coincided with a series of developments and trends giving conservatism new strength. The business and the new, or ideological, right-wing communities developed a shared interest in the candidates of the Republican party, as such organizations as the Chamber of Commerce and the National Conservative Political Action Committee became de facto arms of the GOP. Voting patterns increased the class bias of voter turnout, as the affluent became a stronger force both within the electorate as a whole and within the Republican party.

Conversely, the forces making up the liberal coalition, represented in large part by major segments of the Democratic party—organized labor, civil rights and civil liberties organizations, political reformers, environmental groups, and feminists—were experiencing increasing disunity. The power of organized labor, essential to any coalition of the left, had been steadily declining. Even more damaging was the emergence of growing inflation and unemployment, a continued decline in the rate of productivity growth, and a drop in the take-home pay of the average worker. This economic deterioration not only splintered the fragile coalition of Democrats that had supported policies of equity and redistribution over the previous forty years but created a growing belief that the nation was caught in an economic crisis that the Democratic party could not resolve, a belief compounded by Democratic disarray.

It was this combination of trends, all favoring the right, that provided the opportunity for a major alteration in public policy. The election in 1980 of Ronald Reagan to the presidency and the takeover of the Senate by the Republican party created the political opportunity for this fundamental realignment, but the groundwork had already been carefully laid. This groundwork included an increasingly sophisticated political strategy capitalizing on the conflicts within the fragile Democratic majority, the careful nurturing and financing of intellectual support both in academia and within a growing network of think tanks financed by corporations and conservative foundations, and the advance preparation of specific legislative proposals, particularly of tax legislation.

From the vantage point of those seeking a reversal of past progressive redistributional policies in both tax and spending programs, this drive was an extraordinary success. On the tax side, the following table describes the distributional consequences of the 1981 and 1982 tax bills, changes in the Social Security tax through 1982, and the distributional consequences of inflation. The table traces the change in the income tax and in the Social Security tax burden from the start of 1980 to 1984 for average taxpayers in nine different income groups.

Table 6.1 [2]   SHIFTS IN THE INCOME AND SOCIAL SECURITY TAX BURDEN FROM 1980 TO 1984, FACTORING IN THE EFFECTS OF INFLATION

Income class	Tax increases from Social Security and inflation	Net tax reduction from tax bills of 1981–82	Net (+) gain or (−) loss
Below $10,000	$ 153	$ 58	$ −95
$10–20,000	573	387	−186
$20–30,000	1,020	882	−138
$30–40,000	1,587	1,465	−122
$40–50,000	2,346	2,210	−136
$50–75,000	3,407	3,305	−102
$75–100,000	4,855	5,258	+403
$100–200,000	5,979	8,248	+2,269
Above 200,000	7,579	24,982	+17,403

In terms of the disposition of government revenues, that is, government spending, the Congressional Budget Office has estimated that during the first two and a half years of the Reagan administration, domestic spending on human resources programs was cut by a total of $101.1 billion for the fiscal years from 1982 through 1985. Of the $101.1 billion, $65.4 billion was cut from programs that provide direct cash (unemployment, welfare, etc.) or in-kind (food stamps, school lunches, etc.) benefits that go directly to individuals and families. The Congressional Budget Office then traced how these cuts in programs providing benefits going directly to individuals affected families in different income groups, in effect determining the distributional consequences of the cuts. The following table shows, for 1982–85, the average dollar value of the loss in benefits to families of varying income groups. For example, the total losses for an average family making less than $10,000 is $1,340 over four years, while for a family making $80,000 or more, the cumulative loss is $490.

Table 6.2 [3]   AVERAGE HOUSEHOLD *LOSS* OF BENEFITS BY INCOME AND FISCAL YEAR

Fiscal year	Less than $10,000	$10,000– $20,000	$20,000– $40,000	$40,000– $80,000	$80,000 or more
1982	$ − 200	$ − 100	$ − 60	$ − 50	$ − 110
1983	− 240	− 110	− 40	− 40	− 50
1984	− 430	− 300	− 170	− 140	− 160
1985	− 470	− 360	− 180	− 160	− 170
Total	− 1,340	− 870	− 450	− 390	− 490

Altogether, then, the first four years of the 1980s have produced a regressive redistribution within federal tax and spending policies.[4] This regressivity has resulted in a net loss for every income group except for those making in excess of $100,000, when the calculations from tables 6.1 and 6.2 are combined; clearly the losses are much more severe for those at the bottom of the income distribution, both in terms of dollars and in terms of the loss as a percentage of total income.

These policy changes have been a significant factor behind a recent increase in the poverty rate in the United States. In 1982 the number of people living below the government's official poverty line—which was for a family of four $9,862—rose to 34.4 million, or 15 percent of the population—more than one American in seven—a full percentage point above the 1981 level and the highest rate since 1965.[5]

From a political point of view, what stands out in this major redistribution of tax and spending programs to the advantage of the very affluent at the expense of all others is that these policy changes have been achieved through a political strategy capitalizing on the dissatisfaction of the working and middle class. The Reagan campaign, along with the campaigns of most Republican candidates for the House

and Senate, was focused on discontent over government tax and spending policies among white voters, many with past affiliations to the
Democratic party, and the strategy was highly successful. The switch
from Democratic to Republican voting in the presidential elections of
1976 and 1980 was strongest among manual workers and labor union
families. When Reagan's record among these groups is compared to
Ford's, the overwhelming debt of the Reagan campaign to these groups
becomes apparent. Reagan gained 15 percentage points over Ford
among manual workers, 20 percentage points among labor union families, and 21 percentage points among all Democrats.[6] Despite the fact
that these groups provided essential support to the Reagan victory,
whatever gains they received from the tax cut of 1981 were eroded into
net losses by the combination of inflation and Social Security tax
increases. In contrast, those making more than $75,000 a year ex-
perienced real improvements in their after-tax income.

The ability to win enactment of a distributional policy skewed
sharply toward those in the upper-income brackets, on the basis of a
political victory heavily dependent on the working and middle classes,
required a highly complex set of circumstances. As previous chapters
have demonstrated, throughout the 1970s there was a pervasive deterioration in the political forces supporting the interests of those on the
bottom half of the economic spectrum and a parallel strengthening of
the forces supporting the interests of those on the top. Additionally,
from 1977 to 1981, three very specific intellectual and political forces
began to gain exceptional influence over the making of tax policy:
formation of a corporate alliance to press for business tax cuts, as
described in chapter 3; the emergence of a conservative and academ-
ically respectable wing of the economics profession, most prominently
represented by Martin Feldstein, arguing that the tax rate on capital
income was excessive (described more fully later in this chapter); and,
third, the appearance of a group of supply-side economists, the best
known of whom is Arthur B. Laffer, who argued that significant tax
rate cuts would, contrary to customary expectations, produce increased
tax revenues. The supply-side wing of the economics profession was
widely felt to lack intellectual credibility, but it gained de facto politi-

cal strength when Ronald Reagan adopted in 1981 as part of administration policy the Kemp-Roth, across-the-board individual tax rate cuts, the centerpiece of supply-side theory put into practice.

The success of these scholarly, intellectual, and politically sophisticated forces can best be understood in the context of the economic crisis of the mid- and late 1970s, which developed under the Democratic control of Congress and reached a peak during the tenure of a Democrat, Jimmy Carter, in the White House. This economic crisis was the essential factor in the ideological and intellectual collapse of the Democratic party, creating substantive problems that the party was both unequipped and unprepared to address. The general shape of this crisis is described in the following table covering the fifteen-year period from 1966 to 1980. For each five-year period, the table shows the average rate of inflation, as defined by changes in the Consumer Price Index; the average unemployment rate; the average growth in the productivity rate, defined as the change in output per hour of all workers; and the percentage $(+)$ increase or $(-)$ decrease in the average weekly earnings of production and nonsupervisory workers calculated in 1977 dollars.

Table 6.3 [7]   CHANGES IN KEY ECONOMIC INDICATORS, 1966–80

	Inflation	Unemployment	Productivity	Earnings
1961–65	1.34%	5.5%	3.86%	+ 1.8%
1966–70	4.59	3.9	1.66	+ 1.5
1971–75	7.37	6.1	1.45	− 0.2
1976–80	9.68	6.8	0.33	− 1.4

By each of these measures, the economy was tightening like a noose around the neck of the Democratic party. While causing havoc for the party, these economic developments created fertile terrain for major alterations of past policies, making the legislative agenda vulnerable to policy initiatives beneficial to the rich. It was in the tax arena that this vulnerability became most apparent, as two separate but closely related elements of the economic crisis became central to the national policy debate: the decline in productivity and the effects of inflation upon the rate structure of the tax system.

To understand the effect of inflation on the tax system it is important to trace some of the history of the tax rate structure. Over the past two decades, the shape of the income tax rate structure has changed radically. In the early 1960s, the progressivity of the system—sharply higher rates for those with higher incomes—was concentrated almost entirely in the top 5 percent of the population. In 1961 a married couple making $15,000 a year was in the top 3 percent of the income distribution; over 80 percent of the population made less than $8,000. For 90 percent of the population, there were, in effect, only three marginal tax rates: zero for the bottom fifth of the population, 20 percent for the nearly half the population making from $2,700 to $7,000, and 22 percent for the next quarter of the population making from $7,000 to $11,000. In other words, for the large majority of workers, there was little or no tax penalty either for moving up to a higher-paying job or for increases in pay resulting from inflation. In 1961 a married carpenter making $7,000 a year could get a promotion to foreman, paying $10,000, a 43 percent raise in salary, and his marginal tax rate would remain the same: 22 percent. Similarly, the wife of a warehouse worker making $2,700 a year could take a job making $2,700, doubling their income, and their marginal tax rate would remain at 20 percent.

On the theory that the redistributive elements of the tax system should apply only to the very poor, who paid no tax, and to the very well-to-do, sharply escalating marginal tax rates of 26 to 91 percent applied only to the top 10 percent of the income distribution in 1961. For example, a married couple making from $12,000 to $15,000 fell into the range of taxpayers from the 94.4th percentile to the 96.9th percentile and paid at a marginal rate of 30 percent. Any couple making more than $20,000 was in the top 1 percent of the income distribution, and as income within this top 1 percent moved in steps from $20,000 to $400,000, the marginal rate went up to 91 percent. For those with incomes of $76,000 to $88,000, for example, it was 69 percent; for those in the $140,000 to $160,000 range, it was 81 percent; above $400,000, it was 91 percent.[8]

Over the next eighteen years, through 1978, a series of tax cuts effectively compensated for the effects of inflation, so that the average tax rate for all taxpayers fluctuated only between 11.5 percent and 14.3 percent between 1962 and 1977. Similarly, the average marginal tax rate fluctuated, although the overall trend was a slight, incremental increase.* The major alterations of the rate structure during this period were made at the bottom and at the top. Tax cuts were skewed toward those on the bottom of the scale by raising the standard deduction (or zero-bracket amount) and through creation of the earned income tax credit. The refundable earned income tax credit is available only to the working poor; the zero-bracket amount is used only by those who do not itemize, a population far poorer than those who do itemize. For the tiny fraction of taxpayers at the very top, the highest marginal rates were reduced from 91 percent to 70 percent in 1964 and, in 1969, to 50 percent for earned income (as opposed to unearned income from dividends and interest). The top rate on unearned income was lowered from 70 to 50 percent in 1981.

While tax cuts resulted in lower rates from 1960 to 1980, the income tax brackets remained generally the same for those making from $16,000 to $60,000 a year. When these brackets had been created in the 1950s, however, the taxpayers falling into them were the most affluent, ranging between the 98.29th percentile and the 99.93rd percentile. Between 1960 and 1979, however, the median family income grew from $5,620 to $19,684, in part from inflation and in part from real

---

*The difference between average tax rate and marginal tax rate can be explained with the following example: the federal income tax for a married couple making $47,000 with $12,000 in deductions—$35,000 in taxable income—is computed by adding up the amount of tax incurred at each bracket. On the first $3,400 of income, there is no tax. On income from $3,400 to $5,500, the tax rate is 11 percent, or $231. On income from $5,501 to $7,600, the rate is 12 percent, or $252. On income of $7,601 to $11,900, the rate is 14 percent, or $602. For $11,900 to $16,000, the rate is 16 percent, or $656. For $16,001 to $20,200, the rate is 18 percent, or $756. For the income between $20,201 and $24,600, the rate is 22 percent, or $968. For $24,600 to $29,900, the rate is 25 percent, or $1,325. For the remaining $5,100 of their income, the amount between $29,900 and $35,000, the rate is 28 percent, or $1,428. Adding up the total produces a tax bill of $6,218. This translates into an *average* tax rate for this couple of 13.4 percent (their $47,000 divided by their federal income tax, $6,218). Their *marginal* rate, however, is the rate applied to the last $5,100 they earned, or 28 percent, almost 15 percentage points higher than their average rate.

increases in spendable income.[9] What had been a statistically exceptional income in 1960 became in 1978 the median income.

As a consequence of this process, the sharply rising marginal rates that had been targeted at the very affluent in the early 1960s—while most of the population faced what amounted to a flat tax—became a system in which the vast majority of taxpayers faced sharply increasing marginal tax rates as their incomes grew. The counterpart in the late 1970s to the skilled craftsman who, when promoted to foreman with a 62.5 percent raise in 1961, faced no increase in marginal tax rates, encountered a very different situation in 1979. If, for example, his 1979 annual taxable income as a craftsman was $11,000, and, having been promoted to foreman, his income increased by 62.5 percent to $17,875, his marginal tax rate shot up from 18 percent to 24 percent. If, at the same time that the craftsman was promoted to foreman, his wife went to work, receiving a taxable income of $13,000, making their combined income $30,875, their marginal tax rate shot up to 37 percent, more than doubling the original 18 percent marginal rate. In effect, bracket creep, once the problem of the rich, became the problem of the working man and woman.

This problem was compounded in 1978, 1979, and 1980 by the effects of sharply rising inflation rates: 7.7 percent in 1978, 11.3 percent in 1979, and 13.5 percent in 1980. During this period, both marginal and average tax rates shot up for all taxpayers. During the eight years from 1962 to 1969, the marginal tax rate for all taxpayers was 24.5 percent; during the next eight years, 1970–78, it went up slightly to 26 percent. In 1979 and 1980, however, it sharply increased, first to 30.6 percent and then to 32.2 percent. Similarly, the average tax rate was 12.8 percent from 1962 to 1969 and 13.2 percent from 1970 to 1978. In 1979 and 1980 it rose to 14.6 percent and then to 15.9 percent.[10]

Together, the sharply rising marginal and average tax rates, combined with a progressive rate system that was no longer separating the very rich from the majority of taxpayers but was impinging directly on the well-being of the working and middle classes, created a strong base of deep, anti-tax sentiments, sentiments seeping more and more into basic economic constituencies of the Democratic party. Compounding these pressures on the working and middle classes, one of the most regressive federal taxes, the tax to finance Social Security, grew at a rate rapidly outstripping even the rate of inflation.[11] From 1960 to 1981, the Consumer Price Index rose 207 percent; during the same period, the maximum level of the Social Security tax paid by employees rose by 1,272 percent, from $144 in 1960 to $1,975 in 1981. This tax hits those at the bottom of the income distribution much harder than those at the top, since it is applied on a flat percentage basis to a fixed amount of income. In 1981, a person whose taxable income equaled the median family income, $22,388, faced a Social Security tax rate of 6.65 percent, or $1,489. A person with a taxable income of $100,000, however, would pay 6.65 percent of the first $29,700 in income, or $1,975, with the remainder of his or her income untaxed. The Social Security tax rate for the person at the median family income level is 6.65 percent, while for the person making $100,000 the tax rate is only 1.98 percent.

From another perspective, that of the financing of the federal government, the importance of rising Social Security taxes becomes apparent. Table 6.4 describes the changing base of federal revenues, as individual income taxes have remained, in percentage terms, the same, while the Social Security tax has more than doubled, the corporate tax has declined to just over one third its 1960 share of federal revenues, and the percentage of revenues provided by other taxes has been nearly halved.

Table 6.4 [12]   SOURCES OF FEDERAL REVENUES

Fiscal year	Individual income tax	Social insurance taxes	Corporate income tax	Excise, estate, and other
1960	44.0%	15.9%	23.2%	16.8%
1965	41.8	19.1	21.8	17.4
1970	46.9	23.0	17.0	13.0
1975	43.9	30.3	14.6	11.3
1980	47.2	30.5	12.5	9.8
1984 (est.)	44.8	36.8	7.8	10.5

Altogether, the increasing dependence on regressive Social Security taxes, the growing problem of bracket creep for the working and middle class, and the sharp acceleration in marginal and average tax rates at the end of the 1970s turned the political issue of taxes into one of the most volatile of all questions facing politicians. At the same time, support for the federal income tax, once viewed as the most equitable source of federal tax revenues, sharply fell during the 1970s. This decline in support for the income tax is reflected in a series of surveys by the Advisory Commission on Intergovernmental Relations showing a sharp increase in the 1970s of the percentage of persons identifying the federal income tax as the most burdensome levy.[13]

The political-economic problem created by the growing hostility toward the tax system was particularly acute for the Democratic party for a number of reasons. In the mid-1960s, when the tax system was effectively flat for its working- and lower-middle-class constituents, when incomes were growing in real terms, and when both inflation and unemployment rates were low, the party expanded and created additions to the network of social programs directed specifically toward the poor, such as Medicaid, Aid to Families with Dependent Children, and food stamps. These programs did not benefit numerous Democratic voters in the working and middle class who, over the next fifteen years, began to experience the most oppressive consequences of the tax system. In effect, the Democratic party had permitted a situation to evolve that encouraged hostility between its taxpaying constituents and its nontax-paying, poor constituents, hostility guaranteed to become directed against the party itself.

While the tax situation created a direct political problem, the steady decline in productivity cut to the core of the Democratic party tradition, preventing the party from increasing social benefits, which is politically possible only within a flourishing economy. In technical terms, productivity is the measure of the growth or decline in the value of production for each hour worked. Using business cycles to define periods of time, the value of the output per hour in the nation's business sector increased annually by 3.3 percent from 1947 to 1966; from 1966 to 1973, the annual rate of increase dropped to 2.3 percent; from 1973 to 1977, to 1.4 percent; finally, from 1977 to 1980, it actually *fell* at a rate of 0.4 percent a year.[14]

The political consequences of this decline in productivity have been immense. Increases in the rate of productivity mean, among other things, that more goods can be purchased for lower prices; that salary hikes can be won without inflationary impact and without real cost to the employer; that more money can be saved for investment; or combinations of these three. If, for example, the labor costs of building a car are $3,000 and the productivity of the workers involved in the process is increased by 10 percent, the saving for each car is $300. This $300 can be passed on to the car buyer as a lower retail price; it can be turned over to the workers; it can be used by the corporation either to augment the wealth of its officers or to finance new investment; or it can be passed on to shareholders. Or it can be split up among these recipients.

For the Democratic party, productivity gains were an essential ingredient in a political strategy based on an ever-expanding economic pie. In the private sector, such gains were a major factor in the real growth of earnings in the 1950s and 1960s above the rate of inflation, as the median family income, in 1981 dollars, rose from $12,539 in 1950 to $17,259 in 1960 and to $23,111 in 1970.[15] At the same time, for the public sector, improvements in the productivity rate resulted in increases in taxable income and consequently in a growth in federal tax revenues above the rate of inflation. These increased revenues permitted the continued growth and expansion of the network of domestic social programs initiated by the Democratic party.

As the productivity rate fell to zero, the economic base of Democratic party politics began to collapse. Instead of a steadily improving standard of living, and a system in which there could be many winners and few losers, the political-economic arena increasingly approached a zero-sum competition in which one person winning meant that someone else had lost, or that there was a significant increase in the budget deficit.

The rising concern with the decline in productivity provoked two interrelated questions: whether the federal government had intervened in the economic process in some way so as to encourage the decline, and whether there was some action or set of actions the government had failed to take and could now take that would reverse the decline.

In combination with the general climate of hostility toward taxes, a hostility felt deeply not only by the affluent but by core Democratic constituents in the working and lower-middle classes, there was a sustained and highly successful effort on the part of the business community to seek intellectually respectable analysis of issues concerning productivity, capital formation, and related problems, calling for policy changes advantageous to the interests of corporations and the rich. The issues of inflation, tax rates, and productivity had reached—by any standard, conservative or liberal—a critical point at which the likelihood of a substantial change in the direction of economic policy became a realizable goal. In this highly fluid situation, the prospects for legislative changes producing major alterations in the distributional outcomes of economic policy escalated exponentially, making the prospect of winning far more attractive and of losing far more damaging.

This competition for control over economic policy was conducted both in the political arena—in the terrain discussed throughout the earlier chapters of this book—and in the form of a competition of ideas, or intellectual combat. A massive flow of cash from corporations and conservative foundations to conservative think tanks financed the emergence of a growing body of intellectual justification for both a reduction of domestic social spending and the alteration of the tax system to the distributional advantage of those in the highest income brackets. "At any given moment in history," wrote James Q. Wilson—himself a well-known conservative intellectual—in the summer 1981 issue of *The Public Interest,* "an influential idea—and thus an influential intellectual—is one that provides a persuasive simplification of some policy question that is consistent with the particular mix of core values then held by the political elite." Just as Wilson wrote those lines, there were a number of influential ideas and influential intellectuals whose theories converged with the goals of the political and economic core elite.

For those seeking a major shift of policy toward the right, intellectual credibility as a tool of persuasion was essential. Although economic research relevant to the political policy-making process is produced at a wide range of American universities, four private institutions[16] were particularly critical in the shift of the economic debate to the right: the National Bureau of Economic Research, the Hoover Institution, the American Enterprise Institute, and the Center for the Study of American Business at Washington University. These institutions provided much of the groundwork for the radical change in policy taking place from 1978 through 1981; and many of their findings, while intensely disputed both within the academic community and in the public arena, remain central to the economic and political debate today.

Of the four institutions,[17] the National Bureau of Economic Research has been perhaps the most directly influential. The NBER has historically concentrated on a broad selection of economic issues, many of them of particular concern to the business community, although it has sponsored a wide range of scholarly work taking a variety of political positions. It is financed, as described in chapter 3, by a combination of government grants and corporate and foundation support, with its major corporate donors coming from the Fortune 500. The financial backing of the Hoover Institution, the American Enterprise Institute, and the Center for the Study of American Business comes from further to the ideological right, including money from a wide array of conservative industrialists and foundations.

Each of these four institutions has in recent years contributed influential economic analysis and theory to the making of public policy, conceptual contributions that have coincided with the economic interests of those corporate and private donors underwriting this policy-relevant research. A central intellectual product of the Center for the Study of American Business, which was founded in 1975 by Murray L. Weidenbaum—chairman of the Reagan administration's Council of Economic Advisers from 1981 to 1982—has been a sustained critique of government regulation. For example, among the papers produced under the center's auspices in 1982 were "The Political Economy of the Clean Air Act: Regional Self-Interest In Environmental Regulation," "Bureaucratic or Congressional Control: Regulatory Policymaking by the Federal Trade Commission," and "Reforming the Regulatory Bureaucracy: Declining Budgets and Staffing in the 1980s." The most influential work of the center has been performed by Weidenbaum, both as sole author and in collaboration with an associate, Robert DeFina. These studies[18] contend that by 1979 the cost of government regulation of business reached $102.7 billion. This finding, which has been disputed in numerous quarters,[19] was central to the claim that the sharp expansion of the regulatory role of the federal government in the 1970s had contributed significantly to the decline over that decade in productivity, forcing companies to spend money to reduce pollution and to increase safety measures to meet federally mandated consumer standards, diverting capital resources from productive investments. The Weidenbaum findings provided justification for one of the major policy initiatives of the Reagan administration—that is, the across-the-board drive to reduce the scope and content of the federal regulation of industry, the environment, the workplace, health care, and the relationship between buyer and seller.[20] The Reagan administration's drive toward deregulation was accomplished through sharp budget cuts reducing enforcement capabilities; through the appointment of anti-regulatory, industry-oriented agency personnel; and, finally, through the empowering of the Office of Management and Budget with unprecedented authority to delay major regulations, to force major revisions in regulatory proposals, and, through prolonged cost-benefit analyses, to effectively kill a wide range of regulatory initiatives.[21]

If Weidenbaum's center and its publications were central to the forging of the Reagan administration deregulatory objectives, the Washington-based American Enterprise Institute (AEI) has been influential across a broader range of government programs and initiatives. In the 1970s, the AEI became the base of operations and a forum for the dissemination of the views of a host of prominent Republicans and neo-conservative Democrats, including such conservative economists as Herbert Stein, Arthur Burns, and Rudolph G. Penner, along with other scholars and political commentators who cut across the right half of the political-economic spectrum, such as Jeane J. Kirkpatrick, David R. Gergen, Seymour Martin Lipset, Edward C. Banfield, Nathan Glazer, Norman B. Ture, Weidenbaum, and Paul McCracken. Under the Reagan presidency, the number of AEI fellows employed in the administration has fluctuated, but in 1981–82 AEI identified ten of their former scholars in government service. Furthermore, in 1983, Rudolph Penner, AEI's conservative tax policy expert, became director of the Congressional Budget Office (CBO), a position of central importance in budget decisions, because the economic forecast and budget analysis of the CBO are the only alternatives prepared by a government body to those of the administration. The most significant aspect to the emergence of AEI, however, is that in many ways it has equaled or eclipsed the Brookings Institution, the central Democratic think tank, as a source of information for the media and congressional and agency staffs in Washington. Although AEI proclaims that it "does not take positions on public policy issues," and that the institution's product represents serious intellectual inquiry, the papers by the scholars and fellows associated with AEI, particularly the economic and defense papers, have a strong conservative bent, emphasizing the costs of regulation, the inflationary dangers of federal spending policies, and the need to build up Western military capabilities. In the political arena, AEI has produced aggressively marketed, sophisticated analyses of election trends, the strengths and weaknesses of the two parties, and shifts in the electorate. These analyses have appeared in the widely read bimonthly magazine of AEI, *Public Opinion,* and in a long and heavily promoted series of well-constructed pamphlets and books. These publications are among the most numerous, timely, and accessible of those produced by any think tank or other intellectual resource in Washington.

On an equally broad scale, the Hoover Institution at Stanford has been an intellectual fount of analyses, theories, and proposals critical to the alteration of economic policy. Two of the institution's senior fellows, Martin Anderson and Thomas Sowell, have become central conservative critics of the nation's network of social programs, Anderson arguing that an improved performance of the economy is far more important to the elimination of poverty than federal spending, and Sowell contending that the network of social programs, including affirmative action, has functioned to weaken the ability of blacks to compete and has retarded the achievement by blacks of economic equality.[22] Two other senior fellow economists at the institution, Robert E. Hall and Alvin Rabushka, have become leading proponents of the establishment of a consumption tax to replace the income tax. Studies by Michael Boskin, a senior fellow at the institution and a professor of economics at Stanford, contributed significantly to the argument that the rate of taxation on savings has functioned to reduce the national savings rate, a key element in the thinking behind the 1981 tax bill.[23]

Perhaps most influential as an intellectual force pushing economic policy to the right, however, has been Martin Feldstein, who in 1982, on leave from the National Bureau of Economic Research and Harvard University, became chairman of the Reagan administration's Council of Economic Advisors. As president from 1977 to 1981 of NBER, Feldstein wrote, sponsored, promoted, and provided broad distribution for a wide range of scholarship on economic matters. A significant part of his strength in the economic debate has been based on a willingness to sacrifice political gain for intellectual credibility, as he demonstrated in 1983 and 1984 when he publicly stressed the danger of continued high deficits, openly splitting with the Reagan administration.

The central thrust of much of Feldstein's own work and of much of the work produced under his aegis is, however, a sustained attack on the tax rate as applied to income derived from capital. In the highly controversial and still unresolved debate over productivity, the distinguishing characteristic of Feldstein's work has been the legitimacy and centrality he grants to the following argument: the combination of high inflation and provisions in the tax code has sharply lowered the rate of return on productive capital investment. "The most direct effect of inflation was to reduce the rate of return on investments in plant and equipment. . . . More generally, inflation raised the total tax rate on the capital income of nonfinancial corporations that is paid by the corporations themselves, their shareholders and their creditors," Feldstein wrote in *The Public Interest* in 1982.[24] This theme appears repeatedly. "The total tax rate paid by the corporations, their shareholders, and their creditors in 1979 to governments at all levels was 69 percent of the real capital income of the corporations, including both debt and equity income."[25] "Inflation distorts the measurement of profits, of interest payments, and of capital gains. The resulting mismeasurement of capital income has caused a substantial increase in the effective tax rate on the real income from the capital employed in the nonfinancial corporate sector. . . . We found that the 1979 effective tax rate on the total real capital income of the nonfinancial corporate sector was 69 percent. Thus, taxes now take about three-fourths of the total real capital income on corporate capital."[26]

Feldstein then takes a critical step in the productivity debate, arguing that the high rate of taxation on income from capital produced much of the reduction in investment in plant and equipment over the past two decades: "[The] U.S. tax rules that prevailed in the 1960s and 1970s can account for much of the nearly 40 percent decline in the net investment share in the gross national product that occurred between the second half of the 1960s and the 1970s."[27] Once these assumptions are made, it is a logical step to the conclusion that the high tax burden on capital income has been a major cause of the productivity decline. "Although some part of this decline [in investment in plant and equipment] reflects the generally weak economy, statistical evidence indicates that the low after-tax rate of return on investment was the primary reason. Experts on productivity agree that the reduced rate of growth of the capital stock was one of the reasons for the slowdown in productivity growth."[28]

This argument, which is based on highly controversial premises, was bolstered by economic analyses produced by others in the conservative intellectual establishment, particularly the studies on the after-tax rate of return on savings by Boskin and by those on the fringes of the economics establishment, particularly the proponents of supply-side concepts suggesting that tax revenues would increase as rates went down. While these two wings of the profession did not agree on specifics, as the supply-siders concentrated on the individual income tax and as the more established wing focused on the tax rates applied to income from savings and capital, including the corporate income tax, together they provided both an intellectual attack on the existing tax system and an intellectual justification for a substantial change in the distribution of the tax burden.

The focus of the debate on the tax rate of capital income had major distributional consequences. Income from capital, as opposed to earned income from wages and salary, is far more concentrated among the very rich. Capital income is received from stocks, bonds, real estate, trusts, life insurance, and savings. In effect, much of capital income comes from the ownership of wealth, as opposed to the receipt of salary or wages. The difference between ordinary wage and salary income and income from capital can been seen, in part, through the following two tables. Table 6.5 shows the 1980 distribution of all after-tax *income,* both earned and unearned, among the population divided into quintiles. Table 6.6 shows the amount of all *wealth* held by far smaller fractions of the population, the top 1 percent, and the top one-half percent. The wealth chart is for 1972, the most recent year for which such figures are available.

Table 6.5 [29]   THE DISTRIBUTION OF AFTER-TAX INCOME, EARNED AND UNEARNED, AMONG THE POPULATION DIVIDED INTO FIFTHS, AND THE PERCENTAGE OF INCOME GOING TO THOSE IN THE TOP 5 PERCENT OF THE POPULATION, 1980

Income quintile	Percentage of share of after-tax income
Lowest fifth	4.9
Second fifth	11.6
Middle fifth	17.9
Fourth fifth	25.1
Top fifth	40.6
Top 5 percent	14.1

In other words, in the case of the distribution of income, the top fifth of the population receives 40.6 percent of the total income while the bottom fifth receives 4.9 percent. While this is a significant disparity, a ratio of eight to one, it is modest when compared to the distribution of wealth:

Table 6.6 [30]   PERCENTAGE OF TOTAL WEALTH AND DIFFERENT TYPES OF WEALTH HELD BY THE ENTIRE POPULATION, BY THE TOP 1 PERCENT, AND BY THE TOP ONE-HALF PERCENT IN 1972; ALL DOLLAR FIGURES ARE IN *BILLIONS*

	Wealth held by entire population	Wealth held by top 1%	Wealth held by top 0.5%	Percentage held by top 1%	Percentage held by top 0.5%
Total wealth	$4,344	$1,047	$822	24.1	18.9
Real estate	1,493	225	151	15.1	10.1
Corp. stock	871	491	429	56.5	49.3
Bonds	158	95	83	60.0	52.2
Cash and savings	749	101	64	13.5	8.5
Mortgages and other debt instruments	78	41	30	52.7	39.1
Life insurance	143	10	6	7.0	4.3
Trusts	99	89	81	90.0	81.0
Miscellaneous	854	83	60	9.8	6.8

In the case of wealth, just under a quarter of all wealth is held by 1 percent of the population. When the distribution of income and wealth is compared, the percentage of after-tax income held by the top 5 percent is significantly less than the percentage of wealth held by the top 1 percent or even by the top half of 1 percent. As a result, shifting the tax debate toward the reduction of the tax burden on income from capital, or unearned income, created the opportunity for a major regressive shift in the tax burden. In effect, the analytic conclusions of a sector of the economics profession coincided with the interests of the holders of wealth, and together they found expression in the legislative policies adopted by the Reagan administration.

There were, however, even in 1981, at the time that the Reagan administration's major tax and budget legislation was adopted, substantive challenges to the theoretical underpinnings of a strategy designed to achieve economic growth through a reduction in government benefits to the poor and through a simultaneous reduction in the tax burden on the wealthy, on corporations, and on those in the upper-income brackets. These challenges have recently intensified.

At the core of the argument in support of the 1981 tax bill, which cut individual and business taxes by $749 billion over five years, was the dual claim that tax reductions would function to increase both the pool of personal savings and the rate of capital investment. According to this economic strategy, individual tax cuts shift money from the public to the private sector, where the beneficiaries—taxpayers—will save a high percentage of their new income. Capital investment, in turn, grows because the legislation sharply increases the tax advantages of capital spending, both through liberalization of the depreciation schedule and through expansion of the investment tax credit. In fact, however, according to data from the Bureau of Economic Analysis in the Department of Commerce, personal savings as a percentage of disposable personal income fell steadily from 1981, the year the legislation was passed, through the second quarter of 1983. In 1981 the savings rate stood at 6.6 percent, in 1982 it fell to 5.8 percent, in the first quarter of 1983 it dropped to 5.4 percent, and in the second quarter of 1983 it went down to 4.0 percent. In the third quarter of 1983 it rose to 4.9 percent, which is, however, a full 1.7 percentage points below the 1981 savings level. Similarly, nonresidential fixed investment, a basic measure of capital investment, stood, in 1972 dollars, at $174.4 billion in 1981, the first year of the tax cut. In 1982 it fell to $166.1 billion and to an annual rate of $159.9 billion in the first quarter of 1983. In the second and third quarters of 1983, the investment rate began to rise, reaching an annual rate of $169.3 billion in the third quarter—still, however, $5.1 billion below 1981 levels.[31] On a larger scale, there is a continuing debate over the sources and strength of the economic recovery that began in November 1982. This recovery clearly, however, was not the result of increased capital investment and a raised savings rates—the twin bases for economic growth, according to supply-side theory. Such increases as have occurred did not materialize until the recovery of late 1982 was well under way. This recovery appears to have largely resulted from increased consumer spending spurred by lower interest rates and by the 1981 tax cuts. Consumer spending rose in 1972 dollars from $956.8 billion in 1981 to $970.2 billion in 1982 and, by the third quarter of 1983, to an annual rate of $1.02 trillion, while all other economic measures stagnated.[32] The drop in the inflation rate, beginning in 1981, cannot be attributed to the 1981 tax cuts, nor to the Reagan administration's domestic spending cuts, which were effectively balanced by increases in defense spending. The sharp decline in the rate of inflation resulted in large part from the 1981–82 recession, the intensity of which is generally attributed to the restrictive monetary policies instituted by the Federal Reserve Board in 1979, while Jimmy Carter was president. Finally, the claim of supply-side theorists that tax revenues would be enhanced by deep tax reductions has not only failed to materialize, with tax revenues dropping from $617.8 in 1982 to $600.6 billion in 1983,[33] but the nation now faces the prospect of annual deficits approaching $200 to $300 billion unless taxes are raised.

The fundamental assumption that a lower tax rate on capital income creates increased investment and increases capital formation has furthermore been thrown into question in an exhaustive international study of the tax systems in the United States, the United Kingdom, Sweden, and West Germany by a group of economists from Princeton University, the National Bureau of Economic Research, the University of Birmingham, Oxford University, the Bank of England, and other European academic and financial institutions.[34] The study ranked each of these countries in terms of effective tax rates on income from capital and then ranked each on two other measures: the growth rate based on the average annual growth of the gross domestic product for the period from 1960 to 1980; and the growth in capital formation, measured as the average annual growth of nonfinancial corporate capital from 1960 to 1980. The results demonstrate that there was no correlation between growth and a low effective tax rate on capital. Instead, growth directly correlated with high tax rates. Table 6.7 shows the pattern:

Table 6.7 [35]   COMPARISON OF EFFECTIVE TAX RATES ON INCOME FROM CAPITAL WITH ANNUAL GROWTH RATES AND ANNUAL GROWTH OF NONFINANCIAL CORPORATE CAPITAL FOR FOUR COUNTRIES

	U.K.	Sweden	U.S.	Germany
Tax Rate	3.7%	35.6%	37.2%	48.1%
Annual economic growth	2.3	3.2	3.5	3.7
Annual corporate capital growth	2.6	4.7	3.7	5.1

As the authors of the study note: "The results are surprising to say the least. If we rank the four countries by the average annual growth in Gross Domestic Product, we obtain exactly the same order as when we rank by effective tax rates. . . . If we look at growth of nonfinancial corporate capital, results are substantially the same. The U.S. and Sweden are reversed, but Germany is still the highest and Britain is the lowest."[36] A second study, conducted under the auspices of the Urban Institute, has found that while the *average* tax rate on capital income has been relatively high, the *marginal* rate on the profits from new investments is low and has been getting lower consistently over the past two decades.[37] This pattern, which reverses the pattern of the individual income tax, where marginal rates are higher than average rates, has emerged because of the increasing number of tax breaks and preferences enacted since 1962, specifically targeted toward new investments. A sharply declining marginal rate of taxation on corporate income would suggest that the tax system is functioning to provide incentives to productive investment and that, conversely, the scope and direction of the blame placed on the tax system for the decline in productivity is inappropriate.

These studies engage only one aspect of an extremely complex debate over taxes and productivity. In the period from 1978 to 1981, however, preparatory to the enactment of the 1981 tax bill, there was room for neither compromise nor debate. Instead, the Reagan administration became the conduit for forces that included those calling for a reduction of tax on capital to spur investment and savings, those who predicted a supply-side burst of productive work effort if individual rates were cut across the board, and traditional Republican conservatives, persuaded that the only method of reducing governmental spending was by reducing tax revenues. In terms of formally organized political backing, these forces gained muscle through the Carlton Group, the alliance of the corporate lobbying community that wrote the business portions of the 1981 tax cut.[38]

The result was an extraordinary victory for those advocating a reduction in the tax rate on capital—or wealth. Under the combined terms of the 1981 tax bill and tax legislation enacted in 1982, the marginal tax rate on corporate income fell from 33.1 percent to 15.8 percent, the lowest level in at least forty years.[39] The only tax in the United States that is applied directly to wealth and that is designed to restrict the concentration of wealth—the inheritance tax—was drastically reduced. The basic exemption for the inheritance tax was raised from $175,625 to $600,000, with the result that the tax will apply only to the top 0.3 percent of estates. Equally important, the top rate, applicable only to that portion of the estate in excess of $3.1 million, was reduced from 70 to 50 percent. Similarly, the maximum personal income tax rate on unearned income from dividends and interest was reduced from 70 to 50 percent, retroactive to June 9, 1981, with a consequent reduction in the top capital gains rate from 28 to 20 percent. All taxpayers were allowed to postpone taxes on up to $2,000 a year for money put into individual retirement accounts, although the benefits of the tax deferral sharply increased for higher income taxpayers: the deferral is far more beneficial to a high-income married couple in the 50 percent marginal bracket than to a couple with a lower income. In an effort to give companies a new method of holding on to top management, the rules governing stock options were altered so that beneficiaries no longer had to treat the bonus as ordinary income, taxable at rates up to 50 percent, but were able both to defer tax liability until the options were sold, and to pay at that time only at the 20 percent capital gains rate.

In effect, the drive to increase the incentive to invest and save through a concentration of tax reductions on income from capital, combined with an across-the-board cut in individual taxes, resulted in the enactment of legislation regressively shifting the tax burden for the first time since the 1920s, as was shown in table 6.1. This redistribution toward those in the upper brackets was, in turn, compounded by the concentration of the budget cuts on programs providing benefits to the poor and working poor, as was shown in table 6.2.

The dual process of cutting both taxes and social programs involved, however, a striking difference in the assumptions of the motivations governing the behavior of the affluent and of the poor. For those in the upper brackets, and for those managing corporate decision-making processes, the underlying assumption of the tax cuts was that the creation of new tax incentives would encourage more work, more investment, and more savings, that the best way to achieve sought-after behavior is to reward it, in this case with lowered tax rates on corporations, savings, executive stock options, and estates.

At the bottom end of the scale, the dominant assumption behind social program cuts was precisely the opposite: the best way to achieve increased work is by making life tougher. In the case of both the basic welfare program, Aid to Families with Dependent Children, and food stamps, cuts were targeted toward those with some earnings. A system permitting a welfare recipient who goes to work part time to keep a declining portion of welfare benefits as income rises—in other words, a method of preventing a dollar benefit reduction for every dollar earned, or the equivalent of a 100 percent marginal tax rate—was severely restricted, with the result that an estimated 225,000 families with some earnings lost eligibility for AFDC. The amount of welfare money lost in many of these cases was often relatively small, but the loss of eligibility for welfare in many states also results in the loss of health coverage under Medicaid, making the penalty for working for a family with health costs significantly higher than the equivalent of a 100 percent tax rate. In the food stamp program, before 1981, recipients lost thirty cents for each dollar in earnings above certain ceilings defined by family size and region. In 1981, however, the cuts mandated the complete elimination of eligibility for any family with an income exceeding 130 percent of the poverty level. In 1982, when the poverty level for a family of four was $9,862, the cutoff from food stamp eligibility occurred when income reached $12,821 for a family of four. The effect of the cutoff at 130 percent and other reductions in the food stamp program was to reduce the total number of recipients by one million.[40]

Underlying the contradictory treatment of the rich and of the poor, the one prodded toward increased productivity through rewards, the other through penalties, there is a political logic. Among voters making less than $10,000 a year—those most heavily penalized by the Reagan agenda—47 percent are Democratic, 17 percent are Republican, and the rest are independent. Among voters making more than $50,000—the most highly rewarded group—44 percent are Republican while 24 percent are Democrats.[41]

The cuts in food stamps and welfare were just a part of a much larger pattern of spending reductions, reductions that functioned more to alter the political balance of power than to reduce the size of the deficit. In programs specifically directed to provide benefits to individuals, and particularly to poor individuals—as opposed, for example, to farm price supports, community development block grants, or defense spending—the Reagan administration has won reductions totaling $112 billion over the period from 1982 through 1985.[42] The programs facing the largest percentage reductions include child nutrition, 28 percent; social services block grants, 22 percent; compensatory education, 17 percent; general employment and training, 35 percent; and public service jobs, 99 percent.

These cuts represent an ideological victory that runs even deeper than the numbers themselves. Perhaps one of the most substantial achievements of the policy changes in the Reagan administration has been to consistently weaken the governmental base of support provided organized labor in its dealing with management—through sharp reductions in unemployment insurance, through the complete elimination of the public service job program, through the weakening of the Occupational Safety and Health Administration, and through appointments of persons hostile to organized labor both to the National Labor Relations Board and to the Department of Labor. In the past, these programs and agencies had provided, among other things, an employment and benefit cushion for those out of work, had insured safety in the workplace, and had required labor and management to abide by the law during organizing contests. The cuts in public service jobs, unemployment compensation, general employment and training, and the Jobs Corps together total $32.2 billion over the four-year period from 1982 to 1985. As chairman of the National Labor Relations Board, the Reagan administration appointed Donald R. Dotson, the former chief management lawyer for the Wheeling-Pittsburgh Steel Corp. Dotson then appointed as the board's solicitor Hugh L. Reilly, a former attorney with the National Right to Work Legal Defense Foundation, an organization specializing in bringing suits against unions.

The thrust of the treatment of organized labor is reflected in a number of ways. The Department of Labor, at a time when it has been forced to absorb extensive budget cuts, has been expanding its role in auditing the financial books of unions and their pension funds. Similarly, the department is currently moving to end a prohibition on government employment offices from referring those seeking jobs to companies where there is a strike taking place, a move that, if successful, would amount to government endorsement of the use of unemployed workers to break strikes.

The ideological tenor of the administration's budget cutting has been equally apparent in the drive to eliminate entirely the relatively minuscule budget for the Legal Services Corporation, the agency providing the poor with representation in dealing both with the courts and with government agencies. The administration has sought to end all funding of the legal services program, although Congress has moderated the effort, permitting the budget for the agency to fall from $344 million to $241 million. On a larger scale, the changes wrought in the network of domestic spending programs have functioned to increase the "cost" of being poor. The sharpest cuts are directed toward the means-tested programs, those directly serving the poor and the working poor, such as public housing, low-income energy assistance, public assistance, Medicaid, Aid to Families with Dependent Children, and food stamps; and those largely benefiting the poor, including Title I of the Elementary and Secondary Education Act of 1965, which targets money toward schools in deprived areas, vocational education, child nutrition, and social services block grants. The Reagan administration has also capitalized on 1980 legislation requiring regular review of the eligibility of recipients of the Supplemental Security Income program for four million aged, blind, and disabled individuals, to eliminate 600,000 recipients from the rolls, many of whom suffered from debilitating mental and physical illnesses and were incapable of appealing termination decisions. Under intense pressure from the media and from constituents, both Congress and the courts have attempted to protect the appeal rights of terminated recipients, permitting them to continue to receive support throughout the appeals process. The administration, however, remains committed to the overall policy of reducing federal transfer programs, in terms both of numbers of recipients and of the size of benefits.

The Future Distribution of Power

THE combination of events leading up to the overall tax and spending reductions of 1981 was unique—events leading up to what might be described as a moment of combustion for the conservative and economic right. Ronald Reagan emerged as an effective national political figure just when the balance of power between business and labor had shifted sharply in favor of business; when voter turnout patterns were giving increased leverage to the rich; when the progressive rate structure of the income tax and inflation-induced bracket creep had begun to whipsaw Democratic constituents; when the Democratic party had created a system of primaries granting disproportionate strength to the affluent; when the failure of the economy to grow in the 1970s turned working- and lower-middle-class Democratic constituencies into sharply hostile critics of programs targeted toward the poor; when the more effective fundraising techniques and the more affluent constituency of the Republican party gave it a major advantage over the Democratic party in a system of politics increasingly dependent upon expensive technology; when the Democratic party had spent much of the 1970s in the false comfort of a Watergate-supported majority, while failing to address the substantial political conflicts among its own constituents over tax and domestic spending programs; and when a number of conservative groups had coalesced around the Republican party.

This unique combination of events providing momentum for the political right began to some degree to deteriorate within months after Reagan won enactment of his budget and tax legislation. Perhaps most importantly, the claimed revival of the economy did not immediately materialize; rather, there was the most severe recession of the postwar period. Reagan, in turn, failed to consolidate the gains he and many fellow Republicans had made among traditional Democratic constituencies. For those who had been drawn to the GOP on the basis of cultural and social issues—abortion and school prayer—the Ninety-seventh Congress produced defeat, as Reagan placed all his political capital on the enactment of his economic program and chose not to place the full weight of his office behind enactment of abortion and school prayer constitutional amendments, allowing them to go down to defeat. In 1976, fundamental and evangelical Christians had voted for Carter over Gerald Ford by a margin of 53 to 47; four years later, these same voters favored Reagan over Carter by a margin of 64 to 36.[43] For those in the working and lower-middle class, drawn to the GOP on economic grounds, Reagan pushed through a program significantly beneficial only to the rich, reviving near-dormant views of the Republican party as the party of big business and of the affluent, a view compounded by the 1981–82 recession. The Reagan administration became, as the 1982 election results showed, at least temporarily, the basis for a revival of the Democratic coalition.

From another vantage point, however, the Reagan administration achieved a number of key, long-range victories, changes that will survive to influence policy significantly no matter what the elective future of the GOP, and regardless of the scope of the economic recovery. The most important of these victories was, first, the use of the tax cut and, second, the use of increased defense spending, to force what amounts to continued conservative domination of the federal agenda. The huge loss of federal revenues resulting from the tax reductions of 1981, only partially replenished by the tax bill of 1982,[44] and a sharp increase in defense spending, which Congress may modify but not halt, have turned the issue of the federal deficit into an inescapable and central question facing the House, the Senate, and the White House, whether control of any or all of these is held by the Republican or by the Democratic party. Milton Friedman's prediction that tax cuts would force spending cuts has failed to materialize; instead, domestic spending cuts have been canceled out by military spending increases, and deficits are widely predicted to remain in the $200 billion range.

The presence of such a large deficit severely restricts any spending initiative by the Democratic party. A deficit of this proportion also places strong political pressure on elected officials of both parties to build up a record of votes showing an intention to reduce spending, in order to demonstrate fiscal responsibility to constituents baffled by deficits of unprecedented size. At the same time, the centrality of the deficit in the national debate inherently provides a strong conservative tenor to that debate, forcing Democrats to choose between raising taxes or more red ink. Even if the Democratic party were to regain power, the centrality of the deficit will obstruct all efforts to seek to provide benefits to such key Democratic voting blocks as blacks, women, and workers in distressed industries. In turn, the prospect of raising taxes has been made more difficult by the failure of the Reagan tax cuts to relieve the overall burden on the working and lower-middle classes. This failure may have contributed to increased hostility toward the GOP, but at the same time, it has functioned to maintain the anti-tax sentiments of these two largely Democratic constituencies.

Conversely, it would be extremely difficult to withdraw the rewards provided by Reagan, through the tax code, to essentially Republican constituencies. The lowering of the top rate on unearned income from 70 to 50 percent, the gutting of the inheritance tax, the tax advantages of IRA and Keogh retirement accounts and of executive stock options, have become integral parts of the tax code, and any efforts to increase taxes in these areas would run up against intense, well-organized opposition. The corporate tax reductions are more vulnerable, as the withdrawal of some of the preferences enacted in 1981 by the 1982 tax bill reflected.[45] But Democrats will be under considerable self-imposed pressure to prove that the party is not anti-business, and it is very unlikely that the Democrats would initiate a drive to increase corporate taxes. The prospect that business political action committees will increasingly support Republican candidates has acted as a major inhibiting force upon Democratic willingness to raise business taxes. In fact, it was the Republican party, under pressure in 1982 to prove that it was not overly probusiness, that initiated and pushed through the 1982 tax bill reversing some of the corporate reductions enacted in 1981.

In the long run, the scope and content of economic policy will be determined in large part by the balance of power between competing economic interests and classes. This balance of power was critical in the steady shift of the economic debate to the right throughout the past decade. It will remain central as the national economic debate moves to such issues as the creation of a national industrial policy; tax increases and spending cuts to reduce the deficit; and substantial alteration of the tax system, moving either in the direction of lowering existing rates through elimination of many of the existing tax preferences or through creation of a tax on consumption—as opposed to a tax on income. Each of these issues has the potential for producing major shifts in the distribution of wealth and income, and the competition for power to influence the course of government policy will be crucial.

The emergence of these issues reflects a basic change in the nature of the debate and in some fundamental characteristics of the contestants. The legitimacy once granted proponents of redistribution—the consensus behind redistribution—has largely evaporated. Instead, the faltering of the economy since the mid-1970s has resulted in the replacement of arguments in favor of redistribution with more stringent demands that tax and spending policies be guided by the goals of increased incentives for work, savings, and investment and by economic efficiency. Will a change in the tax code function to increase economic activity? What kind of domestic social spending increases the productivity of society, and which programs act as disincentives? Does the creation of a new tax preference encourage favored investment patterns or result in an unproductive distortion of the marketplace? This is new terrain for the national debate and is not familiar to much of the political left in this country, a left that in the past has been able to make much of its case on moral grounds. The themes of efficiency, productivity, and tax incentives are far more familiar to the conservative and business communities; and this familiarity has since the latter part of the 1970s helped the conservative and business communities to dominate the economic debate.

In this economic debate, the substantive differences between the Republican and Democratic parties—the economic status of constituents, fundraising tactics, voter turnout, ideological cohesion, and the strength of the party structure—are becoming major determinants in the formulation of economic policy. There are two parallel sources of pressure on both parties. The first emerges out of the changing economic character of the constituency of each party, the Republicans increasingly tied to the affluent, the Democrats to those in the bottom third of the income distribution. The second grows out of an economic reality severely constricting the scope of political decisions: the awarding of benefits to one group must be done at the expense of another group, since the shrinking of the postwar prosperity that for two and a half decades of steadily rising real incomes and federal revenues permitted all to gain. These twin developments, growing partisan class allegiance and zero-sum political-economic choices, are forcing each of the parties to adopt a stronger role representing the interests of a majority of their constituents in what amounts to a distributional competition. The competition is to develop an economic policy that protects and advances the interests of those who are the core of partisan support—the upper-middle class to the rich for the GOP, the poor to the lower-middle class for the Democrats—while at the same time appealing to a majority of all voters.

To a large extent, the resulting pressures are toward more polarized parties along European lines, conservative versus labor party divisions. These pressures run directly counter to the tradition in the United States of an absence of class-based politics, a tradition arising out of a host of factors: there are far fewer formal class barriers in this country; sustained economic growth has permitted a steady flow from the working class into the middle class; the labor movement has never been strong enough to function as a central force for political mobilization; and the regional, ethnic, and religious heterogeneity of the population has often been as important as class divisions in the outcome of elections. The lack of a class-based tradition has not, however, prevented the Republican party from adopting a set of policies that, by American standards, are highly class-oriented, targeted to the benefit of the top 5 percent of the income distribution, where Republican margins are largest. The willingness of the Republican party to become the representative of its dominant class constituency, while the Democratic party remains ideologically ambivalent, provides the basis for significant insight into the prospective balance of power and the future outcome of economic debates.

In one respect, the ambiguity of the Democratic party grows out of the fact that its ties to various groups in society are diffuse, and none of these groups—women, blacks, labor, the elderly, Hispanics, urban political organizations—stands clearly larger than the others. In many other Western democracies, responsibility for constructive participation in major national debates over tax and industrial policy, while at the same time protecting the interests of the poor, working, and lower-middle classes, generally belongs to organized labor. In order for this representation to be effective, however, the union movement must be strong. In Western European countries there is a strong correlation between a powerful labor movement and the maintenance of low unemployment, a progressive distribution of income, and high expenditures for domestic social programs. All these point to goals sought by those on the bottom half of the income distribution. In addition, however, those countries with a strong union movement were also the most successful, during the period from 1965 to 1980, in keeping the rate of inflation down, a goal sought by rich and poor alike. Labor effectively entered into an arrangement with the government in which unions agreed to keep wages and strike activity down in return for the maintenance of high employment, high social service expenditures, continued support of transfer programs to the elderly and to the poor, and continued progressive distribution of income. In countries where the labor union movement is weak, there were not only higher unemployment rates but higher rates of inflation and greater strike activity. These findings suggest not only that a strong labor movement benefits the workers represented by it, but that such a movement can effectively represent broader interests than its own constituents.[46]

In the United States, the labor union movement is too weak to perform this kind of representation. In political terms, organized labor has since 1981 been gaining strength within the Democratic party and has shown increasing sophistication in the use of campaign money. But increased political power does not translate into the capacity to provide broad representation. The representative weakness of U.S. organized labor is reflected in the very low proportion of the workforce that is unionized, only two out of every ten workers, compared to nine out of ten in Sweden, eight out ten in Denmark, better than four out of ten in Germany, seven out of ten in Belgium, and better than three out of ten in Switzerland.

Labor's difficulties in the United States have been compounded by the shape of its decline, which has been concentrated primarily in one area, the manufacturing industries. These industries, including automobiles, metals of all kinds, machinery production, textiles, paper, apparel, chemicals, rubber, printing, and food, have been the mainstay of the union movement, providing a third of the total U.S. union membership, far exceeding transportation, trades, finance, service, and public employees. Not only is the manufacturing sector failing to grow, but organized labor's share of the remaining workforce is declining. In 1973 unions represented 7.87 million workers in manufacturing, 38.8 percent of the total; just seven years later, in 1980, the number of union members fell by over 1 million to 6.77 million, which in turn amounted to only 32.3 percent of all those working in the manufacturing industries.[47]

The steady decline in union strength has forced organized labor to adopt an inherently defensive posture, a stance in which its principal goal is the protection of its own beleaguered interests rather than the interests of the workforce as a whole. In a country such as Sweden or Denmark, where the entire labor force is effectively organized, significant economic change can be accomplished without threatening the core of the labor union movement, its membership. If, either through the marketplace or through government planning, an automobile plant running into deeper and deeper losses is replaced by a computer facility in a country in which the entire labor force is organized, there is no loss to organized labor, because the workers in the computer facility will also be union members. In the United States, such a shift from autos to computers would inevitably result in a heavy loss of union members.

In this context, a national debate over the creation of an industrial policy, for example, is likely, for much of organized labor, to turn into a protectionist drive. Labor, which supports the adoption of an industrial policy, will enter into the debate with a large vested interest in a policy favoring the revival of the northern, smokestack industries, where its strength is highest, although membership in this sector has been declining rapidly. Pressure for protectionism, as the United Automobile Workers, the Steelworkers, and the Building and Construction Trades have already shown, in all likelihood will extend to import trade barriers on foreign-made steel and cars, and to the preservation of federal regulations requiring contractors to pay prevailing wage scales, which effectively mandates union scale wages for both union and nonunion contractors. One major advantage of an industrial policy for the union movement is that its representatives, under almost any plan, are guaranteed a block of votes on any national or regional board controlling the allocation of loan supports, job training grants, federal subsidies, etc. Even with no increase in the number of workers repre-

sented by unions, organized labor would gain far more control over
the industrial process than it presently has.

The internal pressures within organized labor to protect what little
it has rule out any possibility that the union movement in the United
States will become the dominant force of the left in a system of politics
increasingly shaped by distributional struggles and by pressures to
increase the nation's productivity. Labor will remain a major actor in
this debate, but there is no chance that it will adopt a role in any way
approaching that of labor in much of middle and northern Europe.

Similarly, two other ascendant groups in the Democratic party,
women and blacks, are not currently in a position to assume centrality
as arbiters in the policy-making process. The rising political leverage
of women and blacks is, however, likely to have a direct impact on
the specific issue of whether there should be further cuts in domestic
social spending. Both women and blacks are functioning as forces of
the left. "You put the two [women and blacks] together, and we [the
Republican party] have a serious problem," Susan Bryant, a GOP
campaign consultant, noted, pointing to the prospect of increased voter
turnout among both groups.[48] There is a strong overlapping interest
between blacks and women on the preservation of domestic spending
programs: the beneficiaries of social spending programs targeted toward
the poor include a disproportionate number of women and a disproportionate number of blacks. While the rate of poverty for the nation as
a whole in 1982 was 15 percent, it reached 36.3 percent among families
headed by women of all races, and for blacks of both sexes, the poverty
rate was 35.6 percent.[49]

For the Democratic party, the lack of a single group broad-based and
strong enough to coordinate the increasingly difficult process of developing economic policy is particularly debilitating, as the party itself is
ill-equipped to adopt this role. In one respect, the growing strength of
the bottom third of the income distribution within the Democratic
party would seem to facilitate the ability of the party to identify its
core constituency and to formulate policy with a clear eye toward the
protection of those on the bottom of the income distribution, counter-
ing the opposing tactics of the Republican party. As table 1.3 in chapter

1 shows, the Democratic party, in terms of income, has changed shape from the 1950s, when its support was relatively evenly split among income groups, with 34 percent from the bottom third of the income distribution and 32 percent from the top third, to a party increasingly dependent for support from those on the bottom of the income distribution. By the end of the 1970s, 38 percent of all Democrats were in the bottom third of the income distribution and only 29 percent in the top third.

There are, however, a host of forces pushing the Democratic party in the opposite direction, preventing any coherent representation of those at the bottom of the income distribution. By its sheer advantage over the GOP in total numbers, it has majority support not only among those in the lower and lower-middle classes but almost through the entire middle and upper-middle class. Although this support often does not translate into votes on election day, particularly among Democrats in the upper-income brackets, it acts as a strong restraint on any leftward motion by the party.

Further weakening the identification of the Democratic party with those on the lower half of the income distribution is the upper-class bias of existing turnout patterns, a bias compounded by the Democratic party-created proliferation of primary elections, where class-skewed turnout patterns are more extreme than in general elections. As described in chapter 2, once in office, Democratic incumbents both in the House and in the Senate are dependent upon ideologically conflicting sources of money from labor, business, and trade associations, divided almost equally in a manner designed to encourage legislative paralysis. At the same time, southern Democrats, always more conservative than their northern colleagues, have been forced into an increasingly defensive posture over the past two decades. The result has been a diminution of the economic populism characteristic of many southern Democrats, a populism that provided the basis for some links with northern liberals but that has now yielded to the adoption of more rigidly conservative positions in order to head off any Republican threat from the right.

In direct contrast to the ideologically conflicting forces within the Democratic party, almost all of the pressures in the Republican party are toward the coherent representation of the affluent. Just as the weight of the income distribution within the Democratic party is shifting toward the bottom, within the Republican party it is shifting toward the top. As table 2.3 in chapter 2 demonstrates, the GOP has changed since the 1950s, when 38 percent of its support came from the top third of the income distribution and 29 percent from the bottom third, to, at the end of the 1970s, a party still more strongly dominated by the well-to-do, when 43 percent were from the top third and 25 percent from the bottom third. What had been a 9 percentage point difference doubled to an 18 percentage point difference. In other words, the shape of the Republican party and the location of its strength coincide and point unambiguously toward the representation of the affluent; in terms of the correlation between income and GOP allegiance, there are no contradictory forces encouraging the kind of ambiguity characteristic of the Democratic party.

Most recent political trends have placed the Republican party in a better position to represent the interests of its strongest base of support, the richest third of the population. As long as class-skewed voting patterns endure, they will help the GOP, and the overwhelming advantage of the affluent in primaries means that the income group providing the largest GOP margins dominates the Republican primary process. Republicans in the House and Senate expeience none of the conflict created by ideologically mixed sources of campaign finance. The Republican party structure—the Republican National, Senatorial, and Congressional committees—has benefited from an increasing number of contributors who see the party itself as a vehicle for the expression of their interests. These contributors are willing to put their money into the party, as opposed to donating their money to prominent candidates, and when they support candidates, they are willing to target their money to candidates selected by the party as being particularly in need of money.

Altogether, then, these changes in the composition of the two political parties have enormous consequences for the balance of power in the formulation of economic policy. As the formulation of economic policy increasingly becomes an adversarial process between income groups and classes, as each of the parties increasingly functions as a competing forum for the development of economic and political theories, strategies and legislative proposals, and as the scope of viable economic options remains restricted, forcing politicians to make choices favoring one class at the expense of another, the distribution of power between income groups becomes a critical, if not the critical, issue. Over the past decade, changes in the political process have strengthened the power of the affluent and eroded the power of the poor, the working class, and the lower-middle class. This shift, in turn, has resulted in the adoption of economic policies highly beneficial to the rich, penalizing the poor, and leaving most of the working and middle classes with increased tax burdens.

The shifts in power that have taken place over the last decade suggest that the changes in tax and spending policies put into place over the past four years benefiting the affluent will remain in place regardless of which party takes control of the White House and which gains a majority in the Senate. Continued Republican control of the federal government is likely to produce efforts to expand the distributional shifts favoring the affluent, but it does not necessarily follow that Democratic control would produce a restoration of more progressive distributional policies favoring the bottom third of the population. Rather, under a Democratic administration, liberal initiatives, which might pass in the House, are sure to face insurmountable opposition in the Senate, where even nominal Democratic control will still mean a de facto conservative majority, resulting from a voting coalition of Republicans and southern and western Democrats.

The power shift that produced the fundamental policy realignment of the past decade did not result from a conservative or Republican realignment of the voters; nor did it produce such a realignment after the tax and spending legislation of 1981 was enacted. Rather, these policy changes have grown out of pervasive distortions in this country's democratic political process. These distortions have created a system of political decision making in which fundamental issues—the distribution of the tax burden, the degree to which the government sanctions the accumulation of wealth, the role of federal regulation, the level of publicly tolerated poverty, and the relative strength of labor and management—are resolved by an increasingly unrepresentative economic elite. To a large extent, these changes have turned the Republican party, in terms of the public policies it advocates, into a party of the elite. For the Democratic party, the political changes of the past decade have distorted the distribution of power and weakened the capacity of the party to represent the interests of its numerous less affluent constituents. Even if the Democrats are victorious in capturing the presidency, there is no evidence that the Democratic party is in any way prepared to set an agenda economically benefiting its core constituents in the same way that the Republican-conservative movement has been able to define the political debate in recent years to the advantage of its most loyal supporters. As long as the balance of political power remains so heavily weighted toward those with economic power, national economic policy will remain distorted, regardless of which party is in control of the federal government.

Notes

The Democratic Party

[1]Samuel Lubell, *The Future of American Politics* (Doubleday/Anchor Books, rev. ed., 1955), pp. 212, 214.

[2]Norman H. Nie, Sidney Verba, and John R. Petrocik, *The Changing American Voter* (Harvard University Press, 1976). See especially chap. 12, pp. 194–242.

[3]The data from the polls cited in this paragraph and in the following chart are taken from the December/January 1981 and December/January 1983 issues of *Public Opinion* magazine, American Enterprise Institute, Washington, D.C.

[4]The findings in the ABC and NBC polls, which were also reprinted in *Public Opinion,* December/January 1983, appear below. More detailed information on voting is in chapter 5.

	NBC	
Voter income	*Percentage voting Democratic*	*Percentage voting Republican*
Less than $8,000	71	27
$8,000–14,999	60	38
$15,000–24,999	56	42
25,000–34,999	54	44
Over $35,000	44	54

ABC

Voter income	Percentage voting Democratic	Percentage voting Republican
Under $5,000	73	24
$5,000–9,999	65	32
$10,000–14,999	62	36
$15,000–19,999	56	40
$20,000–29,999	56	41
$30,000–$39,999	54	44
$40,000 and over	47	50

[5]For a detailed description of the parallel rise of Lyndon B. Johnson and Brown and Root, see Robert A. Caro, *The Path To Power* (Alfred A. Knopf, 1982).

[6]See, for example, Richard Scammon and Benjamin J. Wattenberg, *The Real Majority* (Coward-McCann, 1970); Wattenberg, *The Real America* (Doubleday, 1974); and Everett Carll Ladd, Jr., with Charles D. Hadley, *Transformations of the American Party System* (W.W. Norton & Company, 2d ed., 1978). Ladd quotes on p. 301 a 1976 postelection memorandum by Patrick H. Caddell, a Democratic pollster: "We see that the Democratic party can no longer depend on a coalition of economic division. Whatever our short-term economic troubles of the 'haves' versus the 'have-nots,' a tremendous growth in economic prosperity has produced more 'haves' in our society than 'have-nots.' " Ladd argues that Caddell's principal client, Jimmy Carter, "was well advised on the state of contemporary coalitions."

[7]The Watergate scandals also coincided with the final days of the anti-Vietnam War movement and of the counterculture that sprung up around that movement. It was, in effect, the late summer of the greening of America, and the Democratic party was its short-term beneficiary.

[8]Phillips, *Post-Conservative America* (Random House, 1982). Arguing that the preliminary Watergate disclosures toward the end of the 1972 campaign resulted in a failure for the GOP to make major gains in the South and in a failure to establish a majority supported "articulate, populist-tinged conservatism. . . . Absent Watergate, political control of the South could also have passed into into the hands of a new coalition" (p. 59).

[9]To qualify for this appellation, a voter has to be willing to cast his ballot for a yellow dog before he would pull the lever for a Republican candidate.

[10]The significance of organized labor and voter turnout will be discussed in much greater detail in chapters 4 and 5.

[11]Andrew Hacker, ed., *U/S: A Statistical Portrait of the American People* (The Viking Press, 1983).

[12]Economic Report of the President, February 1983, p. 194.

[13]Richard H. Davidson, "Subcommittee Government," in *The New Congress,* ed. Thomas E. Mann and Norman J. Ornstein, American Enterprise Institute, 1981. p. 109.

[14]Walter Dean Burnham, *The Current Crisis in American Politics* (Oxford University Press, 1982), p. 178.

[15]Data for these elections calculated from the pamphlet "Voting and Registration in the Election of November 1980" Bureau of the Census, pp. 2, 8.

[16]Michael Barone, Grant Ujifusa, and Douglas Matthews, *The Alamanac of American Politics* (E.P. Dutton, 1978), for demographic descriptions of the congressional districts.

[17]In order to kill the filibuster, under Senate rules, sixty votes were needed. In two key votes, on June 14 and 15, 1978, proponents of labor law reform could muster only fifty-eight members of the Senate willing to stop Hatch's filibuster. Of these, forty-four were Democrats and fourteen were moderate to liberal Republicans. Seventeen Democrats voted to permit the filibuster to continue. The fight will be discussed in more detail in chapter 4.

[18]Common Cause was founded in 1970 as a citizens' reform lobby, although it gained much of its prominence during the Watergate years from 1973 through 1977. The upper-middle-class composition of Common Cause is reflected in its failure to actively press tax reform proposals that, if progressive, damage the interests of the upper-middle class.

[19]Everett Carll Ladd, Jr., *Where Have All The Voters Gone?* (W. W. Norton & Company, 1977), pp. 40, 41. The findings are from polls conducted by the National Opinion Research Center of the University of Chicago in 1972 and 1976.

[20]Perhaps the best descriptive and analytical material on this period is contained in *Consequences of Party Reform,* Nelson W. Polsby (Oxford University Press, 1983).

[21]Polsby, *Consequences,* p. 114.

[22]All data are from pages 12 and 13 of the report, "Democratic Party's Commission on Openness, Participation and Party Building: Reforms For a Stronger Democratic Party," Washington, D.C., 1978. The commission made

the calculations on the basis of a survey of primary voters by the New York Times and CBS, and a sample of likely general election voters by Cambridge Survey Research. The data for comparative primary and general election turnout among those with college educations or more and for blacks in primary and general elections are as follows:

PERCENTAGE OF DEMOCRATIC VOTERS
WITH A COLLEGE DEGREE OR MORE
VOTING IN THE 1976 PRIMARY AND
GENERAL ELECTIONS

State	Primary	General
California	34	17
Florida	28	17
Illinois	23	6
Indiana	13	6
Massachusetts	36	22
Michigan	20	10
New Hampshire	38	18
New Jersey	35	14
New York	32	19
Ohio	25	10
Oregon	23	20
Pennsylvania	23	15
Wisconsin	22	15

PERCENTAGE OF SAME ELECTORATE
THAT IS BLACK

State	Primary	General
California	12	15
Florida	8	14
Illinois	15	16
Indiana	10	11
Massachusetts	2	3
Michigan	11	22
New Jersey	17	26
New York	15	20
Ohio	11	17
Pennsylvania	8	15
Wisconsin	3	7

[23]Haynes Johnson, *The Washington Post,* July 8, 1972.

[24]Paul T. David, Ralph M. Goldman, and Richard C. Bain, in *The Politics of National Party Conventions* (The Brookings Institution, 1960), did not categorize delegates by specific income classes, but their demographic analysis of the 1948 convention delegates clearly suggested a strong bias toward the upper-middle class. The table on page 338 shows that 55.1 percent of the Democratic delegates were classified as professionals: lawyers, doctors, publishers, educators, etc., and another 23.4 percent were involved in business occupations. The same general pattern applied to both parties, although the percentage of Democratic delegates who were members of unions was far higher— 9.7 percent, compared to 2.7 percent for the GOP. Without specific figures, the authors suggest that union representation significantly increased in the 1952 and 1956 conventions, as the strength of organized labor was on the upswing and the AFL and CIO were moving toward a merger that was consummated in December 1955.

[25]"Democratic Party's Commission on Openness, Participation and Party Building," 1978, p. 20.

[26]This assertion, more applicable to the Senate than to members of the House, is certainly true of a majority of the more aggressive members of both branches of Congress, whose role in setting policy is significant. In 1983 there were twenty-four Senators who had either run for the presidency, were at that time running, had been vice-presidential candidates, or had been given serious consideration in the media as potential presidential or vice-presidential candidates. Presidential candidates from the House in recent years have included Morris K. Udall, John Anderson, and Gerald Ford.

[27]Publications highly influential within the conservative movement, such as *Human Events* and *The Conservative Digest,* function as watchdogs of the right, quick to criticize failures of GOP House and Senate members to toe the line. On June 4, 1983, for example, *Human Events* reported that "such conservatives as [Senators] Roger Jepsen [Republican of Iowa] and William Roth [Republican of Delaware]" had joined "outright leftwingers" in support of legislation creating a Peace Academy. The same issue faulted Senator Pete V. Domenici (R–N. Mex.) for his role in passing a Senate Budget Resolution calling for a $9 billion tax hike in 1984.

[28]*Handbook of Labor Statistics,* Department of Labor, December 1980, p. 412. For more detailed information on organized labor, see chapter 4.

[29]"Voting and Registration in the Election of November 1980," Bureau of the Census, April 1982, p. 2. The census figures are based on interviews, and

as a consequence the turnout figures tend to be exaggerated by 5 to 9 percent.

[30]Economic Report of The President, February 1983, p. 194.

[31]Computed from data in The American National Election Studies Data Sourcebook, 1952–1978, by Warren E. Miller, Arthur H. Miller, and Edward J. Schneider (Harvard University Press, 1980), and from 1980 data supplied by the Center for Political Studies, Institute for Social Research, the University of Michigan. Altogether, the data are based on fifteen separate surveys, each involving well over 1,000 respondents. The distribution of respondents into three income groups by the Center for Political Studies worked well except for the 1950s, when those in the middle third were significantly underrepresented in the sample. Table 1.3 corrects for this.

[32]Ibid.

[33]Ibid., p. 81.

[34]Data taken from the American National Election Study, 1980, conducted by the Center for Political Studies, University of Michigan.

[35]These calculations are based on the tables on page 12 of the 1978 "Democratic Party's Commission on Openness, Participation and Party Building." The average percentage increases in primaries of voters with college educations and with incomes in excess of $20,000 in 1976 for the thirteen states were examined in the report. These increases in primary strength were then applied to the figures in Table II. There are difficulties with these calculations since the bases and time periods are not uniform. The probable error, however, is in the direction of underestimating the strength of elite voters.

[36]Economic Report of The President, February 1983, p. 207.

The Republican Party

[1]Warren E. Miller, Arthur H. Miller, and Edward J. Schneider, American National Election Studies Data Sourcebook, 1952–1978 Harvard University Press, 1980), p. 81.

[2]Following Petrocik's usage, the determination of status is based on education and employment. Petrocik, Party Coalitions (University of Chicago Press, 1981), p. 91.

[3]Computed from Miller, Miller and Schneider, op cit, pages 96 and 97.

[4]Defining specific groups of politicians, Republican or Democratic, as "ideological" rather than "pragmatic" is a difficult and dangerous process, but it can be safely said that the ideological politician sees issues primarily in moral terms, rather than as negotiable questions on which compromise is possible.

A related characteristic of the ideological politician is a belief that his or her own candidacy and participation in the legislative process are part of a larger cause, ranging, for example, from temperance to the emancipation of slaves, from fiscal austerity to the exposure of union corruption. Once in office, the need to seek reelection has often modified the intensity of ideological fervor, as it has in the case of many of the Republican conservatives elected over the past fifteen years.

[5]For additional information on political action committees see chapter 3, pp. 129–136.

[6]Index of Independent Expenditures 1979–1980, Federal Election Commission (FEC), 1325 K Street, N.W., Washington, D.C. 20463, November 1981, pp. 26–30.

[7]FEC, Interim Report No. 4, May 1983.

[8]Index of Independent Expenditures 1979–1980, FEC, p. 31.

[9]Index of Independent Expenditures 1981–1982, FEC, September 1983. Nineteen-eighty was a year of major victories for NCPAC, as it contributed to the defeat of such liberal Democratic senators as McGovern, Bayh, Church, Culver, and Nelson. In 1982 NCPAC's efforts were a failure, as all seventeen of the Democratic House members NCPAC campaigned against won reelection and all but two of the Senate candidates NCPAC campaigned against— Howard Cannon and Edmund G. Brown, of Nevada and California—won election.

[10]The contribution figures come from *The American Almanac of Politics 1982*, Michael Barone and Grant Ujifusa (Barone and Company, 1981). Excluded from the calculations are two cases in which open seats had been filled in special elections in 1981 by Democrats who were then defeated by Republicans in the 1982 general election.

[11]The contribution figures for the 1982 congressional elections all come from FEC, Reports on Financial Activity 1981–1982, Interim Report No. 3, House and Senate Candidates, Washington, D.C., May 1983.

[12]For a detailed series of articles describing the scope of the Energy and Commerce Committee, see David Maraniss, "The Committee," a series in the *Washington Post* appearing on a random basis throughout 1983 and 1984.

[13]The full description of the legislative jurisdiction of all committees can be found in the 1983 Congressional Staff Directory, Congressional Staff Directory, Ltd., Mount Vernon, Virginia, 1983. The Energy and Commerce Committee appears on p. 394.

[14]Figures calculated from FEC Reports on Financial Activity 1981–1982, Interim Report No. 3, U.S. Senate and House Campaigns, May 1983.

[15]The most commonly used formula to correlate economic conditions with election results was developed by Edward R. Tufte, in *Political Control of the Economy* (Princeton University Press, 1978). Using the Tufte formula, Gary C. Jacobson and Samuel Kernell, of the University of California at San Diego, calculated that economic conditions would have produced a fifty-seven-seat loss in the House for the GOP. In fact, the loss was only twenty-six, which Jacobson and Kernell attribute to the effectiveness of the Republican party in recruiting and financing candidates (Jacobson and Kernell, "Strategy and Choice in 1982," in *Strategy and Choice in Congressional Elections* [Yale University Press, 1983]).

[16]FEC Reports on Financial Activity 1981–1982, Interim Report No. 3, U.S. Senate and House Campaigns, Washington, D.C., May 1983.

[17]Calculations of spending in the 1982 election were computed from 1981–1982 Financial Activity for Campaigns of General Election Candidates, FEC release, May 2, 1983, p. 3.

[18]FEC report, April 29, 1983, "1981–1982 PAC Giving up 51%."

[19]FEC release, "Fec Releases Data on 1981–82 Congressional Races," May 2, 1983.

[20]FEC Reports on Financial Activity 1981–1982, Interim Report No. 3, U.S. Senate and House Campaigns, Washington, D.C., May 1983.

[21]FEC, Interim Report No. 3, May 1983.

[22]FEC release, April 26, 1983.

[23]FEC release, "FEC Reports Republicans Outspend Democrats by more than 5-to-1 in '82 elections," April 26, 1983.

[24]Herbert E. Alexander, *Financing the 1980 Election* (Lexington Books, 1983), pp. 447–59.

[25]Based on computation from Symms's first quarter (1980) report of expenditures and receipts to the FEC.

[26]Austin Ranney, *Channels of Power—The Impact of Television on American Politics* (Basic Books and American Enterprise Institute, 1983); Michael J. Robinson, "American Political Legitimacy in an Era of Electronic Journalism," in *Television as a Social Force,* ed. Douglass Cater and Richard Adler (Praeger, 1975); and Robinson, "Television and American Politics, 1956–1976," *The Public Interest,* Summer 1977.

[27]Robinson, *Television as a Social Force,* p. 101.

[28]Ranney, *Channels,* pp. 74–87.

[29]The figures used in this paragraph were taken from "Where the Money Goes," *The National Journal,* April 16, 1983.

[30]U.S. House of Representatives Special Committee to Investigate Campaign Expenditures, 1952, Government Printing Office, 1952, p. 144. Quoted in Alexander Heard, *The Costs of Democracy* (University of North Carolina Press, 1960), p. 18.

[31]Because of the major changes in reporting requirements, comparisons of partisan fundraising strength between the present and earlier periods is very difficult. The most comprehensive study was conducted by Alexander Heard, in *The Costs of Democracy*. Democrats were consistently outspent during the depression years—when they consistently won elective office—by margins ranging from 49–51 in 1932 to 35–65 in 1940. During the Eisenhower victories of 1952 and 1956, the GOP continued to outspend the Democratic party by what Heard estimated to be about a 60–40 ratio, but during these years of Republican tenure in the White House and of Republican advantages in fundraising the Democrats still were able to regain the House and Senate in 1954, after losing control in the 1952 Eisenhower landslide. See Heard, pp. 18–22 and 391–99.

[32]Gary C. Jacobson, *Money in Congressional Elections* (Yale University Press, 1980), p. 65.

[33]The 1974 campaign reforms limited individuals to giving a maximum of $1,000 per candidate in a specific race. Individuals can, however, give up to $20,000 to political parties, and $5,000 to political action committees, and the annual individual ceiling is $25,000, meaning that a couple can give $50,000 a year. In addition, these restrictions apply only to money going to federal elections. Many states permit unlimited contributions to state parties and candidates. See examples of specific contributors later in this chapter.

[34]See Stephen Hess and David S. Broder, *The Republican Establishment* (Harper and Row, 1967), pp. 45, 60, 61.

[35]Herbert E. Alexander, *Financing the 1980 Election* (Lexington Books, 1983), p. 422.

[36]Heard, *Costs of Democracy*, p. 122.

[37]*Fortune* Magazine, "Texas Business and McCarthy," May 1954.

[38]The $25.7 million estimate is based on the following: 1) Republican party committees received a total of $31.5 million in contributions of $500 or more during the 1979–80 election cycle. A study by the author that appeared in the *Washington Post* on April 25, 1983 of large contributions to the Republican National Committee showed that at least 25.9 percent of the contributions of $500 or more were from persons directly tied to the oil industry, and the figure is low because many contributors from such oil states as Texas and Oklahoma

whose source of income could not be determined were not included in the 25.9 percent. Applying the 25.9 percent figure to the $31.5 million raised from large contributors by all Republican committees suggests that at least $8.16 million was from oilmen. In addition, both parties raised what is called "soft" money in 1980. This is money raised to support presidential candidates but channeled into state and local get-out-the-vote, telephone bank, and other activities run by state parties that do not fall under federal regulation. This money, most of which is not publicly reported, amounted to $19 million in the case of the GOP; and Republican officials who helped conduct the soft money drive said that at least a third was raised in oil states from oilmen. This translates into another $6.33 million. This figure is, however, unquestionably conservative. A single fundraising dinner for the Reagan soft money campaign in Houston in September 1981 raised $2.8 million. Political action committees run by companies with oil interests or by organizations dominated by independent oilmen contributed another $6 million to federal candidates in the 1980 election, with Republicans getting at least three out of every four dollars, or $4.5 million. Examination of the campaign receipts of Republicans favored by the oil industry suggests that contributions from individual oilmen are at least double the amount given by oil PACs. Reducing this to a more conservative estimate of 3 to 2 suggests that total contributions from individual oilmen to specific House and Senate candidates amounted to another $6.75 million. Altogether, this totals $25.74 million.

[39]Based on examination of reports of contributors of $500 or more to the National Conservative Political Action Committee and to the Republican National, Senatorial, and Congressional committees during the 1981–82 election cycle, supplied by the FEC.

[40]Details on all individual contributions were obtained from FEC microfilm data listing contributions of all persons who give $500 or more to candidates or committees involved in federal elections.

The Politicization of the Business Community

[1]This quotation is taken from a series of three articles by the author for the *Baltimore Sun* appearing on February 25, 26, and 27, 1980, hereafter referred to as the *Baltimore Sun Series* on business lobbying.

[2]A third group, organized labor, shares with the corporate and trade associa-

tion lobbying communities a sustained interest in much, but by no means as much, legislation. The complexities of labor's efforts to influence the legislative process will be examined in chapter 4.

[3]Milton R. Benjamin, "Natural Gas Lobby Organizes 'Grass-Roots' Decontrol Move," *The Washington Post,* August 13, 1983, p. 1.

[4]Seymour Martin Lipset and William Schneider, *The Confidence Gap* (The Free Press/Macmillan, 1983), pp. 48, 49.

[5]Edsall, the *Baltimore Sun Series* on business lobbying.

[6]Edsall, the *Baltimore Sun Series* on business lobbying.

[7]*Savings and Loan News,* Chicago, Ill., September 1978, p. 66.

[8]Edsall, the *Baltimore Sun Series* on business lobbying.

[9]The profits from the sale of real estate, stock, paintings, gold, and a host of other assets are taxed at a highly favorable rate if the asset is held for a certain minimum amount of time. As of the summer of 1983, this time period is one year. For a taxpayer in the highest income bracket, 50 percent, the tax rate on the profits from the sale of stock held for one year or longer is only 20 percent. At this writing, legislation before Congress would shorten the holding period to six months.

[10]Subcommittee on Commerce, Consumer and Monetary Affairs, of the House Government Operations Committee.

[11]Lipset and Schneider, *The Confidence Gap,* p. 48, and chapter 6, pp. 163–98.

[12]Among the more detailed analyses of the Heritage Foundation are Dom Bonafede, "Issue-Oriented Heritage Foundation Hitches its Wagon to Reagan's Star," *The National Journal,* March 20, 1982, p. 502, and Ann M. Reilly, "Reagan's Think Tank," *Dun's Review,* April 1981, p. 110, both of which provided information on the sources of financial support of the Heritage Foundation.

[13]The information on the contributions made by these foundations is based on publicly available annual reports to the Internal Revenue Service. These reports are retained on microfilm by The Foundation Center in Washington, D.C.

[14]Based on IRS reports and on the findings of Mark Green and Norman Waitzman, *Business War On The Law,* published by the Corporate Accountability Research Group, Washington, D.C.

[15]Based on copies of foundation reports to the IRS maintained by The Foundation Center, Washington, D.C.

[16]The early formation of the Business Roundtable, which became one of

the most influential business lobbies in Washington, went largely uncovered by the press. Some early history was described by the *Engineering News Record,* a construction industry publication put out by McGraw-Hill, New York. *Engineering News Record* published stories on the formation of the Roundtable on October 10, 1972, p. 55; November 16, 1972, p. 19; and June 14, 1973, p. 54.

[17]These figures represent the membership of the Chamber as of July 1983.

[18]Robert W. Merry and Albert R. Hunt, *The Wall Street Journal,* May 17, 1978, p. 1.

[19]Edsall, *The Baltimore Sun Series* on business lobbying.

[20]*Fortune,* March 27, 1978, p. 57.

[21]A concise summary of the legislative history of PACs appears in a monograph published in 1983 by the Public Affairs Council, 1220 16th Street, N.W., Washington, D.C. 20036: "The Case For PACs," by Herbert E. Alexander, director of the Citizens' Research Foundation.

[22]From the Amoco PAC's report of June 1983 to the FEC, Schedule A, pp. 1–11.

[23]FEC Reports on Financial Activity, 1981–1982 Interim Report No. 4, May 1983.

[24]Figures for 1978 and 1982 are from the Public Affairs Council Monograph cited in note 21. The 1982 figures are from an FEC release dated April 29, 1983, titled "1981–1982 PAC Giving Up." In 1972, the breakdown between corporate and trade association PACs was not performed by the FEC, and consequently the available information lumps the two together.

[25]In a number of instances, contributions from a single trade association combined with an intense grass-roots lobbying campaign have produced legislative victories, as in the killing by Congress of proposed Federal Trade Commission regulations requiring used-car dealers to disclose known defects in cars offered for sale; and in the defeat of regulations requiring funeral home operators to disclose full costs and price alternatives for burial. This kind of influence over Congress by a single intensely mobilized interest, such as used car dealers or funeral home operators, only works, however, in the absence of well-organized opposition and, in victory, produces such extensive negative publicity that it can be exerted only infrequently.

[26]Computed from FEC releases on total PAC contributions dated February 21, 1982, and April 29, 1983.

[27]Computations based on figures in FEC release dated April 29, 1983, "1981–82 PAC Giving Up 51%."

[28]All figures on the campaign support going to these candidates are from Edsall, *The Baltimore Sun Series* on business lobbying.

[29]Edsall, *The Baltimore Sun,* November 3, 1980.

[30]Speech entitled "The National Scandal of the '80's: It's Time To Declare War on PACs," February 1, 1983, The National Press Club.

[31]Drew, "Politics and Money—I," *The New Yorker,* December 6, 1982, pp. 54, 149. In addition, see Drew, *Politics and Money—The New Road to Corruption* (Macmillan, 1983).

Labor Unions and Political Power

[1]Handbook of Labor Statistics, U.S. Department of Labor, December 1980, table 165, Union Membership as a Proportion of the Labor Force, 1930–78, p. 412. One consequence of the 1981 budget cuts has been the elimination of subsequent annual calculations by the Labor Department of the proportion of the workforce represented by unions.

[2]The quotations of Jones, Panetta, and Kirkland are taken from the committee records, Hearings before the Committee on the Budget, House of Representatives, Ninety-seventh Congress, First Session, March 3, 4, 9, and 11, 1981, volume 2, pp. 97–201. The quotations, however, barely catch the tone of dismissal and disparagement in the treatment of Kirkland in the hearing room by many of the Democrats on the panel.

[3]Cameron, "Social Democracy, Corporatism, and Labor Quiescence: The Representation of Economic Interest in Advanced Capitalist Society," a paper presented at a conference on Representation and the State: Problems of Governability and Legitimacy in Western European Democracies, at Stanford University in October 1982, table 6.

[4]Both the 1980–81 and 1965–81 unemployment data are from Cameron, cited in note 3, table 1.

[5]Organization for Economic Cooperation and Development, Revenue Statistics of OECD member countries, 1965–81, Paris, 1982, p. 68, table 1.

[6]David R. Cameron, "Politics, Public Policy, and Economic Inequality: A Comparative Analysis," a paper prepared for the Conference on the Role of Government in Shaping Economic Performance, University of Wisconsin–Madison, March 1981, figure 5 following p. 30. The data are for 1972.

[7]Ibid., table 2. The data apply to only twelve of the eighteen countries. The

number in the chart is "the difference in the share of total disposable (i.e., post-tax) income received by two groups which contain equal numbers of households—the top and bottom quintiles (20 percent) of the size distribution of income." In other words, in strong union countries, the affluent top fifth of the population received 28.3 percent more of total after-tax income than the bottom fifth of the population. In weak union countries, the richest fifth of the country received 38.8 percent more of total after-tax income than the poor in the bottom fifth.

[8]OECD, The Taxation of Net Wealth, Capital Transfers and Capital Gains of Individuals, Paris, 1979, pp. 20, 21.

[9]Using Cameron's measures, the United States's labor movement is weak on all three counts. In 1978 the percentage of the nonagricultural workforce belonging to unions in the U.S. was 23.6 percent. Unpublished data from the Department of Labor, division of Foreign Labor Statistics and Trade, September 1982, show the comparable rate for Australia to be 57 percent; for Canada, 37 percent; for Denmark, 81 percent; for Germany, 44 percent; for Japan, 33 percent; for the Netherlands, 46 percent; for Sweden, 92 percent; for Switzerland, 36 percent; and for the United Kingdom, 59 percent. Secondly, of all the workers in the United States represented by unions and associations (such as the National Education Association) in 1978, only 65.3 percent were members of unions affiliated with the AFL-CIO. Thirdly, in contrast to many other countries, the AFL-CIO has no power either to control or to directly influence the collective bargaining practices of member unions; nor can the AFL-CIO order one union to honor the picket lines of another member union.

[10]Handbook of Labor Statistics, U.S. Department of Labor, December 1980, table 165, p. 412.

[11]For the declining rate of union victories in union representation elections, see a table available from the National Labor Relations Board, Collective Bargaining Elections—Fiscal Years 1936 to Present. For the percentage of the workforce represented by unions, see the Handbook of Labor Statistics, Department of Labor, December 1980, p. 412.

[12]The same declining interest in organized labor is present in academic circles. Richard B. Freeman and James L. Medoff, writing in The Public Interest, "The Two Faces of Unionism," point out that the percentage "of articles in major economic journals treating trade unionism dropped from 9.2 percent in the 1940s to 5.1 percent in the 1950s to 0.4 percent in the early 1970s" (p. 69).

[13]U.S. News and World Report, February 21, 1972, pp. 27, 28.

[14]Calculated from NLRB annual reports for 1965, 1970, 1975, and 1980, U.S. Government Printing Office, Washington, D.C.

[15]Freeman, "Why Are Unions Fairing Poorly in NLRB Representation Elections?" National Bureau of Economic Research, Cambridge, Mass., pp. 14–16.

[16]The figures in this paragraph and in the following three paragraphs are calculated from tables supplied by the NLRB titled: Final Outcome of Representation Elections, Fiscal years 1936 to Present; Collective Bargaining Elections—Fiscal Years 1936 to Present; Outcome of Decertification Elections, 1948–1980; and "Voting in Decertification Elections—Fiscal Years 1948–1980."

[17]Paula Voos, "Labor Union Organizing Programs, 1954–1977," Harvard University doctorate thesis, June 1982, quoted in Freeman, "Why Are Unions Faring Poorly in NLRB Representation Elections?" Voos calculated that twenty major unions spent an average of $3.91 per member on organizing in 1953 and, after adjustment for inflation, $3.94 per member in 1974.

[18]From a table supplied by the NLRB called: Outcome of Decertification Elections, Fiscal Years 1948–1980.

[19]Ibid.

[20]Archie Robinson, *George Meany and His Times* (Simon & Schuster, 1981), p. 295.

[21]The Labor Law Reform bill was a major revision of the National Labor Relations Act of 1935. Among the provisions of the defeated legislation were 1) a requirement that once a majority of employees in a company signed a petition for a vote on union representation, the election would have to be held within thirty to seventy-five days; 2) the penalty for a company found to have illegally fired an employee for union activities would have been raised from the employee's lost wages minus any income earned at other jobs, to 150 percent of the lost wages, minus other income; 3) once a union won recognition, the NLRB could penalize a company refusing to enter into good faith bargaining.

[22]A. H. Raskin, "Big Labor Strives To Break Out of Its Rut," *Fortune*, August 27, 1979, p. 33.

[23]*Business Week*, "Building Trades Lose Ground," November 9, 1981, pp. 103, 104.

[24]Robinson, *George Meany and His Times*, p. 294.

[25]Ibid., p. 322.

[26]U.S. Department of Labor, Earnings and Other Characteristics of Organized Workers, May 1977, issued in 1978.

[27]In the 1972 presidential election, the votes of the working class were only 4 percentage points more Democratic than those of the middle class. Since 1944, when this difference was first calculated, the previous low point in disparity between the working and middle-class Democratic vote was in 1956, 11 percentage points, when Dwight D. Eisenhower won reelection. In 1976 and in 1980, the differences were 21 and 15 percentage points, respectively. See Paul R. Abramson, John H. Aldrich, and David W. Rohde, *Change and Continuity in the 1980 Elections* (CQ Press, 1983), p. 105.

[28]"[Union members] are becoming relatively more, not less, Democratic," John R. Petrocik found in *Party Coalitions* (University of Chicago Press, 1981), p. 90.

[29]Robinson, *George Meany and His Times,* p. 323.

[30]While more ambiguous, disputes in the early 1980s over the appropriate role of American military intervention in Central America, the Middle East, and the Caribbean are likely to cause similar conflicts between the reform wing of the Democratic party and the old guard of organized labor.

[31]The most exhaustive study of the legislation produced from 1953 through 1966 is James L. Sundquist's *Politics and Policy* (The Brookings Institution, 1968). The book includes many references to labor's role during that period, including considerable detail on the formation of the senior citizen and golden age clubs and of the National Council of Senior Citizens. Michael Barone, principal author of the *American Almanac of Politics* and editorial writer at the *Washington Post,* noted in the December 22, 1982, *Washington Post:* "Organized labor has been a major political force not because of its prowess in campaigns but because of its skill as a lobby. In the 1950s, 1960s, and most of the 1970s, labor was the one major Democratic-oriented lobbying force on Capitol Hill. . . . Labor set and enforced the agenda for the Democratic party."

[32]*The New York Times,* November 9, 1980, and release from the Gallup Poll, "Dramatic Changes Seen in Vote Given Carter in '76 and '80," December 21, 1980.

[33]The campaign contribution figures in this and the next two paragraphs were computed from the May 1983 reports published by the FEC covering the period 1981–82.

[34]FEC, Interim Reports on the 1981–1982 Election Cycle, May 1983.

[35]For one of the best available summaries of the efforts of unions and other labor organizations to revive their legislative and political strength, see a

two-part series by Bill Keller in the August 28 and September 4, 1982, issues of the *Congressional Quarterly*.

[36]Membership figures from charts supplied by the AFL–CIO, Comparison of National and International Union Membership, January 26, 1983.

[37]FEC, final report on the 1979–80 election cycle, released February 21, 1982, and the release of April 29, 1983, "1981–82 PAC Giving Up 51%."

[38]*Congressional Quarterly,* September 4, 1982, p. 2195.

[39]Senators with relatively strong prolabor records who were replaced by senators unlikely to support labor are: James Abourezk, Democrat of South Dakota; Wendell R. Anderson, Democrat of Minnesota; Dick Clark, Democrat of Iowa; Floyd K. Haskell, Democrat of Colorado; William D. Hathaway, Democrat of Maine; Thomas J. McIntyre, Democrat of New Hampshire; Birch Bayh, Democrat of Indiana; Frank Church, Democrat of Idaho; John C. Culver, Democrat of Iowa; Mike Gravel, Democrat of Alaska; John A. Durkin, Democrat of New Hampshire; Jacob K. Javits, Republican of New York; George S. McGovern, Democrat of South Dakota; Warren G. Magnuson, Democrat of Washington; Gaylord Nelson, Democrat of Wisconsin; and Howard G. Cannon, Democrat of Nevada. Only one Senate seat has changed hands in a direction favorable to labor: Carl Levin, Democrat of Michigan, replaced Robert P. Griffin, Republican.

[40]Peter T. Kilborn, *The New York Times,* May 16, 1983, p. 1.

[41]Calculated from membership lists supplied by the AFL–CIO, dated January 27, 1982. The calculation of the decline takes into account the decision of the UAW and the AFL–CIO to reunite in 1981.

[42]Peter Perl, "Unions Lose Jobs, Clout in Construction", *The Washington Post,* November 2, 1983, p. 1.

[43]Steven Stark, "Labor's Kiss of Death," *The New York Times,* May 22, 1983.

[44]Robert M. Kaus, *Harper's,* June 1983, pp. 23–35.

[45]Jonathan Alter, "With Friends Like These . . . O'Neill, Manatt, And What's Wrong With The Democrats," *Washington Monthly,* January 1983, pp. 21, 22.

[46]Seymour Martin Lipset and William Schneider, *The Confidence Gap* (The Free Press/ Macmillan, 1983).

[47]George Lardner, Jr., *The Washington Post,* June 5, 1981; Joe Pichirallo, *The Washington Post,* September 25, 1981; and a report by the Federal Bureau of Investigation titled "Labor Racketeering Cases Resulting in Prosecution or Judicial Disposition, January 1981 through December 1982."

[48]Lipset and Schneider, *The Confidence Gap,* pp. 48–49 for the rating of union leaders, p. 203 for the approval rating of unions, and p. 219 for views on labor ties to racketeers and abuse of pension funds.

[49]See chapter 2, pp. 80–81, for details on the fundraising ability of incumbent Democrats.

Voting Patterns

[1]Computed from "Voting and Registration in the Election of 1980," Current Population Reports, Bureau of The Census, April 1982.

[2]Raymond E. Wolfinger and Steven J. Rosenstone, *Who Votes?* (Yale University Press, 1980), p. 118, based on voter validation studies by the University of Michigan Center for Political Studies.

[3]Ibid.

[4]Rhodes Cook, *Congressional Quarterly,* July 23, 1983, p. 1504.

[5]Comparative data have been computed from the Bureau of the Census voting and registration reports issued every two years, known as Series P–20.

[6]Ibid., 1968–80.

[7]Charles E. Johnson, "Nonvoting Americans," special study, Series P–23, No. 102, Bureau of the Census, April 1980, p. 15.

[8]Michael Barone and Grant Ujifusa, *The Almanac of American Politics 1984* (The National Journal, 1983), pp. 829, 836.

[9]Based on Series P–20. The data for off-year, congressional elections parallel the findings for presidential election years:

CONGRESSIONAL ELECTION YEARS

Occupation	1966	1970	1974	1978
White collar	67.2%	65.4%	55.0%	55.1%
Blue collar	49.8	47.7	37.1	34.6
White-collar advantage or bias	35	37	48	59

[10]The basic calculations were made by Thomas E. Cavanaugh, "Changes in American Voter Turnout, 1964–1976," *Political Science Quarterly,* Academy

of Political Science, New York, N.Y., Spring 1981, p. 60. The calculations are extrapolated from Warren E. Miller, Arthur H. Miller, and Edward J. Schneider, *American National Election Studies Data Sourcebook* (Harvard University Press, 1980), p. 317. The method of calculating the income or class bias is the same as used in calculating the white-collar bias in tables 5.4 and 5.5 as described in the footnote on p. 187.

[11]Data on partisanship by income, race, and education are taken from the combined 1982–83 General Social Surveys of the National Opinion Research Center of the University of Chicago, supplied by The Roper Center at the University of Connecticut.

[12]*The New York Times,* November 9, 1980.

[13]Based on combined exit polls of CBS, NBC, and ABC as compiled by *Public Opinion,* The American Enterprise Institute, Washington, D.C., December/January 1983, pp. 28, 29.

[14]National Opinion Research Center data for 1982–83, as in note 11.

[15]See tables 1.3 in chapter 1 and 2.3 in chapter 2.

[16]Based on Series P–20.

[17]"The Political Report," Stuart Rothenberg, ed., Free Congress Research and Education Foundation, December 10, 1983.

[18]See section in chapter 1 on the generational split among Democrats in the House of Representatives, pp. 44–51.

[19]Barry Sussman, *The Washington Post,* September 3, 1983.

[20]See, for example, David S. Broder, "Reagan's 'Gender Gap' Seen Widening," and "GOP's 'Gender Gap' Gets Scrutiny," *The Washington Post,* August 8, 1983, and September 5, 1983.

[21]Figures taken from James L. Sundquist, *Dynamics of the Party System* (The Brookings Institution, 1982), pp. 198–240.

[22]The voter turnout figures from 1848 to 1896 are from Walter Dean Burnham, *The Current Crisis in American Politics* (Oxford University Press, 1982), p. 29, and the figures for 1980 are from *Congressional Quarterly,* June 23, 1983, p. 1504.

[23]G. Bingham Powell, Jr., "Voting Turnout in 30 Democracies: Partisan, Legal and Socio-Economic Influences," in *Electoral Participation,* (Sage Publications, 1980), p. 6. Powell developed a "class index" for the countries studied. The index was determined by first taking the percentage of manual workers in a country voting for the "left" political party (or parties) and then subtracting from that figure the percentage of workers in other, generally middle-class, occupations voting for the left party or parties. In the United States, for

example, 78 percent of manual workers voted for the Democratic party presidential candidate, while 61 percent of workers in other occupations voted for the Democratic candidate, yielding a "class index" of just 17 percent. In Sweden, in contrast, 84 percent of manual workers supported the Social Democratic and Communist parties, while only 32 percent of those in non-manual occupations did so, yielding a class index of 52 percent. Powell found a very strong correlation between countries with a high class index and countries with a high voter turnout. The finding strongly suggests that the more political parties represent clearly defined strata of society, the higher the voter turnout will be. To a certain extent, this is obvious: voters who are able to perceive a direct link between the interests of their own class or ethnic or religious group and the elective success of a specific political party are much more likely to vote to protect those interests—even in those cases where service (nonmanual) laborers make up increasingly larger proportions of the working and lower-middle classes. Similarly, a political party dependent upon a specific group for the core of its support will do all that it can to propel members of that group to the polling booth on election day.

[24]James L. Sundquist, *Dynamics of the Party System* (The Brookings Institution, 1983), p. 218.

[25]Burnham, *Current Crisis,* p. 29.

[26]Wolfinger and Rosenstone, *Who Votes?* (Yale University Press, 1980), pp. 94–101. The ten patronage states were Indiana, Maryland, Massachusetts, Missouri, New Jersey, New York, Pennsylvania, Rhode Island, and West Virginia. The ten reform states were California, Idaho, Minnesota, Nebraska, North Dakota, Oregon, South Dakota, Utah, Washington, and Wisconsin.

[27]Fred L. Greenstein, "The Changing Pattern of Urban Party Politics," The Annals of the American Academy of Political and Social Science, volume 353, 1964.

Consequences in Economic Policy

[1]As a result of inflation, family work patterns, and other developments in the private marketplace, redistributive tax and spending policies have not substantially changed the share of income going to the top and bottom quintiles of the population in the United States over the past forty-five years.

The poorest 20 percent received 5.1 percent of all family income in 1947, 5.4 percent in 1972, and 5.1 percent in 1980. The top 20 percent received 43.3, 41.4, and 41.6 percent of family income in 1947, 1972, and 1980, respectively. Redistributive governmental policies have prevented a regressive alteration in the shares of income from going to various segments of the population.

[2]Computed from tables prepared by the Joint Committee on Taxation for a June 16, 1983, hearing of the House Ways and Means Committee. Data for the impact of increases in the Social Security tax enacted in 1983 were not available at the time the Joint Committee completed the table.

[3]Congressional Budget Office, "Major Legislative Changes in Human Resources Programs Since January, 1981," Staff Memorandum, Washington, D.C., August 1983, p. 79.

[4]The regressivity of the changes in federal tax and spending policies has been compounded by actions at the state and local levels. Many states, facing state constitutional requirements to maintain balanced budgets, have raised taxes and cut social services. This shift in the tax burden from the federal to the state level is inherently regressive, as most states depend for tax revenues on sales taxes and on income taxes that have very little, if any, of the progressivity of the federal income tax.

[5]Spencer Rich, "Poverty Rate Rises to 15 percent," *The Washington Post,* August 3, 1983, p. 1.

[6]Gallup Poll press release, December 21, 1981, "Dramatic Changes Seen in Vote Given Carter in '76 and '80."

[7]Figures are computed from the Economic Report of the President, February, 1983.

[8]The data for this section are taken from Eugene Steuerle and Michael Hartzmark, "Individual Income Taxation 1947–79," Office of Tax Analysis, Department of the Treasury; from tax tables in the "General Explanation of the Economic Recovery Tax Act of 1981," the Joint Committee on Taxation, December 29, 1981; and from I.R.S., *Statistics of Income, Individual Income Tax Returns,* 1961

[9]Economic Report of The President, February 1983.

[10]Joint Committee on Taxation pamphlet, "Background and Issues Relating to Individual Income Tax Reductions," April 27, 1981.

[11]Detail on the changes in the Social Security tax is from the Statistical Abstract of the United States, 1980, Bureau of the Census, Washington, D.C., pp. 338, 339.

[12]Based on figures from the 1983 Economic Report of the President, page

251, and from the Office of Management and Budget publication *Federal Government Finance, 1984 Budget Data,* (February, 1983).

[13]Advisory Commission on Intergovernmental Relations, *Changing Public Attitudes on Governments and Taxes,* 1983.

[14]Economic Report of The President, February 1983, p. 208.

[15]Ibid., p. 194.

[16]For more details on the financing and structure of these institutions, see chapter 3, pp. 117–120.

[17]For further details on these four private research institutions, see chapter 3. "

[18]Weidenbaum, *The Future of Government Regulation* (Amacom, 1978) and "The Costs of Government Regulation of Business," Joint Economic Committee, U. S. Congress, April 10, 1978.

[19]See John E. Schwarz, *America's Hidden Success: A Reassessment of Twenty Years of Public Policy* (W.W. Norton & Company, 1983), and Green and Waitzman, "Business War on the Law," cited in chapter 3.

[20]The recent history of regulation and deregulation involves two very separate activities by the federal government. Both President Carter and Senator Edward M. Kennedy, Democrat of Massachusetts, advocated deregulation, but they focused their activities on regulatory agencies and rules largely created in the early twentieth century, which, by the 1970s, were seen to encourage monopolies, increase consumer costs, and benefit the wealthy holders of monopoly rights in such areas as airline and trucking routes. The Reagan administration, in contrast, has focused much of its deregulatory fervor on those agencies and rules largely created in the 1970s to protect the environment (the Environmental Protection Agency), worker health and safety (the Occupational Safety and Health Administration), and the consumer (the Consumer Product Safety Commission).

[21]For a detailed analysis of the alteration of the federal regulatory process during the Reagan administration see Susan and Martin Tolchin, *Dismantling America* (Houghton Mifflin Company, 1983).

[22]Anderson, *Welfare* (Stanford University Press, 1978); and Thomas Sowell, *Ethnic America* (Basic Books, 1981).

[23]Boskin, "Taxation, Savings and the Rate of Interest," *Journal of Political Economy,* April 1978.

[24]Feldstein, "Income and The American Economy," *The Public Interest,* Spring 1982, p. 69.

[25]Feldstein, *Capital Taxation* (Harvard University Press, 1983), p. 5.

26Feldstein, *Inflation, Tax Rules and Capital Formation* (University of Chicago Press, 1983), pp. 1, 4.

27Feldstein, *Capital Taxation,* p. 22.

28Feldstein, "Income," *The Public Interest,* Spring 1982, p. 70.

29"Estimating After-Tax Money Income Distributions Using Data from the March Current Population Survey," Bureau of the Census, Series P-23, No. 126, August 1983, p. 11.

30Statistical Abstract of the United States 1980, Bureau of the Census, p. 471.

31Savings rate and nonresidential fixed investment rate figures are from the Department of Commerce, Bureau of Economic Analysis, report dated November 22, 1983, BEA 33–61.

32Ibid.

33Budget of the United States Fiscal Year 1984, p. 4–3.

34Mervyn A. King and Don Fullerton, eds., *The Taxation of Income from Capital: A Comparative Study of the U.S., U.K., Sweden, and West Germany* (University of Chicago Press, forthcoming).

35Taken from table 7.14 in King and Fullerton.

36Ibid.

37Charles R. Hulten and James W. Robertson, "Corporate Tax Policy and Economic Growth: An Analysis of the 1981 and 1982 Tax Acts," a working paper, The Urban Institute, Washington, D.C., December 1982.

38In an extraordinary delegation of power, Congress, with the full support of the Reagan administration, permitted key representatives of the business lobbying community to write the provisions of the 1981 tax cut as they affected the corporate income tax. As part of his tax bill, President Reagan accepted what was known as 10–5–3, legislation written by a small group of business lobbyists, generally tax specialists representing the most influential of America's corporations, increasing the value of the investment tax credit and sharply accelerating the depreciation schedule on new investments. The lobbyists took advantage of this delegation of power to write a tax cut for business that reduced federal revenues by $154 billion over six years and by close to $500 billion over ten years. The lobbyists, who met Tuesday mornings in the Sheraton Carlton hotel (hence the name Carlton Group), included Charls E. Walker, whose clients included AT&T, Caterpillar Tractor; Standard Oil (of Ohio); Ernest S. Christian, Jr., whose clients included Chrysler Corp. and the American Retail Federation; the U.S. Chamber of Commerce; Cliff Massa, IV, of the National Association of Manufacturers; Phillips S. Peter, of General

Electric; John M. Albertine, director of the American Business Conference; and James D. McKevitt, of the National Federation of Independent Business. For additional details on the Carlton Group see Edsall, *The Washington Post,* "Three Who Sow Tax Provisions Reap Its Business Bonanza," October 5, 1981, p. A1, and "How a Lobbyist Group Won Business Tax Cut," January 17, 1982, p. G1.

[39]Hulten and Robertson, "Corporate Tax Policy." Their calculation includes the effects of the 1982 tax bill that reduced the scope of some of the business tax preferences enacted in 1981.

[40]For detailed analyses of the 1981 and 1982 budget cuts, see "Major Legislative Changes in Human Resources Programs Since January 1981," Congressional Budget Office staff memorandum, August 1983, and *The Reagan Experiment,* John L. Palmer and Isabel V. Sawhill, eds. (The Urban Institute Press, 1982).

[41]Party and income correlations are taken from the combined 1982 and 1983 General Social Surveys of the National Opinion Research Center of the University of Chicago.

[42]This figure, along with spending reduction figures for specific programs, is taken from the Congressional Budget Office staff memorandum cited in note 39.

[43]Thomas Ferguson and Joel Rogers, eds., *The Hidden Election* (Pantheon Books, 1981), p. 130.

[44]The Economic Recovery Tax Act of 1981 reduced taxes by a total of $609 billion for the period 1982–86. The Tax Equity and Fiscal Responsibility Act of 1982 raised taxes by a total of $149.9 billion over the same period, for a net tax reduction over those five years of $459.1 billion. See p. 4–4 in the Budget of the United States Government, Fiscal Year 1984, Office of Management and Budget, Washington, D.C.

[45]In 1982 Congress eliminated the most controversial provision in the 1981 tax bill, the section that allowed corporations to buy and sell tax breaks. In addition, the investment tax credit was modified in an effort to prevent a situation in which corporations received a "negative" tax rate on the profits from new investments. With a negative tax rate, a company makes more money from an investment after taxes than before taxes.

[46]David R. Cameron of Yale University has performed a detailed analysis comparing economic trends in countries with strong and weak labor unions in "Social Democracy, Corporatism, and Labor Quiescence: The Representation of Economic Interest in Advanced Capitalist Society," a paper presented

at the Stanford University Conference on Representation and the State, October 1982.

[47]Directory of U.S. Labor Organizations, 1982–83 edition, Courtney D. Gifford, ed., Bureau of National Affairs, Washington, D.C., 1982.

[48]David S. Broder, "Reagan's 'Gender Gap' Seen Widening," *The Washington Post,* August 8, 1983, p. 1.

[49]Spencer Rich, "U.S. Poverty Rate Rises to 15 Percent," *The Washington Post,* August 3, 1983, p. 1.

Bibliography

Abramson, Paul R.; Aldrich, John H.; and Rhode, David W., *Change and Continuity in the 1980 Elections* (CQ Press, 1983).

Aaron, Henry J., ed., *Inflation and the Income Tax* (The Brookings Institution, 1976).

Aaron, Henry J., and Boskin, Michael J., *The Economics of Taxation* (The Brookings Institution, 1980).

Aaron, Henry J., and Pechman, Joseph A., eds., *How Taxes Affect Economic Behavior* (The Brookings Institution, 1981).

Alexander, Herbert E., *Financing the 1980 Election* (Lexington Books, 1983).

Barone, Michael, and Ujifusa, Grant, *The Almanac of American Politics 1984, 1982, 1980, 1978, 1976,* various publishers.

Bluestone, Barry, and Harrison, Bennett, *The Deindustrialization of America* (Basic Books, 1982).

Bowles, Samuel; Gordon, David M.; and Weisskopf, Thomas E., *Beyond The Wasteland* (Anchor/Doubleday, 1983).

Broder, David S., *The Party's Over* (Harper & Row, 1971).

Brownstein, Ronald, and Easton, Nina, *Reagan's Ruling Class* (Pantheon, 1982).

Burnham, Walter Dean, *The Current Crisis in American Politics* (Oxford University Press, 1982).

Calleo, David P., *The Imperious Economy* (Harvard University Press, 1982).

Caro, Robert A., *The Path to Power* (Knopf, 1982).

Crawford, Alan, *Thunder on the Right* (Pantheon Books, 1980).

deLone, Richard H., *Small Futures* (Harcourt Brace Jovanovitch, 1979).

Dodd, Lawrence C., and Openheimer, Bruce I., eds., *Congress Reconsidered* (Praeger, 1977).

Drew, Elizabeth, *Politics and Money—The New Road to Corruption* (Macmillan, 1983).

Fenno, Richard F., Jr., *The Power of the Purse* (Little, Brown and Company, 1966).

———, *Home Style* (Little, Brown and Company, 1978).

Ferguson, Thomas, and Rogers, Joel, eds., *The Hidden Election* (Pantheon Books, 1981).

Green, Mark, *Who Runs Congress?* (The Viking Press, 1972).

Hacker, Andrew, *U/S, A Statistical Portrait of the American People* (The Viking Press, 1983).

Hofstadter, Richard, *The American Political Tradition* (Vintage, 1948).

Heard, Alexander, *The Costs of Democracy* (University of North Carolina Press, 1960.

Heilbroner, Robert L., *The Economic Problem* (Prentice-Hall, Inc., 1968).

Hess, Stephen, and Broder, David S., *The Republican Establishment* (Harper & Row, 1967).

Jacobson, Gary C., *Money in Congressional Election* (Yale University Press, 1980).

Kent, Frank R., *The Great Game of Politics* (Economica Books, 1959).

———, *The Story of Maryland Politics* (Tradition Press, 1968).

Key, V. O., *Public Opinion and American Democracy* (Knopf, 1961).

———, *Southern Politics* (Vintage, 1949).

———, *American State Politics* (Knopf, 1956).

Kirkpatrick, Jeane, *The New Presidential Elite* (Basic Books, 1976).

Ladd, Everett Carll, Jr., *Where Have All the Voters Gone?* (W. W. Norton & Co., 1977).

Ladd, Everett, with Hadley, Charles D., *Transformations of the American Party System* (W. W. Norton & Co., 1978).

Ladd, Everett, *American Political Parties* (W. W. Norton & Co., 1970).

Lindblom, Charles E., *Politics and Markets* (Basic Books, 1977).

Lipset, Seymour Martin, *Political Man* (Johns Hopkins University Press, 1981).

Lipset, Seymour Martin, and Schneider, William, *The Confidence Gap* (The Free Press/Macmillan, 1983).

Lubell, Samuel, *The Future of American Politics* (Anchor/Doubleday, 1955).

Magaziner, Ira C., and Reich, Robert B., *Minding America's Business* (Harcourt Brace Jovanovitch, 1982).

Manley, John F., *The Politics of Finance* (Little, Brown and Company, 1970).

Mann, Thomas E., and Ornstein, Norman J., eds., *The New Congress* (American Enterprise Institute, 1981).

Mayhew, David R., *Congress—The Electoral Connection* (Yale University Press, 1974).

Miller, Warren E.; Miller, Arthur H.; and Schneider, Edward J., *American National Election Studies Data Sourcebook 1952–1978* (Harvard University Press, 1980).

Nie, Norman H.; Verba, Sidney; and Petrocik, John R., *The Changing American Voter* (Harvard University Press, 1976).

Orfield, Gary, *Congressional Power: Congress and Social Change* (Harcourt Brace Jovanovich, 1975).

Ornstein, Norman J., and Elder, Shirley, *Interest Groups, Lobbying and Policymaking* (Congressional Quarterly, Inc., 1978).

Ornstein, Norman J., ed., *Congress in Change* (Praeger, 1975).

Palmer, John L., and Sawhill, Isabel V., eds., *The Reagan Experiment* (Urban Institute Press, 1982).

Page, Benjamin I., *Who Gets What From Government* (University of California Press, 1983).

Peabody, Robert L., *Leadership in Congress* (Little, Brown and Company, 1976).

Peabody Robert L., and Polsby, Nelson W., eds., *New Perspectives on the House of Representatives* (Rand McNally & Co., 1969).

Pechman Joseph A., and Okner, Benjamin A., *Who Bears the Tax Burden?* (The Brookings Institution, 1974).

Pechman, Joseph A., *Federal Tax Policy* (The Brookings Institution, 1977).

Petrocik, John, *Party Coalitions* (University of Chicago Press, 1981).

Phillips, Kevin P., *Post-Conservative America* (Random House, 1982).

Polsby, Nelson W., and Wildavsky, Aaron, *Presidential Elections* (Scribners, 1976).

Polsby, Nelson W., *Consequences of Party Reform* (Oxford University Press, 1983).

Powell, G. Bingham, "Voting Turnout in 30 Democracies," in *Electoral Participation,* ed. Richard Rose (Sage Publications, 1980).

Ranney, Austin, ed., *The American Elections of 1980* (American Enterprise Institute, 1981).

———, *Channels of Power—The Impact of Television on American Politics* (Basic Books and the American Enterprise Institute, 1983).

Reich, Robert B., *The Next American Frontier* (Times Books, 1983).

Robinson, Archie, *George Meany and his Times* (Simon and Schuster, 1981).

Sabato, Larry J., *The Rise of Political Consultants* (Basic Books, 1981).

Scammon, Richard, and Wattenberg, Benjamin J., *The Real Majority* (Coward-McCann, 1970).

Smith, James D., *Modeling the Distribution and Intergenerational Transmission of Wealth* (University of Chicago Press, 1980).

Sundquist, James L., *Dynamics of the Party System* (The Brookings Institution, 1983).

———, *Politics and Policy: The Eisenhower, Kennedy and Johnson Years* (The Brookings Institution, 1968).

Tolchin, Susan and Martin, *Dismantling America* (Houghton Mifflin, 1983).

Thurow, Lester C., *The Zero-Sum Society* (Basic Books, 1980).

———, *Generating Inequality* (Basic Books, 1975).

Tufte, Edward R., *Political Control of the Economy* (Princeton University Press, 1978).

Wolfinger, Raymond E., and Rosenstone, Steven. J., *Who Votes?* (Yale University Press, 1980).

Index